SHAMING JUSTICE

The Arizona State Bar and Supreme Court

Shaming Justice

The Arizona State Bar and Supreme Court

by

Bartus Trust

2015

First (paperback) edition July 4, 2015
Visit website: www.azaacpr.org
For email inquiries, visit:
http://www.azaacpr.org/contact-azaacpr.html

Library of Congress Cataloging-in-Publication Data
Trust, Bartus
Shaming Justice: The Arizona State Bar and Supreme Court
274 pp.   15.24 x 22.86 cm.
ISBN-13   978-0692478189

1.   Attorneys—U.S.A. (Arizona)   2. State Bar
Organizations—U.S.A.
3.   Professional Licensing—U.S.A.
4.   U.S. Department of Justice   5. Americans With
Disabilities Act (ADA)

PRINTED IN THE UNITED STATES OF AMERICA
10 9 8 7 6 5 4 3 2 1

ACKNOWLEDGMENT

Acknowledged with appreciation are numerous
contributions to the www.azaacpr.org website
by legal researcher
Michele Flick.

Table of Contents

[C]ivil servants have a wide, and sometimes even unlimited, administrative discretion, therefore creating fertile ground for patterns of corruption to spring up when licenses are issued for specific types of activity which require them, or when state inspections are held, or when enforcement measures are taken as a result of the inspections.

Yelena Ovcharova, "Patterns of Corruption in Licensing and State Regulation in Russia," *The Moscow Times,* May 25, 2011. *Available at:* http://www.themoscowtimes.com/business_for_b usiness/article/patterns-of-corruption-in-licensing -and-state-regulation-in-russia/437417.html.

1. Introduction

[I]f you can never evade the watchful eyes of a supreme authority, there is no choice but to follow the dictates that authority imposes. ... All oppressive authorities—political, religious, societal, parental—rely on this vital truth, using it as a principal tool to enforce orthodoxies, compel adherence, and quash dissent.

> Glenn Greenwald, NO PLACE TO HIDE: EDWARD SNOWDEN, THE NSA, AND THE U.S. SURVEILLANCE STATE 173. Metropolitan Books (2014).

Sympathy for the victims, however brutally they had been abused, was tempered because, after all, they were criminals.

> Douglas A. Blackmon, SLAVERY BY ANOTHER NAME: THE RE-ENSLAVEMENT OF BLACK AMERICANS FROM THE CIVIL WAR TO WORLD WAR II 5. Doubleday (2008).

The US Constitution confers upon citizens a right, as against the government, to be left alone—an impunity from intrusions upon one's beliefs, thoughts, and emotions; a protection from depredations upon one's inviolate personality; in sum, a right to privacy.[1] Federal statute, the Americans with Disabilities Act,[2] prohibits denial of governmentally regulated privileges where bureaucrats regard an individual as mentally ill, unless they can show a connection between the individual's ability to exercise the privilege and the actual or perceived mental illness.[3] Thus the US Constitution and federal law, together, prohibit governmental actors, such as administrative agencies regulating the practice of a profession, from certain kinds of conduct. In particular, they are restricted from labeling an individual otherwise qualified for a profession—whether or not there is a factor of actual or perceived mental

---

[1]   Greenwald, NO PLACE, pp. 172-173.
[2]   42 U.S.C. § 12101 *et seq.* (1990).
[3]   Job Accommodation Network, "Accommodation and Compliance Series: The ADA Amendments Act of 2008," n.d., *available at:* http://askjan.org/bulletins/adaaa1.htm.

illness—as characterologically unfit for the pursuit of that profession, without due process, including the right to a hearing.[4]

In the United States, our own governmental corruption is less widely reported than that of foreign governments. America loves to lecture the rest of the world about public virtues that, too often, are honored in the breach upon our own shores. For instance, every year, the US Department of State issues a report about slavery (human trafficking) in numerous countries.[5] The United States is not a stranger to slavery. Not only did the United States formerly host slavery officially—with the sanction of law—but for decades after the official prohibition of slavery under the US Constitution's Thirteenth Amendment, slavery—false arrest and prison-camp interment of Blacks—continued to be practiced due to the perversion of local and state laws by corrupt law enforcement officials, with the connivance of courts.[6] In the United States, there still occurs trafficking in persons, especially women and youth.[7]

The United States has criticized foreign regimes for intruding on their citizens' privacy, dignity and right of public expression. Yet official bodies, including the Congress, and its members individually, are immune from legal action to redress gross wrongs. A notorious example was the House Un-American Activities Committee (HUAC)'s depredations upon

---

[4]   "Press Release: Settlement Agreement Between the United States of America and the Louisiana Supreme Court under the Americans with Disabilities Act," August 14, 2014, *available at*: http://www.ada.gov/louisiana-supreme-court_sa.htm.   *See also* Melissa Moody, "When Courts Do Not Protect the Public: How Administrative Agencies Should Suspend Professionals' Licenses on an Emergency Basis," X FLA. COASTAL L. REV. 551 n. 2 (2009), *available at*: https://www.fcsl.edu/sites/fcsl.edu/files/Moody_Web.pdf.

[5]   *See, e.g.* U.S. Department of State, "Trafficking in Persons Report June 2014," *available at*: http://www.state.gov/documents/organization/226844.pdf.

[6]   Blackmon, SLAVERY BY ANOTHER NAME.

[7]   The Advocates for Human Rights, "Trafficking in Women" (2010), *available at*: http://www.stopvaw.org/trafficking_in_women_3.

the privacy and First and Fifth Amendment rights of American citizens, which occurred only a few decades ago.[8]

Americans boast to the world of the US Constitution's First Amendment as a model of enlightened freedom for public expression. In pretending the public enjoys free speech, Americans tend to overlook abuses such as the White House's harassment of ex-Ambassador Joseph C. Wilson and his wife, CIA operative Valerie Plame, over Wilson's unwillingness to collude in the administration's public deception about Iraqi stockpiling of weapons of mass destruction—weapons ultimately proved fictitious.[9]

The United States also loves to lecture third-world governments about the purportedly inferior social and legal status of their women. But the Congress has done virtually nothing to redress the rapes of American servicewomen by fellow military personnel.[10]

If we as Americans can acknowledge that our democratic system not only permits but requires that we consider, investigate, and contemplate corrective action where we fall short of the ideals enshrined in our laws and Constitution, then the justification for this book is self-evident. This book is an examination of lucrative abuse of power by public entities in one U.S. state and its effect on an entire profession.

For years, the Supreme Court of Arizona and its satellite organization, the State Bar of Arizona, has engaged in organizing panels of lawyers—not medical professionals—to label selected applicants for admission as mentally ill and in need of supervised "therapy." The Bar has done the same thing with large numbers of already admitted members. For such supervised "therapy," by Supreme Court edict, the Bar charges the victims enormous sums of money. Over the years, both the Bar and the Supreme Court have been enriched in the hundreds of thousands of dollars by collecting "fees," either for the Bar's putative costs of administratively supervising the therapy or, in some instances, for the services of one of the Bar's own employees in administering the "therapy." Although it does

---

[8]   1970 Academy Award acceptance speech by James Dalton Trumbo, *cited in*: *Trumbo* (documentary film) (Filbert Steps Productions, Reno Productions, and Safehouse Pictures 2007).

[9]   *Fair Game* (feature film) (River Road Entertainment 2010).

[10]   *The Invisible War* (documentary film) (Chain Camera Pictures 2012).

3

not hold itself out as a provider of mental illness treatment, for years, the State Bar of Arizona has employed a "therapist" for these purposes.

The Bar has denied hearings to Bar applicants flagged for this type of screening. In violation of state statute and the Arizona Constitution, the Bar has libeled members it has flagged for "therapy" by publishing information as to their purported mental problems. Moreover, once having submitted to forced mental intervention, as long as they practice law, victims may be bullied serially by the Bar with charges of professional misconduct, the proof of which the Bar represents to be their prior acquiescence with an official order imposing "therapy." This bullying sometimes culminates in disbarment—even where not a single client has ever lodged any Bar complaint against the attorney.

Where victims of the State Bar of Arizona's disciplinary mental illness program are Bar members (as opposed to Bar applicants), almost invariably, they are individuals in solo practice, as contrasted with attorneys serving large, influential law firms. Furthermore, whether Bar members or Bar applicants, most of the targets are women, many belonging to racial or religious minorities.

Many individuals who the Supreme Court and the Bar have flagged and treated as requiring mental health intervention had no mental history before joining the Bar. Some attorneys who have resisted the disciplinary psychiatry program on grounds of its illegality, as will be extensively discussed *infra*, or who have protested the corruption and mistreatment, have been pretextually sanctioned and even disbarred. This too is discussed *infra*.

As mentioned *supra*, for years, the State Bar of Arizona has employed a "therapist" to oversee its coerced mental intervention program ("Member Assistance Program"). This individual is a disgraced former law enforcement officer, a felon, and the subject of multiple allegations of professional misconduct, including sexual assault. As Director of the State Bar of Arizona MAP program, his duties have included engaging privately in "therapy" with Bar members and applicants.

Since 2012, an organization, Arizona Attorneys Against Corrupt Professional Regulation (AZAACPR), has sponsored a website[11] protesting corruption in Arizona Bar admission and disciplinary practices. To obviate the risk of administrative and/or legal reprisal, AZAACPR's organizers and participants avoid disclosing their identities. For everyone's protection, the AZAACPR website has been set up with aliases and fictitious contact information, as has been AZAACPR's email account. This book cites numerous AZAACPR revelations about Arizona's corrupt lawyer admission and disciplinary policies.

The Supreme Court of Arizona has established the State Bar of Arizona under its "direction and control:"

> [T]he Supreme Court of Arizona does hereby perpetuate, create and continue under the direction and control of this court an organization known as the State Bar of Arizona, such organization which may be a non-profit corporation under Chapter 5 of Title 10 of the Arizona Revised Statutes, and all persons now or hereafter licensed in this state to engage in the practice of law shall be members of the State Bar of Arizona in accordance with the rules of this court. The State Bar of Arizona may sue and be sued, may enter into contracts and acquire, hold, encumber, dispose of and deal in and with real and personal property, and promote and further the aims as set forth herein and hereinafter in these rules.
>
> Arizona Revised Statutes (A.R.S.) Volume 17A, Title V, Rules of the Supreme Court of Arizona R. 32 (a) "Organization of State Bar of Arizona."

Both the Supreme Court and its satellite, the State Bar, are part of the Arizona Judicial Department.[12] Although as an official body, the Supreme Court of Arizona is immune from

---

[11]   The website of Arizona Attorneys Against Corrupt Professional Regulation is www.azaacpr.org.

[12]   The Arizona Judicial Department (aka Arizona Judicial Branch) consists of the Supreme Court of Arizona; its satellite bodies such as the State Bar of Arizona, the Committee on Character and Fitness, and the Arizona Commission on Judicial Conduct; and the Administrative Office of the Courts, which acts under authority of the Supreme Court to supervise the administration of all courts in the state.

lawsuit and liability (under the usual restrictions, arising from common law, prohibiting suits against governmental institutions for malfeasance in the course of their official functions), for the wrongdoing of its satellite, the State Bar of Arizona, the Court is clearly accountable to the public, since it not only has established, but it also governs, the Bar—and it has declared the Bar liable to legal action.[13]

Unfortunately, it would be mistaken to assume that Arizona Bar and Supreme Court excesses affect only Arizona-licensed attorneys. Attorneys licensed in jurisdictions other than Arizona must beware too. Consider an Arizona Bar disciplinary matter PDJ-2013-9077 (reported in the July/August, 2014, *Arizona Attorney* magazine, a Bar publication). Here, Attorney N, a member of the military (and a JAG), was licensed in State B and by the federal bar. A dissatisfied ex-client residing in Arizona complained to the Arizona Bar about the outcome of an immigration case. The Bar seized on this—an unjustified complaint—to confabulate false allegations against Attorney N. But it is not the allegations that are at issue here. What is to point is that the State of Arizona *did not have jurisdiction* to discipline this attorney because the attorney *was not licensed* in Arizona. To practice in federal courts, all that is required is membership in any state bar (even if it is not the bar of the same state in which one operates one's practice) and admission to the federal bar. Attorney N had the right to practice immigration law in federal courts in Arizona without being subject to the jurisdiction of Arizona judicial authorities because these standards were satisfied.

A responsible bar organization might have simply passed on its information about such an attorney to the federal attorney licensing body and to the bar authority in State B. Instead, in a bizarre show of megalomania and excess, the State Bar of Arizona convened a formal hearing, which the respondent was unable to attend because of the obligations of military service. (The Bar likewise struck the response to the

---

[13]   Practically speaking, however, only federal authorities, such as the U.S. Department of Justice, could sue the Arizona Bar. Any Arizona-licensed attorney who associated himself or herself with a lawsuit against the State Bar of Arizona would almost certainly be disciplined with interim suspension and, ultimately, disbarment. Interim suspension is explained in Ch. 2 ii *infra*.

complaint on the pretext of lateness; the respondent did not timely receive the complaint, again, because of the obligations of military service.) As an outcome, the Bar pretended to impose a "sanction," including monetary charges—charges which the Arizona Bar has no authority to impose, and which the Arizona Supreme Court would have no lawful means of enforcing. And thereafter, in a colossal act of deception, SBA reported to the State B and federal authorities that it had "disciplined" Attorney N. As a result, Attorney N now faces reciprocal discipline in State B as well as involuntary separation from the military and loss of military retirement benefits. As this shows, the excesses of the Arizona Bar are not merely to be feared by Arizona Bar members.

At the outset of this work, it is important to fully demonstrate for the reader how the Arizona Bar and Supreme Court have treated their own rules as inconsequential when interacting with members and the public. For years, Arizona lawyer discipline has been capricious and politically motivated and has favored power cliques over ethics, as well as over the responsibility that the Bar and Court bear to the public. Beginning with the following chapter, this book will provide many examples.

This book is copiously footnoted. With apologies to readers for whom this feature may diminish its appeal, let it be said that most of the information cited from footnoted sources is publicly accessible. The corruption of the Bar and its sponsor, the Supreme Court, has occurred in plain view, even though in many cases, journalistic sources seem to go out of their way not to report everything they might when it comes to these entities' chicanery.[14] The purpose of the footnotes is not only to allow the reader to check the sources for himself or herself but also, to allow the reader to see that some of the more bizarre cases of Bar and Court misbehavior, a number of which appear so strange as to stretch credulity, are neither

---

[14] For example, in the following chapter, the disciplinary history of a suspended Arizona Bar member is recited, as is the eventual reinstatement of that individual to the practice of law. But there has heretofore been almost no public discussion of the impropriety and violation of its own Rules of Court in which the Arizona Supreme Court engaged by reinstating the lawyer in question. *See* Ch. 2 i *infra.*

being misrepresented nor distorted herein, but are reliably documented.

To begin, the following chapter demonstrates the willingness of the Arizona State Bar and Supreme Court to mire themselves in sleaze as it recounts the story of how an Arizona lawyer, after a lengthy suspension, got herself reinstated to active Bar membership thanks to her sexual relationship with the state's foremost law enforcement official—the Arizona Attorney General.

2.   The Arizona Attorney General's Attorney-Mistress and the Old Lady

> But the importance of privacy is evident in the fact that even those who devalue it, who have declared it dead or dispensable, do not believe the things they say. Anti-privacy advocates have often gone to great lengths to maintain control over the visibility of their own behavior and information. The US government itself has used extreme measures to shield its actions from public view ... .

Greenwald, NO PLACE, pp. 170-71.

Titillation is not the objective of this book. Nevertheless, from time to time, information will be included that to some readers, may be titillating, because the State Bar of Arizona and the body of which it is a satellite, the Supreme Court of Arizona, have not consistently avoided sleaze when there has been a political purpose to be served, or an effort to avoid adverse publicity and public censure for failure to protect the public interest and maintain appropriate, dignified judicial decorum.

Below, examples are given in which the Court and the Bar have misconducted themselves in two respects.

First, they ignore their own rules and regulations when the purpose suits them.

Second, the Court has promulgated, and the Bar has enforced, unconstitutional and unjust rules.

As the Rules of the Supreme Court of Arizona are part of the state's statutory code, they come under the limitations against unjust laws enunciated in the US Constitution. The discussion below reveals that certain of the Court's Rules merit investigation into their constitutionality.

i.   Politician Tom Horne's Lover's Bar Reinstatement

Volume 17A of the state's lawbook, Arizona Revised Statutes (A.R.S.), comprises Rules of the Supreme Court of

Arizona.[15] These rules are the instrument whereby the Court has established and constituted the State Bar of Arizona as the licensing and regulatory body for the legal profession.

Title V of the Rules, "Regulation of the Practice of Law," includes R. 64 "Reinstatement; Eligibility." It concerns the reinstatement of attorneys after suspension of Bar privileges. The Supreme Court, usually acting in accordance with the Bar's recommendation, may order a lawyer suspended from practicing law. If after five years or more, the lawyer applies for reinstatement, then by R. 64 (c), "in addition to other requirements of these rules relating to reinstatement, the applicant shall be required to apply for admission and pass the bar examination." Furthermore, by R. 64 (e) (3), the period of the attorney's suspension does not end until the date that the Supreme Court orders reinstatement.

Together, the two provisions of R. 64 mandate that after five years or more, the suspended lawyer must start the entire Bar membership application process anew—by resubmitting the voluminous membership application, and by taking the bar examination, offered in Arizona twice annually. This condition seems unobjectionable, given that five years after last practicing law, an individual is unlikely to be capable of simply picking up where he or she left off.

But the Court and the Bar ignore this rule if the suspended lawyer just happens to be having sex with an important politician.

In Arizona, the top law enforcement officer of a county is the County Attorney and, of the state, the Attorney General. From 2011, a politician of very dubious credentials occupied the Attorney General's office. The following details are public record, easily reviewed in online sources.[16]

Thomas Charles Horne is a Canadian-born Arizona politician who attended Harvard Law School. He held a SEC securities trading license in the 1960's and ran an investment

---

[15]   The Rules of the Supreme Court of Arizona are online, *available at*: https://govt.westlaw.com/azrules/Browse /Home/Arizona/ArizonaCourtRules/ArizonaStatutesCourtRules?gui d=N96EE7620715511DAA16E8D4AC7636430&transitionType=Categ oryPageItem&contextData=(sc.Default)&bhcp=1.
[16]   *See, e.g.* http://en.wikipedia.org/wiki/Tom_Horne. *See also* https://votesmart.org/candidate/biography/13558/tom-horne#.VYyDnRfxjR0.

firm, T.C. Horne & Co. However, around 1970, Horne was banned for life from trading by the SEC owing to willful violations of securities laws.

From 1970, Horne partnered in a private law practice (Horne, Ducar, Lorona & Slaton, P.C.), then entered politics. A Republican, he was elected to the Arizona House of Representatives and served from 1997 to 2001. He then was elected Superintendent of Public Instruction in the Arizona Department of Education and served from 2003 to 2011.

Among other controversial acts as Superintendent, Horne instituted a test required for high school graduation, the "Arizona Instrument to Measure Success" (AIMS) test, which was imposed beginning in 2006. It was abruptly abolished by the state legislature in 2015.

As Superintendent, Horne also curried controversy by concluding his tenure with action to abolish a highly popular Mexican-American Studies component of the curriculum of the Tucson Unified School District, one that Horne regarded as racially offensive. Previously, Horne had been instrumental in inducing the state legislature to pass a *post hoc* law tailored to the TUSD curriculum, which Horne could then conveniently cite in abolishing the component.

Horne was elected Arizona Attorney General in 2010. The voters turned him out with the next election in 2014, in part because of public disgust with his frequent embroilments over the period of his tenure with law enforcement, including multiple citations for traffic violations.

Among these incidents, the most spectacular occurred on March 27, 2012, when Horne, driving with a female passenger, committed a hit-and-run in a downtown Phoenix parking garage. The incident was witnessed by two FBI agents who had Horne under surveillance due to an investigation into Horne's possible violation of state campaign finance laws when running for Attorney General.[17] The City of Phoenix brought a criminal hit-and-run charge to which Horne pleaded guilty (and paid a fine). After purportedly investigating, the State Bar of Arizona declined to discipline him, either in connection with the ethics of his alleged campaign-finance rule bending, or in

---

[17]   Jeremy Duda, "Feds, Phoenix Police Said Horne Left Accident Scene to Hide Affair," *Arizona Capitol Times*, October 30, 2012, *available at*: http://azcapitoltimes.com/news/2012/10/30/tom-horne-left-accident-scene-to-hide-affair-feds-sa/.

connection with the hit-and-run charge.[18] As deplorable as was the Bar's indifference to the Attorney General's unlawful conduct, the focus here is on the female companion who was Horne's accomplice in the hit-and-run, an attorney named Carmen A. Chenal.

When Horne was in private practice of law, Chenal became, for a period, one of his firm's partners. At the time, both were married, although not to one another. (Horne, at the time of this writing, remains married to his original wife and has four children; Chenal divorced in 1999.) In 2006, after he became Superintendent of Instruction, Horne hired Chenal for a position in the Arizona Department of Education, a position for which, it has been alleged, she lacked suitable qualifications.[19]

Shortly before Chenal undertook duties at the Department of Education, the Supreme Court had ordered Chenal's suspension from the practice of law owing to a wide array of ethical lapses, including acts of financial misconduct against clients.[20]   The Arizona Supreme Court's August 30,

---

[18]   Yvonne Wingett Sanchez, "Arizona Bar Dismisses 2d Charge Against Horne," *The Arizona Republic*, July 11, 2013, *available at*: http://www.azcentral.com/news/politics/articles/20130710arizona-bar-dismisses-charge-against-horne.html.

[19]   Stephen Lemons, "Who Gets to Chop Off the Head of Tom Horne's Zombie-Like Campaign?", *Phoenix New Times*, May 22, 2014, *available at*: http://www.phoenixnewtimes.com/2014-05-22/news/tom-horne-attorney-general-corruption/. *See also* www.azaacpr.org, webpage "Inquisitional Discipline" [3] [a] [C] [i], citing Stephen Lemons, "Attorney General Horne Hired Carmen Chenal to a Highly Paid Top Post – 'Cause She's His Goomba," *Phoenix New Times*, July 14, 2011, *available at*: http://www.phoenixnewtimes.com/news/attorney-general-horne-hired-carmen-chenal-to-a-highly-paid-top-post-cause-shes-his-goomba-6449672.

[20]   *See* www.azaacpr.org, webpage "Inquisitional Discipline" [3] [a] [C] [i], citing Dave Biscobing, Mark LaMet, and Lauren Gilger, "Attorney General Tom Horne's Accident Raises Questions about His Relationship with Female Employee," *ABC 15 Arizona News*, October 3, 2012, *available at*: http://www.abc15.com/news/local-news/investigations/attorney-general-tom-hornes-fender-bender-leads-to-questions-about-his-relationship-with-employee.

2005, suspension order in Chenal's disciplinary matter, SB-05-0104-D, is public record.[21]

For the next five years, during which she continued to work for Superintendent Horne in the Department of Education, Chenal did not apply for Bar reinstatement. Then, having been elected Attorney General, Horne initiated efforts to get Chenal reinstated so that he could hire her again. In 2011, he did hire her, at an annual starting salary of $108,000.[22]

Chenal's hiring by the Attorney General's office followed Arizona Supreme Court action to reinstate her to the Bar. In this matter, Supreme Court No. SB-11-0034-R, Arizona Supreme Court Chief Justice Rebecca White Berch signed an order reinstating Chenal on April 19, 2011, more than five years and six months after the date of Chenal's order of suspension. The document says not one word about the Supreme Court's own rules, cited above, requiring an applicant for reinstatement to retake the bar examination and re-apply for Bar membership.[23]

Nor did the Arizona Bar ever investigate Chenal's role as Horne's accomplice in the criminal hit-and-run.[24] At the time of this writing, the State Bar of Arizona's website,[25] through its "Find a Lawyer" function, lists Chenal as a Bar member in good standing.

As l'affaire Chenal shows, the Bar and Court are pleased to overlook their own rules for political expediency or in deference to powerful politicians, the public interest be damned.

One question that, evidently, has not been investigated, but which bears investigation, is: Aside from her employer and lover Tom Horne, what persons or parties benefited materially from the Bar's and the Court's flouting the Supreme Court rule

---

[21]   See "Judgment and Order," *available at*: http://www.azcourts.gov/portals/36/2005_scanned/JOandOrders/ChenalJO.pdf.

[22]   According to the *Phoenix New Times*; *see* Lemons, "Attorney General Horne," n. 19 *supra*.

[23]   See "Order of Reinstatement," *available at*: https://casetext.com/case/in-re-app-for-reinstatement-st-bar *and see* alternative cite in www.azaacpr.org, webpage "Inquisitional Discipline" [3] [a] [C] [i].

[24]   According to the *Arizona Capital Times*, Horne had left the scene of the accident to avoid detection of his affair with companion Chenal. *See* Duda, "Feds," n. 17 *supra*.

[25]   The website of the State Bar of Arizona is www.azbar.org.

in their rush to return this questionably qualified lawyer to active status? Absent an investigation, the public can only wonder whether the Bar or the Court, or Justice White herself, may have received consideration for the favoritism shown to Horne and his mistress.

ii.   The Supreme Court's R. 61 (Interim Suspension) and the Probate Court Scandal

For the sake of exposition, it will be useful here to contrast two of the rules in Title V, "Regulation of the Practice of Law," of the Rules of the Supreme Court of Arizona.

R. 62 "Summary Suspension by the Board of Governors of the State Bar" states that the Bar can summarily suspend a member from the practice of law, but only upon the Bar's offering the member a chance to reply to charges, and only on one or more enumerated grounds. The grounds, listed in the statute, are specifically: failure to pay an fee assessed by the Bar; failure to pay dues; failure to comply with mandatory continuing legal education requirements; failure to maintain a trust account for client funds and property; and failure of a new admittee to complete a professionalism course.

On the other hand, R. 61 "Interim Suspension" concerns a device the Bar can wield against members called interim suspension. The rule enables the Bar to summarily, without a hearing, and for an indefinite period, suspend the practice privileges of any member who may have committed or be suspected of having committed wrongful acts.

But in the case of interim suspension, such acts need not be any one or more enumerated acts, as in R. 62. Rather, the Bar can recommend an order of interim suspension against a lawyer if he or she is merely thought by the Bar to be "engaging in conduct that has caused or *is likely to cause* substantial harm to clients, the public, or the administration of justice." [emphasis added] In other words, the lawyer does not have to have done anything (or be suspected of having done anything); the Bar can get an order issued to compel the attorney to desist from practicing law merely on suspicion of having evil intentions.

The relevant passage of R. 61 is:

(a) Grounds for Interim Suspension. An interim suspension may be entered upon a showing of probable cause that a lawyer has been convicted of a misdemeanor involving a serious crime, as defined in Rule 54 (g), or is engaging in conduct that has caused or is likely to cause immediate and substantial harm to clients, the public, or the administration of justice. ... (b) Period of interim suspension. A lawyer may be suspended from the practice of law for an indeterminate interim period, pending further order of this court.

By R. 61 (c) (2) (B), the order suspending the lawyer is entered by a judge—an official appointed by and answerable to the Supreme Court of Arizona, but employed by the Bar, called the "Presiding Disciplinary Judge." (About this PDJ, more will be said in Ch. 3 *infra*.) The PDJ can enter such an order upon notice to the subject attorney, but is not obliged to offer an opportunity for the attorney to respond to the allegations (i.e., a hearing)—even if there is no reasonable basis in belief that the attorney has committed any crime.[26]

R. 61, being part of the state statutory code, has the imprimatur of the Arizona legislature. As such, and being unconstitutionally vague, if a federal court were to scrutinize it, the court would very likely strike the rule as unconstitutional. It amounts to a Bill of Attainder as contemplated (and prohibited as an exercise of state powers) in the US Constitution, Art. 1 § 10.

A R. 61 order of interim suspension is a device recommended by the Bar when it wants to summarily prevent a licensed individual from practicing law without the benefit of a hearing.[27] Obviously, a rule of this power, allowing a solitary Bar official to suspend an attorney without a hearing, on the mere supposition that he or she *may* intend to interfere (whatever that means) in the administration of justice, can be wielded for political and/or corrupt reasons, such as to satisfy

---

[26] If a lawyer has been convicted of a crime, even a misdemeanor, that involves "moral turpitude," interim suspension under R. 61 becomes mandatory and "the sole issue to be determined shall be the extent of the discipline to be imposed," according to R. 54 (g) "Grounds for Discipline" of the Rules of the Supreme Court of Arizona. By this rule's terms, the Bar does not have discretion about charging the attorney; interim suspension is mandatory. *See* "Arizona Lawyers Who Get DUIs," n.d., *available at*: http://arizonadui.com/arizona-lawyers-who-get-duis/. This gives rise to another example of the authorities making of the Court's rules whatever they wish, for in only some lawyer DUI cases does the Bar investigate. In other cases, at its whim or out of political considerations, the Bar has taken no disciplinary action. For instance, State Bar of Arizona disciplinary File No. 08-1118 arose due to a report to the Bar against Tucson attorney Vernon Edward Peltz. In 2001, Peltz was sentenced in Oracle, Arizona, Justice Court (and did jail time) for DUI. Although it opened a disciplinary file, the Bar neither recommended discipline nor pursued an investigation. At the time of this writing, the Bar website's "Find a Lawyer" function lists Peltz as a member in good standing. It may be added that over a period of years, the Bar has received some fifteen complaints against Peltz. On just one occasion, the Bar disciplined him—by imposing an "informal reprimand." *See* www.azaacpr.org, webpage "Inquisitional Discipline" [4] [xi]. *See also* n. 114 and accompanying text *infra*.

[27] *See* www.azaacpr.org, webpage "Inquisitional Discipline" [2] paragraph 20.

personal vendettas or biases of Arizona Supreme Court or Arizona Bar officials.

In 2010, a public scandal brought infamy on the Arizona Judicial Department. *The Arizona Republic* newspaper published a series of stories by reporter Laurie Roberts between mid-March and mid-May of that year concerning alleged collusion of Arizona courts in the financial abuse of elderly wards under conservatorship. Particular attention was focused on alleged misconduct by an Arizona Supreme Court-certified corporate fiduciary, a company called Sun Valley Group.

Among others, the stories concerned demented, 88-year-old Marie Long. Upon being ordered a ward of Sun Valley by Maricopa County Superior Court Probate Commissioner Lindsay Ellis, Long was deprived of nearly all her assets of $1.3 million in a year's time. Ellis was never disciplined. She retired from the bench and, at the time of this writing, is listed on the State Bar of Arizona's website under its "Find a Lawyer" function as a Bar member in good standing. Long, on the other hand, was left destitute; she died a ward of the state.[28]

With egg on its judicial face, the Supreme Court of Arizona entered reaction and damage-control mode. On April 30, 2010, Chief Justice Rebecca White Berch established a "Committee on Improving Judicial Oversight and Processing of Probate Matters."[29] Its final report appeared in June, 2011.[30]

---

[28] Laurie Roberts, "Probate Victim Spoke Softly but Was Heard," *The Arizona Republic*, May 7, 2014, a*vailable at*: http://www.azcentral.com/story/laurie-roberts/2014/05/07/marie-long-probate/8638289/.

[29] The Committee members were Hon. Ann A. Scott Timmer, Hon. Gary Donahoe, Hon. David L. Mackey, Hon. Robert D. Myers, Hon. Denise Lundin-Newton, Faustina Dannenfelser, Jay M. Polk, Esq., Mark Salem, Denice Shepherd, Esq., Sylvia Stevens, Hon. Julia Connors, Hon. Charles V. Harrington, Hon. Rosa Mroz, Hon. Robert Carter Olson, Diana Clarke, Esq., Thomas L. Davis, Pamela Johnston, Catherine Robbins, and Jacob Schmitt. *See* http://www.azcourts.gov/Portals/83/pdf/PCCCommitteeMembershipListUpdated01182011.pdf.

[30] See Arizona Supreme Court Committee on Improving Judicial Oversight and Processing of Probate Matters, "Final Report to the Arizona Judicial Council June 2011," *available at*: www.azcourts.gov/Portals/83/FinalReportProbateCourtCommittee062011RED.pdf.

The ensuing changes in probate rules, taking effect in 2012, force applicants for guardianships and conservatorships to engage in amplified reporting requirements, thus jumping through more bureaucratic hoops than previously. But none of the new probate rules alters the fact that a presiding officer in a probate proceeding, such as Commissioner Ellis, may—at his or her own discretion—approve a fiduciary's requests for disbursements from the ward's estate—as Ellis approved Sun Valley's—and likewise, may issue orders in derogation of motions filed by blood relatives when they perceive their incapacitated relative's estate being depleted by a court-appointed fiduciary—as Ellis struck down motions filed by Marie Long's sisters against Sun Valley Group.[31]

Meanwhile, in 2010, a Phoenix attorney, Grant Goodman, filed racketeering lawsuits in federal court on behalf of Marie Long, as well as two other Sun Valley wards, Helga Mallet and Edward Abbott Ravenscroft.[32] The suits raised allegations of conspiracy to defraud, not only against Sun Valley Group, but

---

[31]   Sarah Fenske, "In Debt and Under Fire, Attorney Grant Goodman Has Found an Unusual Pool of Clients: The 'Victims' of Probate Court," *Phoenix New Times*, April 15, 2010, *available at*: http://www.phoenixnewtimes.com/2010-04-15/news/feeding-frenzy-in-debt-and-under-fire-attorney-grant-goodman-has-found-an-unusual-pool-of-clients-the-victims-of-probate-court/full/.

[32]   Laurie Roberts, "Old Lady Goes to Federal Court (and Now She Has Company)," *The Arizona Republic*, January 29, 2010, *available at*: http://archive.azcentral.com/members/Blog/LaurieRoberts/72790. In Phoenix, Arizona, Federal District Court, Goodman filed a suit *Raynak v. Olen, et al.*, Case No. 2:2010cv00146, to which both Frenettes (Sun Valley's owners) and Sun Valley Group, Inc., were defendants (and in which he represented the Raynak family, relatives of Marie Long), on January 24, 2010; *see* https://dockets.justia.com/docket/arizona/azdce/2:2010cv00146/4 96078. Goodman also filed in the same court, and also including the Frenettes and Sun Valley Group, Inc., as defendants, the following suits: *Mallet v. Zimmermann, et al.*, Case No. 2:2010cv00161, on January 26, 2010; *see* https://dockets.justia.com/docket/arizona/azdce/2:2010cv00161/4 96561; and *Ravenscroft v. Sun Valley Group, Inc., et al.*, Case No. 2:2010cv00183, on January 27, 2010; *see* https://dockets.justia.com/docket/arizona/azdce/2:2010cv00183/4 97012.

also against various probate lawyers representing Sun Valley or its principals.[33]

Unlike reporter Roberts, who had no Bar license, Goodman was vulnerable to Bar discipline. By calling attention to the failings of the Arizona Judicial Department, Goodman put himself in the crosshairs of the State Bar of Arizona. On July 21, 2011, the Presiding Disciplinary Judge, William J. O'Neil, slapped Goodman with an order of interim suspension.[34] On February 24, 2014, this was followed by Goodman's disbarment.[35]

Regardless of the relative lightness of an offense, progressively more and more severe punishments are the norm whenever the Arizona Bar instigates discipline against an attorney. This is because prior discipline (including being forced into "therapy" under the "Member Assistance Program" at the time of the lawyer's admission) is automatically treated as an aggravating factor in determining the disciplinary sanction. Whenever the Arizona Judicial Department has been threatened with exposure of its negligence—or culpability for active wrongdoing—by any action of an Arizona Bar member, after the Supreme Court and the Bar have reacted to the immediate threat, the Bar will generally wait a convenient period, then trump up new charges and may, eventually, secure the lawyer's disbarment.

This book will further discuss Arizona retaliatory

---

[33]   Fenske, "In Debt," n. 31 *supra*.

[34]   *See* PDJ-2011-9030 "Temporary Restraining Order of Temporary [*sic*] Suspension and Report [File No. 11-1872]," *available at*: https://www.scribd.com/fullscreen/60682730?access_key=key-98z9dd33inbm7y3b723. *See also* www.azaacpr.org, webpage "Inquisitional Discipline" [2] paragraph 20, citing Joe Ducey and Maria Tomasch, "Attorney Grant Goodman Suspended Without a Hearing," *ABC 15 Arizona News*, August 30, 2011, *available at*: http://www.abc15.com/news/local-news/investigations/attorney-grant-goodman-suspended-without-a-hearing.

[35]   "PDJ-2013-9065 Judgment of Disbarment" is *available at*: http://www.azcourts.gov/LinkClick.aspx?fileticket=1hxhHe-c_-E%3D&tabid=7259&mid=10580. *See also* www.azaacpr.org, webpage "Inquisitional Discipline" [2] paragraph 22.

disbarment in Ch. 3 and in Ch. 6 "Lawyer D" *infra.*[36]

Meanwhile, the tale of the probate scandal opens a second chapter with the enactment of the new probate rules, for the miseries imposed on Grant Goodman are only one dimension of the drama; the fate of Sun Valley Group and its wards merits discussion too. This is because, in Arizona, an individual or business entity that engages for profit in fiduciary services (accepting a court appointment as guardian and/or conservator for a vulnerable ward) requires a license. And it is the Arizona Judicial Department that licenses private fiduciaries.[37]

This raises a question of the Arizona Judicial Department's collusion in the misconduct of Sun Valley Group, for it is impossible that this entity could have acted as a fiduciary for wards had neither it, nor its principals, held a state-issued license.

---

[36] For instance, in Pima County, Arizona, Superior Court in 2010, a grandchild of a demented Tucson nursing home resident petitioned for guardian-conservatorship, although priority to petition would have resided with the subject's siblings, who held the subject's power of attorney and who were contributing financially to her living arrangements. Before the proceedings concluded, the petitioner and her father (the prospective ward's son) attempted without authorization to relocate the subject, evidently to take her into an adjoining county in order to effect a change of venue. The subject's counsel showed the court that the prospective ward's son was a drug dealer and convicted felon, and that through his daughter, the nominal petitioner, he was seeking to wrest control of his mother's income for personal benefit. The counsel asked the court to appoint a guardian and conservator, possibly the Public Fiduciary, since the siblings resided out of state. For the attorney's pains in trying to protect the prospective ward, the judge in this case, Hon. Charles V. Harrington, then a panelist on the "Committee on Improving Judicial Oversight and Processing of Probate Matters," ordered her to pay a sanction. He also appears to have reported her to the State Bar of Arizona, resulting in her suspension, followed a few years later (as in Grant Goodman's case) by her disbarment. This case is further discussed in n. 111 and accompanying text *infra* and in Ch. 6 "Attorney D" *infra.* For a detailed account, *see* Joyce Holly, AN INCONVENIENT OLD WOMAN, Thirteenth Amendment Publishers (2014).

[37] *See* http://www.azcourts.gov/cld/FiduciaryLicensing Program.aspx.

The online database of the Arizona Corporation Commission[38] shows that such an organization as Sun Valley Group, Inc. (as the name is still listed in some sources, including online summaries of the Maricopa County Superior Court cases alluded to *supra*) never registered its existence as a business entity. Sun Valley Group ceased operation on February 28, 2011.[39] According to at least one source, it closed not because of any state action, but because it lost its insurer.[40] The owners of Sun Valley Group, named in public sources as husband and wife Peter and Heather Frenette, started a new business called Desert Care Management. This new business does have a Corporations Commission existence[41] although neither it, Sun Valley Group, nor either of the Frenettes, are officially listed as licensed Arizona fiduciaries at the

---

[38]   *See* http://ecorp.azcc.gov/Search/Details?Category=3& Type=0&Term=sun+valley+group.
[39]   Robert Anglen, "Major Fiduciary Firm is Going Out of Business," *The Arizona Republic*, February 8, 2011, *available at*: http://archive.azcentral.com/arizonarepublic/news/articles/201102 08arizona-fiduciary-firm-closing.html. *See also* Chris Scholl, "Guardian Firm Closes Business in Arizona," *CBS Evening News*, February 8, 2011, *available at*: http://www.cbsnews.com/news/ guardian-firm-closes-business-in-arizona/.
[40]   *See* www.azaacpr.org, webpage "Inquisitional Discipline" [2] paragraphs 21-24. *See also* Kim Owens, "Press Release: Sun Valley Group Closes One Door, Opens Another," National Organization to Stop Guardian Abuse, February 7, 2011, *available at*: http://nasga-stopguardianabuse.blogspot.com/2011/02/press-release-sun-valley-group-closes.html *and* Robert Anglen, "Shuttered Sun Valley Group Fiduciary Blames Hype," *The Arizona Republic*, February 20, 2011, *available at*: http://archive.azcentral.com/arizonarepublic/ business/articles/2011/02/20/20110220sun-valley-shuttered-fiduciary-blames-hype.html.
[41]   Arizona Corporations Commission File No. L-1617112-6. *See* http://ecorp.azcc.gov/Details/Corp?corpId=L16171126.

time of this writing.[42]

When Sun Valley Group went out of business, it came to light that it had not only been sued by Grant Goodman, but that other dissatisfied wards' relatives had also been fighting it in court.[43] Hon. Rosa Mroz, then presiding probate judge at Maricopa County Superior Court, Phoenix (and a member of the "Committee on Improving Judicial Oversight and Processing of Probate Matters"), had to convene proceedings in February, 2011, to distribute Sun Valley's cases to other fiduciaries. Reportedly, Sun Valley's caseload was eighty wards.[44] This is a staggering number of cases under the supervision of one husband-and-wife partnership. The assignment of so many cases to one fiduciary could not have occurred without the approval of probate judges and/or commissioners, since it is up to them to grant letters of guardianship and/or conservatorship. Likewise, it is up to them to approve all disbursements from a ward's income or assets.

Moreover, upon the Bar's introducing itself as a champion of Sun Valley Group against its challenger, attorney Goodman, over a half-dozen Maricopa County Superior Court civil cases (not all brought by Goodman) against Sun Valley

---

[42] *See* "Licensed Fiduciary Alphabetical Listing Updated 10/14/14," *available at*:
https://www.azcourts.gov/Portals/26/fiduciary/101414FIDDIRECTO RY.pdf. However, as of November 18, 2009, both Frenettes and Sun Valley Group, Inc., were listed in an official Arizona certified private fiduciary directory; Peter Frenette under certificate no. 20077; Heather Frenette under certificate no. 20323; and Sun Valley Group, Inc., under certificate no. 20078. *See*
http://www.azcourts.gov/portals/26/fiduciary/pdf/2009/WebDocs/ 111209FiduciaryDirectory.pdf.

[43] Anglen, "Major Fiduciary Firm," n. 39 *supra*. *See also* Owens, "Press Release," n. 40 *supra*; *and* "Sun Valley Group Has the Nerve to Ask Judge to Sanction Marie Long's Attorneys," National Association to Stop Guardian Abuse, April 12, 2010, *available at*: http://nasga-stopguardianabuse.blogspot.com/2010/04/sun-valley-group-has-nerve-to-ask-judge.html.

[44] *See* Anglen, "Major Fiduciary Firm," n. 39 *supra*.

Group were either dismissed or deemed "abandoned."[45] It is unusual for a case to be deemed "abandoned" or to be dismissed for want of prosecution. Obviously, however, as regards these cases against Sun Valley Group, once the Bar made an example of Grant Goodman by subjecting him to extraordinary sanctions, no other Arizona-licensed attorney was inclined to risk likewise being sanctioned by filing a notice of appearance on behalf of the plaintiffs. In other words, a plaintiff such as Marie Long had to die a public charge and her family could not pursue compensation for her financial losses in court. And this was because the State Bar of Arizona engaged in willful interference in the administration of justice—aka obstruction of justice—a charge with which, ironically, in disciplinary actions, the Bar frequently slaps its *members.*

A question that bears investigation and public explanation is: Why did the Arizona Judicial Department, which licenses fiduciaries, not to speak of the probate courts and their judges and commissioners—which are likewise constituents of the Arizona Judicial Department—countenance such a situation? and who profited by it?

Where did all the money from the wards' estates go? There is no report that the State of Arizona ever investigated, let alone sued, the Frenettes, nor Sun Valley Group, to recover on behalf of the wards—nor to fund the activities of the Arizona Judicial Department's "Committee on Improving Judicial Oversight and Processing of Probate Matters" (whose existence became necessary because of the Frenettes and their Sun Valley Group). As noted above, the Frenettes survived financially to live another day, starting a new elder-care-oriented business. How was this possible?

Why was the Arizona Judicial Department, through the State Bar, desperate to punish and silence a lawyer whose activities contributed to public awareness of the plight of victims of the state's misadministration of fiduciary services? It bears investigation whether the Department has engaged in actionable racketeering. At least one Phoenix-area lawyer has

---

[45]   Case summaries can be accessed by entering "Frenette" or "Sun Valley Group" into the search box on the online Maricopa County Superior Court Civil Cases public search function, *available at*: https://www.superiorcourt.maricopa.gov/docket/CivilCourtCases/caseSearch.asp.

expressed his opinion that the Arizona Judicial Department was mounting a cover-up and has called for a federal grand jury investigation.[46]

The constituting and the activities of the "Committee on Improving Judicial Oversight and Processing of Probate Matters" have shed no light on what happened nor who gained from it all. Indeed, it might as well have been called "The Cover-Up Committee" because it obfuscated the real nexus of the corruption, while posturing as if something were being done to prevent future problems. Nothing has been done to prevent judges or commissioners from colluding against the interests of the aged and vulnerable.

Yet the Arizona Judicial Department's shaming justice stems not predominantly from the Bar's persecuting attorneys who seek to redress the harms in which the Department has colluded (not only Grant Goodman; *see e.g.* n. 36 *supra*); nor in its covering up the negligence and/or malfeasance of its judges and commissioners; nor even in its refusal to take responsibility—its outsourcing blame, such as by introducing amplified reporting requirements for fiduciaries—new requirements that principally burden relatives of vulnerable adults who, in good faith and, usually, without substantial resources, seek court approval to assist their kin. The single most egregious and shameful harm that has come out of the Arizona probate fiasco has been the Department's showing consistently and unmistakably that its accords no priority whatsoever to its number one obligation and *raison d'être*: the protection of the public.

---

[46]   Laurie Roberts, "Probate Judge Violates Ethics Code," *The Arizona Republic*, May 17, 2010, *available at*: http://archive.azcentral.com/members/Blog/LaurieRoberts/83603 *and at*: http://www.nosue.org/guardian-abuse-of-the-elderly/.

3.   Follow the Money: The State Bar of Arizona and Its Allies

Would you like a man who told on his friend?   There would not be one ... who would answer yes. But show me the man who informs on friends who have harmed no one, and who thereafter earns money he could not have earned before, and I will show you not a decent citizen, not a patriot, but a miserable scoundrel who will, if new pressures arise and the price is right, betray not just his friends but his country itself. ... Wherever there's fear there's hysteria and wherever are people who whip up fear for their own purposes they will produce the hysteria—and they will do it again.

James Dalton Trumbo, 1970 Academy Award acceptance speech (*see* n. 8 *supra*).

Disciplining lawyers is a lucrative business. In 2010, the "Lawyer Regulation" revenue of the State Bar of Arizona was about $174,000, exclusive of about $55,000 revenue from the so-called "Member Assistance Program" (the Bar's disciplinary forced-mental-treatment program). By 2011, the Bar's "Lawyer Regulation" intake increased to about $205,000,[47] exclusive of

---

[47]   For the Bar's 2010 and 2011 Independent Auditor's Report and Financial Statements, *see* http://www.azbar.org/media/752487/state_bar_of_arizona_2011_au dit.pdf. *See also* www.azaacpr.org, webpage "State Bar of Arizona: About" [2].

over $54,470 revenue from MAP.[48] There is evidence that the number of members that the Arizona Bar annually subjects to disciplinary investigations is on the increase (*see* n. 144 *infra*).

When he or she used to apply to various state bars, all that an applicant had to do in order to be disciplined (under the rubric of "conditional admission") was admit on an admission application of having ever been treated, however remotely or briefly, by a mind science professional (psychiatrist, psychologist, or "therapist"-social worker). Many state bars have programs similar to the Arizona Bar's "member assistance" apparatus. Like Arizona's apparatus, they have demanded payment from conditional admittees for "supervising" their admission and monitoring their initial period of practicing law. This has changed in some states lately due to U.S. Department of Justice action (discussed in Ch. 4 iii *infra*).

As will be shown *infra*, the Supreme Court of Arizona, through its Committee on Character and Fitness, has taken this practice a nasty step further. Not only has it flagged applicants with previous mental or substance histories, but it has also taken applications from persons having *no* prior history of mental illness (including substance abuse) of any kind and, notwithstanding, at the Committee's whim, has flagged some of these applicants as mentally ill and in need of referral to the Bar's "Member Assistance Program." No hearing is permitted.

---

[48] At the time of this writing, the most recent published State Bar of Arizona Consolidated Financial Statements document is for calendar year 2013; *see* http://www.azbar.org/media/6936/2013__state_bar_financial_state ments.pdf. It discloses net assets of about $11.7 million. Of this figure, the contribution from the combined disciplinary functions of "Lawyer Regulation" and "Law Office Management Assistance Program" comes to about $227,000. The 2013 Statement also acknowledges revenue from the "Member Assistance Program," but only in the amount of $50.00. Notwithstanding, MAP has not been abolished; *see* "FAQs About Member Assistance Program," *available at*: http://www.azbar.org/professionaldevelopment/map/ resources/faqsaboutmemberassistanceprogram; "Member Assistance Program," http://www.azbar.org/professionaldevelopment/map; *and* "Member Assistance Committee," http://www.azbar.org/ sectionsandcommittees/committees/memberassistance (all three sites last accessed 6/2/15). On the ongoing activities of MAP, *see* this chapter, c iii *infra*; as to this Committee, *see* n. 191 *infra*.

As a condition of practicing law in Arizona, the victim is forced to seek out a mind science practitioner in order to *procure* a mental illness diagnosis.

And to enforce the scheme, the Bar has even employed a "therapist"—about whom much more will be said *infra.* For the moment, it bears note that not only has this "therapist" imposed his attentions on numerous lawyers, but there are even reports that in some cases he has required a lawyer to persuade a *spouse* to accede to mental treatment or evaluation as a condition of the lawyer's licensure.[49]

Some readers may be surprised to encounter the concept of "conditional admission" (discipline before the fact, i.e., before any possibility of professional misconduct) because they may suppose that bar organizations discipline attorneys upon receiving complaints from their clients. In the case of the State Bar of Arizona, nothing could be further from the truth. At the time he was slapped with interim suspension, Grant Goodman, the Arizona Bar member discussed in Ch. 2 ii *supra*, had no client complaints; the Bar had no basis in any report of client dissatisfaction to restrict his practice. (For proof of this, *see* the order of interim suspension, which mentions zero client complaints, *cited in* n. 34 *supra.*) Similarly, the lawyer alluded to in n. 36 *supra* was subjected to conditional admission with forced mental treatment, repeated sanctions, including suspension, and ultimately, disbarment, without any of her own clients ever having complained. (This case is further discussed in Ch. 6 "Attorney D" *infra.*)

One of the most objectionable aspects of this situation, in the case of applicants admitted conditional to forced mental treatment, is that the Arizona Bar makes the fact of its imposing forced mental intervention as a condition on the lawyer's admission a matter of public record (as discussed *infra*). Yet the Arizona Judicial Department hides from the victim all documentation that would reveal the grounds for the order of conditional admission. Neither the Supreme Court's Committee on Character and Fitness nor the State Bar of Arizona, nor the "therapist"-employee of the Bar who presides over the "Member Assistance Program," has acceded to inquiries by victims seeking their records. This is discussed in detail in Ch. 5 (5) and in Ch. 6 "Attorney D" *infra.*

---

[49] *See* www.azaacpr.org, webpage "SBA 'Member Assistance Program'" [1] paragraph 4 *and see* Ch. 6 "Attorney B" *infra.*

When a victim asks to see such records, the State Bar, as well its "therapist"-employee, each responds by insisting that the records are secret and that there is no obligation to disclose them to the victim—and each refers the inquirer to the other (a practice which elsewhere has been deemed a "shell game.")[50] When inquiries are directed to the Committee, they are ignored or, when its staff members deign to answer, they refuse the request while addressing the inquirer rudely. Appendices 5-2 to 5-5 *infra* cite verbatim from inquiring members' correspondence to and/or from each of these entities—the Bar, its employee-"therapist," and the Committee.

More generally, the Bar's lack of transparency in communicating with its members as well as the public violates state's public records laws, as will be discussed in this chapter *infra*.

Obviously, in hiding information as to the grounds for imposing conditions on admission, the objective is to prevent victims from examining the evidence, true or false, accurate or distorted, whereby they have been shamed and libeled at the very start of their legal careers.

As mentioned *supra*, the procedure for "character and fitness" screening of Arizona Bar applicants begins in the Supreme Court of Arizona with its Committee on Character and Fitness. It decides which applicants to flag for conditional admission and consequent referral to the Bar's "Member Assistance Program," pursuant to Rules of the Supreme Court of Arizona R. 36 (g) "Procedure Before the Committee on Character and Fitness." By this rule, applicants flagged for conditional admission have *no right to a hearing.* This is the case even though, under R. 36 (e) (5) (B), applicants who the Committee recommends against admitting automatically get a hearing.

---

[50]   Rules of the Supreme Court of Arizona R. 37 "Miscellaneous Provisions Relating to Admissions" concerns, *inter alia,* Bar admissions records. Regarding the Bar's and its "therapist's" misuse of one of these rules, R. 37 (c), to illicitly hide "therapy" records from aggrieved Bar members, see Ch. 5 (5) infra. On the "shell game," *see* www.azaacpr.org, webpage "SBA 'Member Assistance Program'" [1] paragraph 20 *and* [6].

Absent an opportunity for a hearing, obviously,[51] the applicant flagged for conditional admission cannot wrest from the Committee the faintest idea of why he or she was flagged.

It is highly suspect that decisions on the mental status of bar applicants are taken by members of a Committee none of whose members (most are lawyers) have an iota of medical qualification.

Even more concerning is the Supreme Court's and the Bar's willingness to abuse Arizona constitutional and statutory protections by disclosing publicly that an applicant for admission is being flagged as mentally ill. When the Bar receives information from the Supreme Court's Committee on Character and Fitness about an applicant flagged for either documented *or* possible (i.e., speculative) mental illness, and when the individual has been given a MAP "evaluation" resulting in an edict that the individual undergo mental therapy as a condition for a license, then the Bar prepares what is called a "Findings of Fact and Recommendation of Conditional Admission." On receiving such "findings," routinely, without the applicant getting an opportunity for a hearing, the Supreme Court issues an order stating, "REVIEW DECLINED. The Bar's Recommendation of Conditional Admission is Final." (For an example, *see* Appendix 6-9 *infra*.) These documents are public record.

Accordingly, if any member of the public asks about a particular Bar member's circumstances of admission, the Bar willingly discloses that the member was admitted subject to monitoring by the "Member Assistance Program." Also, a summary of each case appears online on a Supreme Court of Arizona webpage, so that the applicant is publicly labeled with

---

[51]   Although under Rules of the Supreme Court of Arizona R. 36 (h) (1) (A), an applicant who opposes any decision of the Committee on Character and Fitness can petition the Supreme Court for "review," in the case of an applicant flagged for conditional admission, this exercise is pointless. Even upon review, the applicant will still be unable to access his or her Character and Fitness file, or otherwise discover what evidence the Committee used as the basis for its decision—and, moreover, since a "review" is not a hearing, the applicant is not allowed to attend when the Court convenes. The Arizona Bar guards everything about conditional admission as a secret to which the victim is not privy. The setup is analogous to Lewis J. Carroll's *Alice in Wonderland* Ch. 12 ("Sentence first—verdict afterwards.")

a judicial pronouncement that he or she suffers from a mental problem.[52]

Such practices violate Arizona's Open Records laws. These laws exclude from public scrutiny all medical records that a governmental administrative body compiles about an individual; they state no exemption for an administrative body that is not an authorized medical provider, yet purports to offer "therapy" through some staff "therapist."[53]

It bears note that, when conditionally admitted, a Bar applicant is required to sign a State Bar of Arizona document which the Bar disingenuously calls a "Therapeutic Contract." In this document, the victim agrees to waive confidentiality in respect of treatment professionals, the Committee on Character and Fitness, the Member Assistance Program's personnel, etc., but nowhere therein does the applicant sign *carte blanche* permission for the Bar or Supreme Court to publicize the fact of an individual's conditional admission, nor

---

[52]   In Arizona, for years, the lawyer admissions apparatus has been publicizing its findings of alleged mental problems of Bar applicants.   For instance, summaries of 2015 Supreme Court disposition of appeals of orders of conditional admission, Supreme Court of Arizona Case Nos. SB-15-0012 and -0013, are *available at*: http://www.azcourts.gov/portals/21/minutescurrent/mot_042115.p df (last accessed 9/3/15). Likewise, this chapter, i c 3 *infra* shows that at the time of this writing, for already admitted attorneys as well, when a disciplinary order specifies forced mental intervention under the supervision of MAP, that order, too, becomes public record.

[53]   The privacy of medical records is a well-defined exception to open records.   It is enunciated in A.R.S. § 12-2292 (A) "Confidentiality of Medical Records and Payment Records," *available at:* http://www.azleg.gov/ars/12/02292.htm: "Unless otherwise provided by law, all medical records and payment records, and the information contained in medical records and payment records, are privileged and confidential.   A health care provider may only disclose that part or all of a patient's medical records and payment records as authorized by state or federal law or written authorization signed by the patient or the patient's health care decision maker." *See* www.azaacpr.org, webpage "SBA 'Member Assistance Program'" [6]. For more exegesis about exceptions to open records in Arizona, see Daniel C. Barr and Jerica L. Peters, Reporters Committee for Freedom of the Press, OPEN GOVERNMENT GUIDE: OPEN RECORDS AND MEETINGS LAWS IN ARIZONA 5-6 (6th ed. 2011), *available at*: www.rcfp.org/rcfp/orders/docs/ogg/AZ.pdf.

to describe the nature of the conditions on the individual's Bar admission to the public at large.[54]

The Bar's revealing publicly that its staff "therapist" evaluates or treats an applicant or member arguably flouts federal law, the Health Insurance Portability and Accountability Act of 1996 (HIPAA) (Pub. L. 104-191, 110 Stat. 1936 [1996]). It also flouts the individual protection of privacy afforded by the Arizona Constitution, "Right to Privacy: No person shall be disturbed in his private affairs, or his home invaded, without authority of law."[55]

Not only has the Bar been violating Arizona Constitution and statute by disparaging the privacy of its applicants and members, but its Presiding Disciplinary Judge, William J. O'Neil, has been inappropriately issuing orders dispensing *medical advice.* An example is discussed in detail in this chapter, i c 3 *infra.*

At this point, an objection may arise as follows: the Arizona Supreme Court signs off on every conditional admission through a formal order; aren't court orders public documents? The answer is that, well, yes, in *criminal* proceedings a court may publicly order an individual to be "evaluated," and in *civil* proceedings a court may publicly declare an individual mentally incapable (such as in probate proceedings or Title 36 involuntary commitment proceedings). However, the proceedings appurtenant to Bar admission are *administrative* actions dressed in the garb of formal court "orders." Putting it another way, what other administrative agency in Arizona treats applicants for licensure like this, publicly libeling them as mentally ill? Can any reader cite any example in which any other Arizona professional licensing body has stated, for the public record, that it considers as mentally impaired some individual who has applied for a license to deal in real estate, insurance, investment advising, etc.?

Why is it that of all professional licensing bodies in Arizona, the premises of the State Bar, which is not a medical services entity, have been used to conduct purported mental

---

[54] For the text of the standard MAP "Therapeutic Contract," *see* www.azaacpr.org, website "SBA 'Member Assistance Program'" [9]. For further discussion, *see* this chapter, iii, *and* Ch. 6 "Attorney D" *infra.*

[55] Ariz. Const. art. II, § 8.

"therapy" and mental "evaluations?"—and how does it happen that the Arizona Bar, which is not an authorized medical provider, has employed a mental "therapist?"[56]—and further, how much money have Bar members paid over the years for the Bar to employ, compensate, and *provide legal defense* (as is discussed in this chapter, i b 2 *infra*) to this "therapist?"

Furthermore, why does any licensing agency need to employ its own "therapist?" Arizona has an Arizona Medical Board that licenses M.D. physicians and an Arizona State Board of Nursing that licenses nurses. Both of these professions are well known for having some practitioners with mental or substance abuse problems, with which these licensing bodies have to deal. Yet neither of these Arizona licensing bodies employs its own in-house "therapist." Why not? Well, one might think, that would be the licensing board steering its own members to one of its own members, so it would be a conflict of interest, right? And that is the answer. Bar associations employ in-house "therapists" (*see* n. 56 *supra*) because they are so eager for the revenue generated from a "member assistance program," or its equivalent, that they disregard the fact that, in forcing lawyers to submit themselves and their pocketbooks to the staff "therapist," they are in a conflict of interest. Anyway, what can the lawyer do about it—sue the very agency (s)he depends on for a license and livelihood?

Before further discussing what amounts to illicit practice of medicine and unlawful withholding of patient records,[57] violation of privacy rights and state public records

---

[56]   The State Bar of Arizona, in having employed a "therapist," is not alone. Another example is the so-called "Lawyers and Judges Assistance Program" of the State Bar of Michigan. *See* https://www.linkedin.com/pub/tish-vincent/5/210/311.

[57]   Arizona statute, A.R.S. § 32-2076 "Unauthorized Practice of Medicine" and the Arizona Administrative Code, Title IV, ch. 16, art. 2 "Licensure" prohibit the unauthorized practice of medicine. Arizona statute, A.R.S. §12-2293 (A) "Release of Medical Records and Payment Records to Patients and Health Care Decision Makers; Definitions" requires medical practitioners, therapists, etc., to turn over a patient's records upon the patient's request: "[O]n the written request of a patient or patient's health care decision maker for access to or copies of the patient's medical records ... the health care provider in possession of the record shall provide access to or copies of the records to the patient or the patient's health care decision maker."

laws, and violation of the US Constitution's Fourteenth Amendment guarantees, all routinely sponsored by the Supreme Court of Arizona, the State Bar of Arizona, and their minions, it is imperative to consider why lately, even as regards persons who do have a mental illness history prior to seeking admission, the U.S. Department of Justice has taken measures to restrict bar admissions abuses such as conditional admission. That will be the subject of the following chapter. First, it is vital to assess the extent of the corruption in Arizona Bar admissions and discipline.

To begin, this chapter discusses the players. The first player, the State Bar of Arizona, has, for years, been in the lucrative business, under the guise of "discipline," of shaming and libeling Bar applicants for alleged mental health imperfections. The Bar is discussed in this chapter, i *infra*.

Other players that figure in this business are external to the Arizona Bar and either have a pecuniary interest in illegal bar admissions and discipline or an avowed interest and a role to play in promoting it. One example is the American Bar Association. It and other external entities are discussed in this chapter, ii *infra*.

In addition, this chapter examines the costs imposed on Arizona lawyers subjected to unfair and extortionate Bar discipline, including being libeled as mentally ill. That is discussed in this chapter, iii *infra*.

i.   The State Bar of Arizona and The Culture of Entitlement

Other than the Supreme Court of Arizona of which it is a satellite, the State Bar of Arizona is accountable to no one. Its operations are funded by impositions on lawyer members and do not depend on the vagaries of the Arizona state budget nor on legislative allocations. [58] Membership is mandatory for individuals wishing to practice law in Arizona.

For years, concerns have been voiced about two notorious aspects of State Bar of Arizona corruption: avarice combined with a lack of accountability to members; and

---

[58]   *See* www.azaacpr.org, webpage "State Bar of Arizona: About" [2] paragraph 2, citing John Phelps, "State Bar is Regulatory Agency, Not Advocacy Group," *The Arizona Republic*, July 15, 2012, *available at*: archive.azcentral.com/arizonarepublic/opinions/articles/ 2012/07/13/20120713state-bar-regulatory-agency-phelps.html.

favoritism, mismanagement and lack of transparency. Each of these is now examined in turn.

a.   Avarice and Lack of Accountability

Recently, without its membership's consultation or approval, the State Bar of Arizona has announced an annual dues increase. At the time of this writing, it is being implemented progressively over the period 2015-2018.[59]
However, even before the increase was announced in 2014, State Bar of Arizona annual dues were among the highest in the nation—and have been so for years. This fact has aroused open criticism by Bar members, including a president of one of the Arizona county bar associations.[60]
Bar impositions come not only in the form of dues, but also other charges, such as fees that the Bar exacts from lawyers. For instance, the Bar has an annual Continuing Legal Education requirement. The Bar sells accredited programs of its own devising to enable lawyers to meet the requirement. For 2013, the latest year for which budgetary figures are available, the Bar took in not quite $2million from Continuing Legal Education fees.[61]
The Arizona Bar also charges extortionate discipline-related penalties. This is discussed in this chapter, iii *infra*.

---

[59]   For an active member of the Arizona Bar in practice (in any jurisdiction) for at least three years, annual Bar dues were raised to $475 as of March 2, 2015, and by 2018 will increase to $520. *See* "Dues Increase FAQ," *available at:*
http://www.azbar.org/aboutus/leadership/boardofgovernors/impor tantissues/duesincreaseeffective2015/duesincreasefaq   (last accessed 6/11/15); http://www.azbar.org/membership/
feesdeadlines (last accessed 6/11/15); *and,* for the April 1, 2014, Supreme Court order increasing dues (Administrative Order No. 2014-32), *see* https://www.azcourts.gov/Portals/22/admorder/
Orders14/2014-32.pdf.
[60]   *See* www.azaacpr.org, webpage "State Bar of Arizona: About" [2] paragraph 4, citing Joey A. Flynn, "From the President's Desk," *The Writ* [publication of the Pima County, Arizona, Bar Association], July, 2009, p. 3. *See also* Rachel Alexander, "Exposing the Myth that a Mandatory State Bar Will Cost More Money," *The Stream*, March 5, 2015, *available at:* http://www.icarizona.com/2015/03/exposing-myth-that-eliminating-state.html.
[61]   For budget figures *see* cites in nn. 47, 48 *supra*.

Meanwhile, it may be noted that if a discipline-related penalty goes unpaid, the Supreme Court of Arizona issues a judgment against the debtor (the Bar member) and records the judgment as a lien in the county of the debtor's residence.

Another form of Bar imposition is its obliging lawyers to render legal services by fiat. In 1986, the State Bar and the Arizona Supreme Court persuaded the Arizona legislature to mandate forced service of attorneys as arbitrators—in effect, placing all attorneys, whether willing or unwilling, with a certain minimum number of years of experience in any kind of law, on a selection list. From this list, superior court judges are entitled to select individuals and order them to arbitrate disputes deemed suitable for resolution alternative to court proceedings. Attorneys so selected are compensated according to a court-approved scheme.

In the 1980's, an Arizona attorney sued in federal court seeking to have this practice stricken as unconstitutional, but was unsuccessful.[62]

Many Arizona lawyers are unhappy about the mandatory-service policy because they are unqualified for the task of arbitration. In law school, lawyers are not trained in taking on the roles of judges, arbitrators or mediators. Thus the policy is an interesting instance in which the Bar chooses both to enforce certain ethical rules and, simultaneously, also to force attorneys to violate ethical rules, for one of the well-known Arizona lawyer ethics rules enjoins attorneys to forebear from areas of legal practice in which they lack competence.[63]

---

[62]   *Scheehle v. Justices of the Supreme Court*, 120 P.3d 1092 (Ariz. 2005), 315 F.3d 1191 (9th Cir. 2003). *See* Tracy Le, "*Scheehle v. Justices of the Supreme Court*: The Arizona Supreme Court's Right to Compel Attorneys to Serve as Arbitrators," 48 ARIZ. LAW REV. 413 (2006), *available at*: http://www.arizonalawreview.org/pdf/48-2/48arizlrev413.pdf; *and see* www.azaacpr.org, webpage "Inquisitional Discipline" [4] [xvii]. Note that although a court, such as the Arizona Supreme Court, has immunity from being named a defendant in a lawsuit, the individual Justices can be sued, which was how the plaintiff proceeded against his defendants in *Scheehle*.

[63]   In fact, this is the first rule of lawyer ethics. *See* Rules of the Supreme Court of Arizona (introduced in n. 15 and accompanying text *supra*) R. 42 ER 1.1 "Competence."

The State Bar of Arizona owns lucrative real estate. In Phoenix, the Bar owns the building in which it is housed.[64] According to Maricopa County Assessor's records, the State Bar of Arizona has title to the building at 4201 N. 24 St., Phoenix (Deed No. 040793936). The 2016 assessed value is $6.2 million. According to Maricopa County Recorder's records, the Bar acquired these premises, recording no. 20040793936, by a special warranty deed from "Phoenix 24th Place, Inc., an Arizona corporation with a mailing address of 825 N. Broadway Ave., Suite 300, Oklahoma City, Oklahoma 73102." The document recites that "Phoenix 24th Place, Inc." conveyed the parcel on July 12, 2004, for nominal consideration ($10). For calendar year 2014, the Bar paid $136,205.86 in property taxes for this parcel (no. 163-06-104). The Bar also owns property in Tucson.[65]

Even the Arizona Legislature, the Supreme Court and, for that matter, the Arizona governor, cannot claim title to their own premises.

---

[64]   See "Dues Increase FAQ," n. 59 *supra*.

[65]   For the Phoenix property records, *see* the respective Maricopa County Assessor's, Recorder's, and Treasurer's records, *available at*: http://mcassessor.maricopa.gov/?s=163-06-104; http://recorder. maricopa.gov/recdocdata/getrecdatadetail.aspx?rec=20040793936&s uf=; *and* http://treasurer.maricopa.gov/Parcel/Summary.aspx [in the search box, enter parcel no. 163-06-104]. The State Bar of Arizona owns its own Southern Arizona satellite building at 270 N. Church Av., Tucson. This parcel, no. 117-10-075-B, was conveyed by warranty deed from "Church Street Partners" to the State Bar of Arizona for nominal consideration ($10) in a recording dated February 26, 2008, sequence 20080380523 (docket/page 13250/2171). The 2014 Pima County Assessor's valuation for this parcel is approximately half a million dollars. For 2014, the property taxes paid by the Bar for this parcel were $17,329.07. *See* the respective Pima County Recorder's, Assessor's, and Treasurer's records, *available at*: https://service.recorder.pima. gov/publicdocuments/docview.aspx?s=4/1/1987&e=6/10/2015& d=13250&p=2171&o=Sequence&v=GG; http://www.asr.pima.gov/links/frm_Parcel.aspx?parcel=11710075B& taxyear=2016; *and* http://www.to.pima.gov/pcto/tweb/property_inquiry/show/117100 75B/2014. According to records of the Arizona Corporation Commission, the entity that conveyed the Tucson property, Church Street Partners, Inc., was dissolved on March 19, 2009. *See* http://ecorp.azcc.gov/Details/Corp?corpId=%2005273292.

Since the Bar's sole source of funding is impositions paid by its members, these impositions obviously are used to satisfy expenses of maintaining the Bar's buildings. For instance, it would be member impositions that fund the property taxes. The same holds of upkeep costs, down to the price of the dimmest light bulb. The members effectively own the real estate, since they pay for everything associated with it. Yet they have no voice in the way the Bar leadership cabal uses it. The leadership does not invite the members' input, for instance, to discuss whether, to cover the annual property tax bill, an entire unused floor of the $6.2million Phoenix building could be leased to one or more tenants—instead of the leadership allowing it to remain vacant, as is its status at the time of this writing.[66]

A large number of individuals are compensated either as employees of, or as members of legitimizing appendages to, the State Bar of Arizona. These appendages include a Board of Governors with no fewer than thirty members.[67] The Bar allows its members to vote in an election annually to approve a slate of candidates for the Board of Governors. However, by collecting and vetting the applications for candidacy, the Bar carefully controls who is allowed to stand for election.[68] Thus the election for the State Bar of Arizona Board of Governors resembles the sort of show election for political office that was a well-known feature of public life in the former Soviet Union.

In turn, the Board of Governors chooses for the membership a body of officers including a president, president-elect, first vice-president, second vice-president and secretary-treasurer. The Bar's members are not called upon to directly elect any of these officers. The officers—the president

---

[66]   See "Dues Increase FAQ," n. 59 *supra.*
[67]   See http://www.azbar.org/aboutus/ leadership/boardofgovernors2014-2015.
[68]   For some details of the process of arriving at a slate, *see* John F. Phelps, "Call for Board of Governors Candidates," January 30, 2015, *available at*: http://www.azbar.org/media/908650/ 2015_bog_nomination_package.pdf.

of the State Bar,[69] etc.—are also members of the Board of Governors.

Since 2012, Arizona Attorneys Against Corrupt Professional Regulation has corresponded by email with several successive State Bar of Arizona presidents. None has addressed AZAACPR's concerns about official corruption. The one response received after AZAACPR addressed its concerns to a State Bar president is reproduced in Appendix 5-1 *infra.*

The names of certain individuals show up over and over in public announcements as Arizona Bar officers and, what is more, as State Bar officials in other capacities, e.g. as members of the Board of Governors, or members of various panels, commissions, task forces, or committees, such as the Committee on Character and Fitness of the Supreme Court of Arizona. The incestuous nature of the selection of lawyers, and even some non-lawyers (*see* this chapter, i c 1 *and see also* iii *infra*), for top posts indicates that the Arizona Judicial Department trusts and favors certain individuals.

The Board also hires officials and staff. Bar officials selected by the Board, other than those enumerated above, include a CEO; a CFO; a General Counsel; various Staff Bar Counsel headed by a Chief Bar Counsel—hired to carry out the Bar's disciplinary functions; and various other salaried

---

[69]   At the time of this writing, the most recent five holders of the position of President of the State Bar of Arizona are lawyers Bryan B. Chambers (2015), Richard T. Platt (2014), Amelia Craig Cramer (2013), Joseph A. Kanefield (2012), and Alan P. Bayham (2011).

employees or consultants[70]—including a State Bar Lobbyist, whose job is to influence the Arizona Legislature.[71]

It is doubtful that any other Arizona professional licensing organization has a lobbyist. The State Bar of Arizona does not make public the identity of its lobbyist or lobbyists. (*See* n. 71 *supra*.) That said, everyone knows what a lobbyist does. On behalf of the organization (s)he represents, (s)he seeks out members of the legislature, plies them with gifts, alcohol and meals, and tries to influence them to take political positions advantageous to his or her organization.

One can only wonder how much consideration (all derived from funds acquired by impositions on Bar members) might be dispensed via the pockets of the State Bar Lobbyist when there is legislation afoot posing an existential threat to the State Bar of Arizona; legislation such as HB2480 in 2013, and HB2629 in 2015, discussed in this chapter, ii e *infra*.

Although the Bar does not offer information about its lobbyists, Arizona lobbyists cannot easily conceal themselves, since they have to register with the Arizona Secretary of State. The *Arizona Capitol Times* newspaper offers an online Lobbyists' Directory.[72] It lists the lobbyists for various entities. The State Bar of Arizona's lobbyists are Janna B. Day, Ryan O'Daniel, Martin Shultz, and Susie Stevens. (Among these three, Janna B. Day and Susan Stevens are also members of the Arizona Bar, according to the "Find A Lawyer" function on the Bar's website, *cited in* n. 25 *supra*.) The last named individual

---

[70]   An official listing of some Bar employees and their job titles is *available at*: http://www.azbar.org/membership/ informationfornewmembers/staffquickreferencelist (last accessed 6/10/15). The list includes a heading for "Member Assistance Program (MAP)," but at the time of this writing, the name of the incumbent of this salaried position is conspicuously left blank. The Bar acknowledges having its own lobbyist (*see* n. 71 *infra*) although it does not publicly identify the State Bar Lobbyist, and although no such position is included in the aforesaid official listing. The listing includes a Chief Communications Officer and Government Relations staffperson, Rick DeBruhl, but he is not a registered lobbyist. Concerning Arizona Bar lobbying, *see infra*.

[71]   *See* http://www.azbar.org/AboutUs/GovernmentRelations. As a perusal of this document shows, the State Bar of Arizona does not identify its lobbyist. *See infra*.

[72]   *See* http://azcapitoltimes.com/azlobbyists/lobbyists-directory/?bd_q=State+Bar+of+Arizona (last accessed 6/26/15).

has her own practice, while the first three individuals are members of a national firm employing 250 lawyers and "policy consultants" (lobbyists) headquartered in Denver, Colorado, and maintaining offices around the U.S.A., including in Washington, D.C., as well as a branch office in Phoenix, called Brownstein Hyatt Farber Schreck, LLP.

The Bar does not disclose how much it has been worth to the Bar's leadership, in terms of the dollar amount of members' impositions spent, to pay the three well-compensated Brownstein Hyatt lobbyists and their compatriot Ms. Stevens to influence policy in the Arizona Legislature.[73]

According to the latest available figures (the 2013 budget), the Arizona Bar annually spends about $6.6million on lawyer discipline. In fact, the Bar acknowledges that no other regulatory agency imposes a greater number of disciplinary sanctions on members than does the State Bar of Arizona: "No other state regulatory agency can compare to this level of scrutiny."[74] The Bar does not say why this is so. It does not admit that it overdoes discipline, frequently imposing discipline wrongfully, because it is greedy. Rather, the Arizona Bar seems to try to cast a different spin on its excesses. It seeks to persuade the public that it looks out for their interests better than the bar in any other state.

Yet at the time of this writing, the Arizona Bar does not disclose how many lawyers benefit by getting to charge and prosecute other lawyers. That is, the Arizona Bar does not disclose the number of persons employed as Staff Bar Counsel.

As of May, 2011, it was possible to use the Arizona Bar's website's "Find a Lawyer" function, searching by employer, to find the names of Staff Bar Counsel. According to the website of Arizona Attorneys Against Corrupt Professional Regulation, at that time, the number of Arizona Staff Bar Counsel was twenty—nearly three times the number of bar counsel employed by the state bar in the adjacent state of New Mexico. The AZAACPR website also reported, based on State Bar of Arizona employment advertisements, that Staff Bar Counsel

---

[73]   *See* the 2013 State Bar of Arizona budget *cited in* n. 48 *supra*. It includes no line item for expenses of lobbying.
[74]   *See* "HB2629 Attorney Licensing," *available at*: http://www.azbar.org/aboutus/leadership/boardofgovernors2014-2015/importantissues/hb2629attorneylicensing.

just starting out—in some instances, newly minted lawyers— were being offered $80,000 in annual salary. [75]

The State Bar of Arizona subsequently changed the format of its website's "Find a Lawyer" function with the result that, at the time of this writing, neither is it is possible to use that function to identify how many Staff Bar Counsel the Arizona Bar employs, nor does the Bar disclose to its membership any information about the size of the Staff Bar Counsel contingent, nor their identities (other than that of Chief Bar Counsel Maret Vessella), [76] nor about how much money all these staffers are earning.

Given the 2011 figures, it remains questionable that compared with the State Bar of Arizona, for the number of lawyers licensed in the state, any state bar at this time proportionately employs a larger number of Staff Bar Counsel. Yet because of the Bar's lack of transparency, this cannot be ascertained. What is certain is that there is no limit on the Bar's ability to hire more and more Staff Bar Counsel and for them to instigate more and more disciplinary charges against more and more lawyers, because the Bar has an unimpeded capacity to keep raising impositions on its members to pay for it all. There is simply no incentive to dial it down. Likewise, there is no accountability for the bloated disciplinary counsel bureaucracy; the Bar takes the position that it doesn't have to show the peons, its members, why it needs all those lawyers to whip them into line.

The same is true as regards the head of the Bar's disciplinary apparatus, the Presiding Disciplinary Judge. The Arizona government appoints the Justices of the state's Supreme Court, but their salaries derive from the Supreme Court's budget, for which the state legislature allocates the funding.

The Arizona Supreme Court has constituted an office of Presiding Disciplinary Judge pursuant to Rules of the Supreme Court of Arizona R. 46 (f) (19) "Jurisdiction in Discipline and Disability Matters; Definitions." This office was created, however, only as recently as 2010, when the Supreme Court was concerned about making a lavishly publicized show trial case of Andrew Thomas. Thomas, then Maricopa County

---

[75] *See* www.azaacpr.org, webpage "State Bar of Arizona: About" [2].

[76] *See* n. 70 *supra*.

41

Attorney, attempted to bring criminal charges against a number of public officials and judges; he was ultimately disbarred.[77] Afterwards, the Bar kept the PDJ on the payroll and the PDJ has been involved in every subsequent Bar formal disciplinary proceeding.

The Supreme Court of Arizona has diverged from the usual way in which judgeships arise in Arizona by its constituting the PDJ's office through a Rule of the Supreme Court of Arizona R. 46 (f) (19), and by its filling the office through another rule, R. 51 (a) "Presiding Disciplinary Judge." The latter rule authorizes the Supreme Court and only the Supreme Court to appoint an incumbent to the office of the Presiding Disciplinary Judge. These rules are a departure from the usual procedures whereby Arizona judicial offices are established and appointments are made to those offices. They suggest overreaching on the part of the Arizona Judicial Department.

Specifically, in the case of all other judgeships in the state, a different procedure occurs. Arizona courts of record (courts above the level of justice courts)[78] include superior courts. Their judges are either elected or, in the three largest counties, judges are nominated by a merit commission, then appointed by the state governor, and are subject to recall by the public in periodic elections. Appointments to the other courts of record—of judges to the Arizona Court of Appeals and of Justices to the Supreme Court of Arizona—are by the governor, again based on nominations of a selection commission.

In Arizona, except in instances where temporarily, a vacancy requires filling—and that, too, usually not in courts of record—no situation arises wherein a collection of judges gets together and establishes a judgeship, then coronates some individual of their choice to that judgeship. The conflict of interest implications are obvious.

---

[77]   Although as of the time of this writing, no book documenting *l'affaire Thomas* seems to have been published, numerous published news stories and essays on the subject are available. That being so, and the Thomas case being outside the scope of the present work, it will not be further discussed herein.

[78]   In Arizona, courts not of record include city courts, justice courts, and administrative tribunals, such as that of the Motor Vehicle Division.

Since its inception, the office of Arizona's PDJ has had one occupant, William J. O'Neil. Before he took office, volunteer hearing officers presided over disciplinary proceedings, which were convened subject to findings of a volunteer probable cause panelist, and the members of the Bar were obliged to pay nothing for their services.

But the PDJ is a different case. Unlike the Justices of the Supreme Court, who (along with all other employees and agencies of the Arizona Judicial Department) have to economize if the legislature freezes funding,[79] the PDJ's salary and job security is unaffected by legislative action. He is appointed by the Supreme Court, but he is paid out of the budget of the State Bar of Arizona—a separate budget funded by impositions on Bar members; a budget that does not depend on the legislature to fill its coffers, nor to fund its personnel and activities. The PDJ's 2010 starting salary was reported to be $145,000.[80]

In 2015, by comparison, the Arizona Supreme Court's Chief Justice is earning $160,000.[81] Each of these officials, in terms of earning capacity, has even the state governor beat,[82] let alone the state legislators.[83]

---

[79] The Supreme Court has been obliged, on occasion, to issue orders to its personnel to economize, e.g. Administrative Order No. 2009-69, dated June 30, 2009 (enumerating self-imposed economizing measures responsive to the state legislature's inaction to approve the judiciary's 2010 budget); *see* http://www.azcourts.gov/portals/22/admorder/orders09/2009-69.pdf. The State Bar's ability to hire Supreme Court-appointed PDJ William J. O'Neil at a salary of $145,000 in 2010 was not affected because the Bar's budget is separate and is unaffected by legislative considerations. *See* n. 58 *supra* and n. 80 *infra*.

[80] Ray Stern, "Pinal County Judge William O'Neil Becomes Arizona's First Presiding Disciplinary Judge," *Phoenix New Times*, September 14, 2010, *available at*: http://blogs.phoenixnewtimes.com/valleyfever/2010/09/pinal_coun ty_judge_william_one.php.

[81] *See* http://ballotpedia.org/Scott_Bales.

[82] The annual salary of the Governor of Arizona is $95,000. *See* http://ballotpedia.org/Arizona_state_government_salary.

[83] Salaries of Arizona legislators are limited to $24,000 per year plus *per diem*. *See* http://ballotpedia.org/Arizona_State_Legislature. They must furnish the easiest prey imaginable to the State Bar lobbyists discussed *supra*.

The PDJ's compensation only begins with his official salary, for he makes money off disciplinary cases by other means as well. For instance, onto a disciplinary order sanctioning a lawyer, he is free to tack on orders of additional exactions to compensate him—the PDJ—for having to show up for the lawyer's hearing.[84]

Also, it is routine for a PDJ order of sanctions to include an explicit option for Bar discipline to be extended indefinitely without requiring additional proceedings. In the case of a disciplinary order targeting a Bar member, the PDJ usually includes a clause allowing the period of the sanction to be extended at his, the PDJ's, discretion. Extending a sanction entails a likelihood of the Bar being able to charge additional fees, monies to enrich its personnel, including the PDJ.

Alternatively, in the case of new Bar members admitted conditional to forced mental treatment through the "Member Assistance Program," the "Therapeutic Contract," or written agreement to compulsory mental intervention, imposed as a condition for joining the Bar, has a provision that after the specified period of MAP discipline, the MAP regimen can continue at the whim of the Director of MAP.

Thus, whether the person is slapped with a "Therapeutic Contract" as an applicant or, after admission to the Bar, pursuant to a disciplinary order, the result is that the Bar member can be kept indefinitely under monitoring and observation and forced to attend "therapy" ... and can be forced to continue paying the Bar a monthly fee for "MAP administration."[85]

This practice has no parallel in non-administrative courts (e.g. criminal justice courts) in the 21st Century. It smacks of the old post-Civil War system that persisted for decades from the late 19th into the mid-20th Century in

---

[84] Various examples could be cited. For instance, in 2012, after hearing a disciplinary case PDJ-2011-9060, O'Neil sent the sanctioned lawyer a bill for his own "costs," or expenses that he supposedly incurred by adjudicating the case. *See* Appendix 6-13 *infra*. This case is further discussed in Ch. 6 "Attorney D" *infra*. No other judge in Arizona is permitted to charge parties to proceedings for his or her personal "costs" of doing the work (s)he is salaried to do.

[85] This is per sec. IV of the "Therapeutic Contract," *cited in* n. 54 *supra*.

Southern U.S. states, whereby citizens going about their business (usually Black males), upon an encounter with law enforcement, might be convicted of unsupported charges without benefit of counsel in kangaroo proceedings, then kept in indefinite involuntary servitude on farms, in factories and on chain gangs.[86]

At the time of this writing, besides his additional compensation, the PDJ may enjoy a salary greater than his 2010 starting salary of $145,000. However, one cannot say with certainty if that is so or not so. In fact, it is not possible to say not only what the PDJ earns, but it is also impossible to say what the Bar's CEO earns, what its General Counsel earns, what its disciplinary counsel (Staff Bar Counsel) earn, what members of its Board of Governors earn, what compensation is paid to Bar officials (such as the president of the Bar), what has been the salary history of its single most corrupt non-lawyer employee—the Director of the "Member Assistance Program"—and so on. All this is not possible because the Bar does not disclose its officials', employees,' or committee members' salaries. There is no line item in the Bar's annual budget to show what amount of compensation it pays out.

One 2015 source ascribes to the State Bar of Arizona's CEO, John F. Phelps, an annual "$180,412 reportable compensation from the organization plus $39,518 other compensation from the organization and related organizations," but does not provide a source for this data.[87] Official data that might verify or refute the stated figures is not to be had because of the Bar's lack of transparency about what it pays employees and other feeders at the trough.

The most concerning aspect of this situation is that the Bar members, who pay all the impositions necessary for what amounts to a gang of overseers, are not privy to any information. The State Bar of Arizona's CEO has publicly avowed that the Bar has no mission of advocacy on behalf of its members.[88]

---

[86]   Blackmon, SLAVERY BY ANOTHER NAME.

[87]   Rachel Alexander, "Exposing the Myth," n. 60 *supra*.

[88]   *See* n. 58 *supra*.

b.   Favoritism, Mismanagement and Lack of Transparency

This arena of State Bar of Arizona corruption is so prolific that one hardly knows where to begin. Below are summarized only a few prominent instances.

As a preliminary, serious State Bar corruption seems to have developed in the mid-2000's, starting about 2004. In 2004, the Bar began to employ as an employee (not as an independent contractor or non-lawyer volunteer) Howard Murray "Hal" Nevitt, a "therapist," to direct its "Member Assistance Program" (*see infra*); and John A. Furlong as its General Counsel and Deputy CEO.[89] Also in 2004, the Bar acquired its premises at 4201 N. 24th St., Phoenix (discussed in this chapter, i a *supra*). In 2009, the Board of Governors created the position of CEO of the State Bar of Arizona and hired lawyer John F. Phelps to fill it.[90] In 2009, moreover, prominent Arizona lawyers began to openly complain about Bar policies and fees (*see* n. 60 *supra*). In 2011, for the first (but not the last) time, the state agency that licenses "therapists" processed a complaint against the Director of the Bar's "Member Assistance Program." It sanctioned him for professional misconduct. (This will be discussed in Ch. 5 *infra*.) And in 2013, for the first (but not the last) time, state legislators deliberated on a bill intended to abolish the State Bar of Arizona. (*See* this chapter, ii e *infra*.)

1.   Misuse of the State Bar of Arizona Premises

John A. Furlong and John F. Phelps, the Bar's respective General Counsel and CEO, have allowed the Bar's premises to be misused in a manner reminiscent of a brothel and a party house.

---

[89]   *See,* respectively, www.azaacpr.org, webpage "SBA 'Member Assistance Program'" [7] *and* https://www.linkedin.com/pub/john-furlong/27/73a/717.

[90]   *See* Mike Sunnucks, "Profile: John Phelps, CEO State Bar of Arizona," *Phoenix Business Journal,* March 22, 2009, *available at*: http://www.bizjournals.com/phoenix/stories/2009/03/23/story14.h tml?page=all *and* Tim Eigo, "A New Bar Leader," *Arizona Attorney,* May 2009, pp. 16-20, *available at*: http://www.myazbar.org/ AZAttorney/PDF_Articles/0509JohnPhelps.pdf.

By "reminiscent of a brothel" is meant certain encounters at 4201 N. 24th St., Phoenix, of Howard Murray "Hal" Nevitt, Director of the Bar's "Member Assistance Program" (MAP), with various Bar members and applicants for membership. Since the Bar hired him as MAP Director in 2004, Nevitt has met alone behind closed doors at the Bar premises with a number of these individuals. In these encounters, Nevitt's purported purpose has been to do "therapy" on Bar members, or to do "initial therapeutic screening evaluations" of Bar applicants flagged by the Supreme Court's Committee on Character and Fitness.

The outcome of one such encounter on December 23, 2005, was a complaint (not the first complaint filed against Nevitt as MAP Director; for the first complaint, *see* this chapter, i b 2 *infra*). The complaint was filed with the agency that licenses Nevitt as a "therapist," the Arizona Board of Behavioral Health Examiners.

The complainant alleges that she was flagged for conditional admission and instructed to make an appointment to be "evaluated;" that Nevitt sent her a letter (*see* Appendix 6-5 *infra*) before the "evaluation," demanding an advance "evaluation" charge of $350, which she paid to the Bar; and that in the private meeting room on the Bar's premises where he directed her to go for "evaluation," Nevitt asked numerous questions having no conceivable relationship to fitness to practice law, including questions about her sexual history, habits and partners. The complainant further alleges that Nevitt assaulted her as she was trying to make her departure from the premises. The case, Arizona Board of Behavioral Health Examiners Disciplinary File No. 2013-0002,[91] is further discussed in Ch. 5 ii and in Ch. 6 "Attorney D" *infra*.

By "reminiscent of a party house" is meant Phelps' and Furlongs' treating the Bar premises as a place for the convenience and use of certain private law firms, as well as certain lawyers in private practice (not Bar-employed). The Bar has offered its premises as a gesture of favoritism to assist

---

[91]   *See* "Arizona Board of Behavioral Health Examiners Meeting Minutes December 5, 2013," *available at*: http://azbbhe.us/sites/default/files/agendas/December%205%20Min utes%20-%20Draft.pdf. The summary therein does not identify the nature of the allegations against Nevitt. *See also* www.azaacpr.org, webpage "SBA 'Member Assistance Program'" [1] paragraphs 12ff.

these firms and lawyers to succeed in their objectives in court actions *to which the Bar was not and is not a party.* In other words, the Bar's premises are not only used for Bar business, but for the business and pleasure of Phelps' and Furlongs' personal favorites among the Bar's members.

Here is one example. On May 27, 2009, to oblige a lawyer—Georgia A. Staton, Bar Member No. 004863, a partner at the large and influential Phoenix law firm Jones, Skelton & Hochuli, PLC—the two Johns—Phelps and Furlong—permitted the firm to hold a deposition at the Bar's premises.[92] The notice of deposition listing the Bar's address appears in Appendix 6-11 *infra.*

The State Bar was not a party to the litigation. The suit was by a lawyer, a former employee of an Arizona county, against the former employer. The Bar had no interest in the litigation; Bar discipline was not at issue in the litigation; and if a lawyer or law firm wants to examine the disciplinary records of opposing counsel or opposing lawyer-parties, it customarily merely asks for a certified copy of the record from the Bar's Disciplinary Records Manager, who is not hard to contact.

The May 27, 2009, deposition could have been held at a court reporter's offices, or at the Jones, Skelton premises. There was no cogent reason to hold it in the Bar's own premises. Nor is the Bar routinely in the business of turning over its physical premises to any member who wants space for its own purposes, such as a deposition.

Phelps and Furlong allowed this misuse of the Bar's premises to show their favoritism to a favored lawyer, Georgia Staton, and to the Jones, Skelton law firm of which she is a partner. And lawyer Staton wanted the Bar to host the deposition in an effort to humiliate and harass the lawyer-opponent, whose disciplinary history was not germane to the

---

[92]   *See* www.azaacpr.org, webpage "Inquisitional Discipline" [3] [c] [i] [II].

ongoing litigation; the deposition record was never furnished to the finder of fact.[93]

It is noteworthy that, while Staton arranged for but did not personally attend the deposition (she preferred to send a junior associate in her place), State Bar General Counsel Furlong personally attended. While in attendance, moreover, he ordered one of the Bar's staff, Disciplinary Records Manager Sandra M. Montoya,[94] to give testimony, although she had not been subpoenaed—and although Montoya is paid to maintain files and keep track of discipline-related correspondence, period.

This incident raises the question what else the Bar is allowing its premises to be used for by Phoenix law firms and their lawyers who maintain a cushy relationship with Bar officials like Phelps and Furlong—and what consideration Bar officials get from firms like Jones, Skelton in return.

While there are many other instances in which the Bar has allowed its premises to be misused (such as its misuse by a Bar employee misconducting himself with female Bar members, discussed *supra*), is hard to imagine a more blatant example of State Bar corruption than this one, wherein the Bar offered its premises and personnel to be misused in a matter having

---

[93]   If the Bar wishes to play favorites, lawyer Staton is a curious choice because she has been the subject of multiple Bar complaints. In each case, the evidence against her has been compelling. In Bar disciplinary File No. 06-0734, she was accused by the La Paz County, Arizona, Attorney, which she had served, of violating an ethics rule (ER 1.7 "Conflict of Interest: Current Clients") against attempting to represent both sides in a controversy. In File No. 09-2078, she was accused by the attorney-opponent (the one Staton had subpoenaed to appear at the Bar's premises for the May 27, 2009, deposition) of violating a statute, A.R.S. §33-420 "False Documents; Liability; Special Action; Damages; Violation; Classification," by recording a false lien on the attorney-opponent's *home*. The statute classifies the recording of a false lien as a misdemeanor. In each of these files, there was incontrovertible evidence that Staton had done exactly what she was accused of doing, and what is more, in neither instance did Staton even dispute the factual evidence. *See* n. 92 *supra; and see* Ch. 6 "Attorney D" *infra*. Immunity from complaints of Staff Bar Counsel being one of the advantages accorded to Arizona Bar pet attorneys, Staton has never been disciplined.

[94]   At the time of this writing, Montoya is still listed as Disciplinary Records Manager. *See* n. 70 *supra*.

nothing to do with Bar business. In this instance, Bar officials deviated from the policies whereby records are normally accessed, and did so by way of interfering in ongoing litigation, a form of obstruction of justice.

Phelps' and Furlong's role in the May 27, 2009, deposition incident smacks of racketeering. It is similar to the way the Bar interfered in ongoing litigation to silence counsel seeking redress for financially abused parties in the Arizona probate scandal discussed in Ch. 2 ii *supra*.

2.   Generous and Unusual Employee Perquisites

The Bar has been providing employees, and itself, with legal defense in official investigations and proceedings.

In 2010, a non-lawyer and one-time assistant to Howard Murray "Hal" Nevitt, Director of the Bar's "Member Assistance Program," complained against him to law enforcement and to the agency responsible for Nevitt's "therapist" licensing, the Arizona Board of Behavioral Health Examiners. The latter complaint, AZBBHE File No. 2011-0063, resulted in a sanction against Nevitt.[95] This case is also discussed in Ch. 5 ii *infra*.

For the time being, it may be noted that, according to the individual who lodged both the criminal and the administrative complaints, in the police investigation, Nevitt was represented by attorney John F. Lomax of the Phoenix office of the mammoth national law firm Snell & Wilmer, LLP. The complainant received correspondence dated November 30, 2011, from attorney Lomax on Snell & Wilmer stationery confirming that it was involved in the matter, although therein, the firm states that it was representing the *State Bar*. The correspondence appears in Appendix 3-1 *infra*.

In the administrative proceedings before the Board, an attorney Frederick Cummings of the influential Phoenix law

---

[95]   See www.azaacpr.org, webpage "SBA 'Member Assistance Program'" [1] paragraph 6 *and*
http://azbbhe.us/sites/default/files/adverse%20actions/2011advacti on.pdf [scroll to p. 29].

firm Jennings, Strouss & Salmon, PLC, represented Nevitt.[96] According to the complainant, attorney Lomax also showed up.

Arizona "therapists" who operate their own practices may purchase professional liability insurance, although the Board does not require it. It is possible that Nevitt had purchased such insurance for the advantage of having representation in disciplinary proceedings before the Board. However, it seems unlikely that any insurer whose premiums Nevitt paid out of his own pocket would have assigned him counsel from such a pricey firm as Jennings, Strouss. Therefore, whether Nevitt was insured or not, in all likelihood it was his employer, the Arizona Bar, that selected and provided counsel for Nevitt's administrative hearing. In addition, the Bar may have assumed the cost, either by paying directly out of its coffers for the representation, or by purchasing a high level of professional liability coverage for Nevitt. Either way, the Bar would have secretly used its funds—funds it obtains by impositions on its members—to defend an employee who had engaged in questionable activity.

Beyond any speculation is the fact the Bar also chose to protect *itself* against the possibility of *respondeat superior* liability by hiring outside counsel from Snell & Wilmer. Bar CEO John Phelps acknowledged that the Bar had retained Snell & Wilmer in a November 30, 2011, email to the complainant. This correspondence appears in Appendix 3-2 *infra*.

The expense for this, borne of course by the Bar's membership, was evidently perceived by the Bar leadership as justified. It made it possible for the Bar to keep the services of a worthless "therapist" who it relied on to further a scheme of "mental treatment"-related exactions upon rank and file members.

Another example of the Bar's unusual employee perquisites is a type of assistance it provides to individuals it has employed as Staff Bar Counsel: assistance in building their private practices once they leave Bar employment to engage in

---

[96]   *See* "Arizona Board of Behavioral Health Examiners Meeting Minutes November 3, 2011 Amended," *available at*: http://azbbhe.us/pdfs/minutes%20agendas/board%20nov%2011%20 min.pdf. For the roll call vote of the same date resulting in the sanction against Nevitt, *see* http://azbbhe.us/sites/default/files/agendas/11%2011%20Nevitt.pdf.

disciplinary defense. Most former Staff Bar Counsel launch this kind of practice.

Disciplinary defense lawyers are unique among lawyers in that their only clients are other lawyers. The Bar has been only too eager to help them find clients.

The Bar sends a notice to attorneys directing them to respond when it initiates a disciplinary investigation. (This process is discussed in detail in this chapter, iii *infra*.) Around 2007 or 2008, the Bar began accompanying such notices with an additional notice headed "AADC Arizona Association of Defense Counsel FREE CONSULTATION." This is not an offer to help the noticed attorney find representation. Also, despite its wording "FREE," it is not an offer of any monetary subsidy. Former Bar counsel who make their living off other lawyers by representing them in disciplinary matters charge, per hour of their time, $200, $250, $300 and more.

An attorney who responds to the solicitation does not get a list of all the Arizona attorneys who practice disciplinary defense. Instead, he or she receives the name of one or two lawyers—individuals who the Bar, with the cooperation of a separate organization, the Arizona Association of Defense Counsel, has decided to reward for prior service as Staff Bar Counsel by sending clients their way and helping them develop a disciplinary defense practice.

The conflict of interest implications of this are obvious, since a lawyer beholden to the Bar for his or her clients cannot possibly offer the client the loyalty, and the zealous representation *against* the Bar, that are the client's entitlement under the lawyer ethics rules.[97]

c.   Cheating in Bar Disciplinary Proceedings

The definition of a kangaroo court is a proceeding wherein the judge and/or the prosecuting counsel conduct themselves as if they cannot achieve a conviction without cheating—manipulating the proceedings unfairly to the disadvantage of a party.

The State Bar of Arizona's Presiding Disciplinary Judge, William J. O'Neil, with the connivance of the Supreme Court of Arizona, has repeatedly misconducted himself to the disadvantage of respondent lawyers in disciplinary proceedings by packing disciplinary panels with his cronies—O'Neil's personal friends and business associates.

In addition, State Bar of Arizona Staff Bar Counsel have cheated by bringing factually false allegations, by suborning

---

[97]   ER 1.3 "Diligence." For additional details about how the Arizona Bar promotes the careers of ex-Staff Bar Counsel, *see* www.azaacpr.org, webpage "Inquisitional Discipline" [3] [a]. The Arizona Attorneys Against Corrupt Professional Regulation website has aired comments by lawyers who have hired former Staff Bar Counsel to defend them in Bar disciplinary proceedings. The Arizona Bar treats its former Staff Bar Counsel as immune from discipline, a fact which may explain how poorly some of them have performed on behalf of their clients. According to one story on the website, Phoenix-area disciplinary defense counsel Karen Clark was so incompetent that she misspelled the client's name on documents she filed with the Bar. In addition, she and her partner, lawyer Ralph Adams, violated an ethical rule against overcharging, ER 1.5 "Fees," by generating documents not for filing—with neither forewarning nor the client's permission—while charging the client hundreds of dollars for the time spent in their preparation. According to other stories on the website, another Phoenix-area disciplinary defense counsel, Denise M. Quinterri, has been worse than hateful and abrasive with clients, going so far as to violate one of the ethics rules, ER 1.16 "Declining or Terminating Representation," by repeatedly threatening to abandon a client's case at crucial points in the representation, including by walking away from a disciplinary hearing informing the client that she would get a restraining order if the client contacted her with any questions after the hearing panel issued a decision. *See* www.azaacpr.org, webpage "Inquisitional Discipline" [3] [a] [B], [E]. *See also* Ch. 6 "Attorney B" *infra*.

perjury from the Bar's witnesses in disciplinary hearings, and by refusing or ignoring responses urging the Bar to correct the record.

Here are several instances.

1. Dishonesty in the Constituting of Disciplinary Panels

According to the Rules of the Supreme Court of Arizona R. 52 "Hearing Panels," in an attorney discipline hearing, the hearing panel consists of three members, including: the PDJ, who serves *ex officio*; an attorney selected from a "pool of volunteer attorney" prospects; and one non-attorney selected from a pool of volunteer "public members."[98]

Among the rules of the Supreme Court of Arizona is a R. 81 comprising the "Arizona Code of Judicial Conduct." Its various guidelines for judges are termed "canons." Canon 1 states: "A Judge Shall Uphold the Independence, Integrity, and Impartiality of the Judiciary, and Shall Avoid Impropriety and the Appearance of Impropriety."[99]

As regards hearing panels, R. 52 (a) states that the Supreme Court of Arizona, through its Chief Justice, organizes a pool of volunteer lawyers and lay people for service on disciplinary hearing panels. The rule does not explicitly enjoin the public member pool from including the PDJ's close associates. But it would stand to reason that for the PDJ to accompany himself on a hearing panel with a personal friend or business associate would be corrupt—just as it would be corrupt if a judge in a criminal court were to allow someone who functions as his outside business partner to serve on a jury. For the PDJ to do so would, in fact, violate Canon 1 by conveying an appearance of impropriety. It would also be a fraud on the public, since it would comprise a violation of due process in administrative proceedings—proceedings on which the public is entitled to rely for the integrity of the Arizona legal profession.

These things are exactly what Judge O'Neil—evidently with the acquiescence of the Supreme Court, which maintains the panelist pool—has repeatedly done. O'Neil has constituted lawyer discipline hearing panels on which the public member

---

[98]   Rules of the Supreme Court of Arizona R. 52 (a), (b).

[99]   Impropriety and the appearance of same are also enjoined in Canon 1, R. 1.2 "Promoting Confidence in the Judiciary."

turns out to be one of his neighbors, friends and/or business associates. At least two non-lawyer individuals have been misused as hearing panelists in this way.

One of the two is the late Robert M. Gallo of Casa Grande, Arizona (Judge O'Neil's home town). The Arizona Attorneys Against Corrupt Professional Regulation website has pointed out that in at least five disciplinary hearings convened between 2010 and 2012 (the disciplinary case numbers are PDJ-2012-9029; PDJ-2011-9084; PDJ-2011-9051; PDJ-2011-9060; and Bar disciplinary File No. 10-1167),[100] Gallo sat on the panel as the "public member," even though Maricopa County Recorder's records shows that the O'Neils and the Gallos were neighbors and, what is more, that William J. O'Neil and Robert M. Gallo had business dealings going back to the mid-1980's.[101]

Another but more concerning instance involves a Tempe, Arizona individual, a businessman (auto repair shop owner) named Mark Salem. Very sharp-eyed readers will notice that Salem was named to the Supreme Court of Arizona's "Committee on Improving Judicial Oversight and Processing of Probate Matters" (n. 29 *supra*). Salem has also been the "public member" panelist in at least nine disciplinary hearings convened in 2010-2013 (the disciplinary case numbers are PDJ-2010-6012; PDJ-2012-9104; PDJ-2012-9106; PDJ-2012-9018; PDJ-2012-9099; PDJ-2013-9011; PDJ-2013-9083; PDJ-2013-9113; and PDJ-2013-9005).[102]

In 2014, Salem, along with the well-known internet hosting conglomerate GoDaddy Operating Company, LLC, of Scottsdale, Arizona, was sued in Maricopa County Superior Court, case no. CV2014-009269, by a Pinal County man, Mark Dixon. Not a lawyer, Dixon has been embroiled since about 2009 in a controversy with Judge O'Neil, alleging that the latter

---

[100]   For cites to documents listing Gallo as the "public member" panelist in these disciplinary cases, *see* www.azaacpr.org, webpage "SBA 'Member Assistance Program'" [5] [a] paragraph 2.

[101]   *See* www.azaacpr.org, webpage "SBA 'Member Assistance Program'" [5] [a] paragraph 3, citing Fee Nos. 1984-021598; 1984-022904; and 1991-011335, Records of the Pinal County Recorder, *available at*: www.pinalcountyaz.gov/recorder/Pages/documentsearch.aspx.

[102]   For cites to documents listing Salem as the "public member" panelist in these disciplinary cases, *see* www.azaacpr.org, webpage "SBA 'Member Assistance Program'" [5] [a] paragraph 7.

has, to Dixon's disadvantage, engaged in unethical conduct in business and judicial matters.[103]

In his suit against Salem, Dixon alleged that as a favor to Judge O'Neil, Salem launched a website, www.pinaljustice.com, devoted more or less entirely to defaming Dixon. Although the website was taken down when Dixon filed suit, quite a few people who follow Arizona Bar issues saw it before it came down. The website called Dixon "a woman," "liar," "fat," "stupid," "ugly," "a--hole," and other endearments.[104] Salem's name did not appear on the website.

Dixon's counsel used a subpoena of GoDaddy records to produce evidence that the customer who purchased the website hosting, acting in his own name, was Mark Salem.

At the time of this writing, the case has been dismissed. It was not proven that Salem, in attacking Dixon, acted on Judge O'Neil's inducement. However, given Canon 1 of the Arizona Code of Judicial Conduct discussed *supra*, it is not in such terms that a judge can defend himself, since a judge is supposed to avoid even an *appearance* of impropriety.

But so are the Justices of the Arizona Supreme Court. What is a man of Salem's alleged character doing, not only serving on the disciplinary panels of its satellite, the State Bar, but also on an "Improving Probate Matters" committee appointed by the Supreme Court of Arizona, ostensibly for the purpose of *reforming* the courts?

It may be added that, in certain of his disciplinary orders, Judge O'Neil has evinced a lack of integrity by acting in a manner exceeding his authority.

---

[103]   *See* www.azaacpr.org, webpage "SBA 'Member Assistance Program'" [5] [a] paragraph 7 *citing, e.g.,* Dennis Wagner, "Divorce Case Stirs Ethics Allegations about Judge," *The Arizona Republic,* April 16, 2014, *available at:*
http://www.azcentral.com/story/news/politics/2014/04/16/divorce -case-stirs-ethics-allegations-judge/7765749/.

[104]   See Dennis Wagner, "Critic of Arizona Courts Claims Libel, Defamation in Suit," *The Arizona Republic,* March 10, 2015, *available at:* http://www.azcentral.com/story/news/local /pinal/2015/03/10/arizona-courts-critic-claims-libel-defemation/24704559/ *and American Post-Gazette,* "Bar Disciplinary Judge's Appointee Made Anonymous Website to Target Complainant," March 14, 2015, *available at:* http://sonoranalliance.com/2015/03/14/bar-disciplinary-judges-appointee-made-anonymous-website-to-target-complainant/.

To clarify this, consider as follows. Under Rules of the Supreme Court of Arizona R. 60 (a) "Disciplinary Sanctions," the forms of discipline that can be imposed in formal Bar proceedings are limited and enumerated. They consist of: disbarment, suspension, reprimand, admonition, probation, and (order to pay) restitution. Bar disciplinary panels are administrative tribunals, not courts. Accordingly, certain forms of punishment that can be ordered in courts, e.g. physical restraints and corporal punishment, both of which are sometimes ordered in criminal proceedings, are not part of the Bar's disciplinary armamentarium.

And yet there is a record of a Bar discipline case in which, on February 11, 2011, O'Neil ordered a lawyer alleged to have a substance problem to suffer physical confinement by the wearing of an "ankle bracelet."[105]

Can any instance be contemplated or cited in which an Arizona realtor, insurance agent or financial consultant—or any licensee of any professional licensing agency other than the State Bar of Arizona—has been subjected to physical restraints as a condition of licensure, or otherwise slapped with a sanction that exceeds the authority of the agency?

In another matter, PDJ-2011-9064, O'Neil ordered as follows: "The Map Director [Nevitt] will have discretion to reduce Respondent's probation to one year." Here, the judge deputizes a Bar functionary to determine the length of a sanction. This is like a criminal court judge leaving it up to the bailiff to decide how long of a term a convicted defendant must serve in prison. As one investigative source comments, "Would our readers care to hazard a guess as to the size of a wall large enough to have listed on it all the possibilities when it comes to the kind of leverage that Nevitt could exert over a Bar member to reduce a probationary term by a year?"[106]

---

[105]   See www.azaacpr.org, webpage "SBA 'Member Assistance Program'" [10] [iv], citing Bar disciplinary File No. 10-1167, "Report and Order Imposing Sanctions," p. 11: "Respondent shall wear an ankle bracelet until [date] if directed by the MAP Director." (Here, "MAP Director" references Howard Murray "Hal" Nevitt.)   A case summary   is   also   *available*   at: http://www.myazbar.org/AZAttorney/PDF_Articles/0112LawReg.pdf [*see* first page].

[106]   See www.azaacpr.org, webpage "SBA 'Member Assistance Program'" [1] paragraph 17.

Such rulings by Presiding Disciplinary Judge William J. O'Neil do not merely reflect on his lack of honesty but may also reflect on his quality of mentation.

2.   Dishonesty in Staff Bar Counsel Prosecutorial Tactics

Lest there be surprise taken in the revelations about Judge O'Neil of the previous section, or about the acts of dishonesty of Staff Bar Counsel to be revealed in this section, three things should be considered.

First, for every sanction arising out of a formal Bar disciplinary proceeding, there is a prescribed monetary fee that the Bar collects from the member or applicant. If it remains unpaid, the Supreme Court of Arizona records a judgment as a lien against the debtor (*see* this chapter, i a *supra*).

In the mid-2000's, such as in 2006, if an applicant were flagged as mentally ill, and if the applicant did not immediately abandon his or her Arizona Bar application (for which (s)he would have already paid a sizeable application fee), the individual was required, by the terms of the mid-2000's version of the MAP "Therapeutic Contract" (*see* n. 54 and accompanying text *supra*), to pay the Bar a $350 fee for "evaluation" by the MAP Director, Howard Murray "Hal" Nevitt. In addition, the Bar imposed a $50 per month fee for every month thereafter that the individual, after Bar admission, was still under MAP "supervision." Typically, MAP was initially imposed for twelve to twenty-four months, although the term could be indefinitely extended at the MAP Director's discretion (as discussed in n. 85 and accompanying text *supra*).

At the time of this writing, the Bar does not publish what it is currently charging for MAP-related impositions.

Of course, the preceding costs are exclusive of what the newly admitted member has to pay, or had to pay, for regular consultations with the MAP-approved therapist—who in many instances, has been Nevitt himself.

As regards disciplinary proceedings against already admitted Bar members, the Bar does publish a schedule of the charges for each category of discipline. The Bar takes a prescribed fee for each and every "order" imposing discipline if issued at the level of the Bar's "Probable Cause Committee" (about which *see* this chapter, iii *infra*) ($600); for each charge to which an attorney pleads to discipline by consent ($1200);

for the "costs" of any case not resolved by consent ($1200); for each hearing below the level of the Supreme Court ($4000); for a hearing on appeal before the Supreme Court ($6000); and, for the purported "costs" to the Bar (presumably, in the form of lost future impositions from the lawyer that it must forgo) if the attorney is disbarred, fees ranging from $1200 to $6000; etc. The preceding are only some of the fees on the schedule.[107]

All the above is exclusive of what the attorney has to pay in additional costs not on the official schedule. For instance, as noted in this chapter, i a *supra*, the PDJ may impose "costs" for his showing up to a disciplinary hearing; MAP can impose fees if the member is sentenced to MAP; etc.

Also additional to the preceding are legal fees if the member hires a disciplinary defense lawyer. Virtually all lawyers who practice disciplinary defense are former Staff Bar Counsel.

For more about costs to disciplined attorneys, *see* this chapter, iii *infra*.

The point is that the Arizona Bar has a financial incentive both to bring disciplinary complaints and to impose discipline. Correspondingly, there is a disincentive for the PDJ or for Staff Bar Counsel to treat fellow attorneys, fellow Bar members, with fairness and honesty.

Lest it be thought that lawyer discipline is not intended to enrich the more powerful side in the disciplinary contest, but to sting the wrongdoer sufficiently to induce improvement in behavior, it should be noted that no such objective as "rehabilitation" is enunciated in Arizona Bar disciplinary rulings. There are many orders of discipline with a recitation approximately as follows: "The objective of disciplinary proceedings is to protect the public, the profession and the administration of justice and to deter similar conduct by other

---

[107]   For the current version of the official schedule of disciplinary fees, *see* Supreme Court of Arizona Administrative Order No. 2011-17, *available at*: http://www.azbar.org/media/56131/ administrative%20order%202011-17%20re%20costs.pdf.

lawyers."[108] State Bar of Arizona disciplinary orders enunciate no objective of rehabilitating the lawyer.

Yet wiping out a lawyer financially does not teach the lawyer to do better. This should stand to reason. But in the public record one nevertheless finds, nauseatingly, a disciplinary case against an impecunious female solo practitioner who the Arizona Bar punished with an order to pay costs of additional proceedings because she was reduced to such poverty that she could not comply with the Bar's prior order of $225 in "Member Assistance Program" exactions.[109]

The second factor to consider is that all participants in Bar disciplinary proceedings (except the targeted member and his or her counsel, if any)—from the PDJ to the Staff Bar Counsel to any witness called by Staff Bar Counsel—have statutory immunity from being charged with any unethical act committed in connection with disciplinary proceedings, including (in the case of witnesses) lying on the witness stand, or (in the case of Staff Bar Counsel) suborning perjured testimony, or (in the case of the PDJ) packing the panel with fake "public member" panelists who turn out to be the judge's personal cronies. This immunity arises by Supreme Court rule.[110] The lawyer ethics rules are suspended in disciplinary proceedings for the people on the power-holders' side of the case. Thus for these players, including for Staff Bar Counsel, in disciplinary proceedings, there is no incentive not to cheat.

Not holding to account at all times, in all their capacities and activities, all lawyers, as having equal responsibility under the ethics rules, of course, is an Orwellian *Animal Farm* case of lawyers all being pigs and some pigs being more equal than others.

---

[108] More or less, this recitation appears in hundreds of Arizona lawyer disciplinary records. For one, *see* "Report and Order Imposing Sanctions," p. 14, *available at*: http://www.azcourts.gov/LinkClick.aspx?fileticket=bkV7nkO_GQM%3D&tabid=7230&mid=10550.

[109] *See* www.azaacpr.org, webpage "Inquisitional Discipline" [2] paragraph 13, *citing* http://www.azcourts.gov/Portals/36/2009_scanned/HO_Reports/SchafferHOrpt.pdf.

[110] Rules of the Supreme Court of Arizona R. 48 (l), (m) "Rules of Construction." R. 48 (l) exculpates (makes immune from civil action) witnesses for the Bar, including witnesses who happen to be Bar members. R. 48 (m) immunizes every participant on the Bar's side from investigation for unethical conduct.

Third, while the Bar has virtually unlimited resources to bring disciplinary actions against attorneys, defense resources are limited (as the Bar is well aware) because attorneys targeted for discipline, usually being solo practitioners (lawyers serving large influential firms are generally immune), do not have vast coffers to command. After a first disciplinary charge, if the member has been carrying professional liability insurance (the Arizona Bar does not require lawyers to carry it, but many members do), the insurer will cancel the policy and leave the defendant lawyer on his or her own. Then the lawyer cannot long financially withstand battery after battery after battery of proceedings, however ill-substantiated the disciplinary charges may be. (This is further discussed in this chapter, iii *infra*.) The Bar, for its part, due to immunity, does not have to observe any standard of integrity in charging members.

Here are two examples, among many that could be cited, of Arizona Staff Bar Counsel evincing dishonesty and unethical conduct in Bar discipline. Although examples with other Staff Bar Counsel could be cited, the following instances both happen to involve the same Senior Staff Bar Counsel. This individual, Craig D. Henley, began to serve the State Bar in 2011 and immediately displayed dishonest conduct in disciplinary proceedings. Both instances here recited also involve the same defendant attorney, whose history is further discussed in Ch. 6 "Attorney D" *infra*.

The first case is PDJ-2012-9039/Bar disciplinary File No. 11-1698. Henley filed a formal complaint charging the respondent attorney with unprofessional conduct for allegedly having overwhelmed a Superior Court judge with frivolous pleadings, citing about eight pleadings by name.

All but two of the cited pleadings had, in fact, been filed in the court by the *opposing counsel*, not by the attorney Henley was charging with misconduct. In fact, of the eight pleadings, four had been filed by the opposing counsel on the eve of a hearing (thereby angering the judge). As to the two listed pleadings for which the respondent attorney was responsible, neither had been filed on the eve of a hearing. Both had been filed to substantiate the reason for that attorney's requesting the hearing—a request that the judge had granted.

The respondent engaged disciplinary defense counsel who, in a written response, pointed out to Henley the error of his allegations and asked him to correct the record. Henley made no response to this and did not correct the record. Rather, he persisted in presenting the PDJ with untruthful allegations. The disciplined attorney was sentenced to suspension.[111]

Senior Staff Bar Counsel Henley seems to have thought that the Bar's side of this case was so insubstantial that he could not achieve a penalty against the victim without misrepresenting the factual basis of the charges to the Probable Cause Committee and the disciplinary tribunal. And Henley knew he could not be held to account for being untruthful because he has statutory immunity from being investigated for an ethics violation.

The second case is PDJ-2011-9060/Bar disciplinary File No. 10-0329. Here, Henley committed a highly unethical act of suborning perjury.

Henley called into the disciplinary hearing a witness favorable to the Bar, a lawyer who, five years earlier, had temporarily employed the respondent attorney for a period of about ten weeks. The witness lawyer's testimony was neither relevant to the complaint then being considered by the disciplinary tribunal nor was it relevant to any previous disciplinary matter before the tribunal. Nevertheless, PDJ O'Neil allowed the testimony.

The witness, lawyer Nina Lou Caples, of Sierra Vista, Arizona,[112] untruthfully testified that a certain former client of her practice, who she named (he may here be called "Mr. Sesile"), had expressed dissatisfaction with legal services rendered by the respondent. Unbeknownst to Caples, however, the respondent attorney had remained in occasional friendly contact with "Mr. Sesile" subsequent to leaving the Caples law office.

After the hearing, the disciplinary defense attorney secured an affidavit from "Mr. Sesile" wherein "Mr. Sesile" denied any dissatisfaction with the legal services the attorney in question had performed on behalf of the Caples law firm.

---

[111] This case has been alluded to in n. 36 *supra.* For more particulars, *see* www.azaapr.org, webpage "Inquisitional Discipline" [3] [b] [i]. *See also* Holly, AN INCONVENIENT OLD WOMAN.

[112] The peculiar personal and professional career of lawyer Nina L. Caples, a subject of multiple Bar complaints but never disciplined, is outlined in Appendix 7-1 *infra.*

The affidavit also specifically refuted the factual testimony Caples had offered in the hearing.

The defense counsel sent Henley an email attaching the affidavit. The counsel requested Henley to correct the record while the hearing panel was still considering the case. Henley refused to withdraw any part of Caples' testimony. His communications on the subject appear in Appendix 6-12 *infra*.[113] The disciplined attorney was sentenced to suspension.

Further details are provided in Ch. 6 "Attorney D" *infra*.

Henley may have felt no compunction based on respect for the ethics rules against suborning perjured testimony in proceedings and failing to correct a record earlier proffered, but now known to be untruthful,[114] because, again, he knew he could lie to the panel, and induce his witness, as well, to lie, with impunity from the lawyer ethics rules for both himself and his witness.

It deserves emphasis that, notwithstanding the Supreme Court's rules, the Bar is prone to forgo charging an attorney even when his or her offense is serious and, for that matter, even if there is an issue of criminal activity. An instance already cited is that of attorney Vernon Edward Peltz, convicted of DUI, yet never disciplined, alluded to in n. 26 *supra*. Another example is the case of Carmen Chenal and her lover, Arizona Attorney General Tom Horne, discussed in Ch. 2 i *supra*.

The Arizona Bar's disciplinary favoritism gives rise to a class of "untouchable" members of the Arizona Bar that includes judges (the State Bar of Arizona admits publicly that judges are immune from Bar discipline and says that, for this

---

[113] *See also* www.azaapr.org, webpage "Inquisitional Discipline" [3] [b] [iii].

[114] These are ethical violations under ER 8.4 "Misconduct," specifically 8.4 (c) "Conduct Involving Dishonesty, Fraud, Deceit, or Misrepresentation" and (d) "Conduct that is Prejudicial to the Administration of Justice."

reason, judges who are attorneys pay lesser Bar dues than do attorney Bar members);[115] politician-lawyers and their friends (as discussed in Ch. 2 ii *supra*); lawyers the Bar relies on or

---

[115]   The immunity of Bar members who are also judges is noted in "Dues Increase FAQ," *cited in* n. 59 *supra*. One example, among many that could be cited, of a judge who clearly has merited Bar discipline is erstwhile assistant judge (Commissioner) Lindsay Ellis, discussed in Ch. 2 ii *supra*. To cite another example: Santa Cruz County, Arizona, Superior Court Judge Ana Montoya-Paez has been a subject of repeated complaints to the State Bar of Arizona as well as to the Arizona Supreme Court's Commission on Judicial Conduct. In 2001, she was publicly accused of misusing her office for financial fraud. *See* Harold Kitching, "Complaint Unfounded, Montoya-Paez Responds," *Nogales International*, February 4, 2001, *available at*: http://www.nogalesinternational.com/complaint-unfounded-montoya-paez-responds/article_66ed34f3-fc1b-58f0-b433-a7fe6cd0f85b.html. And in 2011, she was cited by Nogales, Arizona, police for domestic violence; *see* Patti O'Berry, "Why is Judge Receiving Special Treatment?" [guest opinion], *Nogales International*, January 6, 2012, *available at*: http://www.nogalesinternational.com/opinion/guest_opinion/why-is-judge-receiving-special-treatment/article_6c1ee46e-387f-11e1-8420-001871e3ce6c.html; Virginia Jensen, "It's Appalling" [letter to editor], *Green Valley News and Sun,* January 10, 2012, *available at*: http://www.gvnews.com/opinion/letters_to_editor/it-s-appallilng/article_4d09bb5e-3bf8-11e1-b7f3-0019bb2963f4.html; "Judge Removes Herself from DV Case," *Nogales International*, September 30, 2011, *available at*: http://www.nogalesinternational.com/news/judge-removes-herself-from-dv-case/article_314593f2-eb76-11e0-85e7-001cc4c03286.html; *and* www.azaacpr.org, webpage "Inquisitional Discipline" [4] [x]. There is no record of any discipline against Judge Montoya-Paez. At the time of this writing, the State Bar of Arizona website's "Find a Lawyer" function states that she is still a judge of the Santa Cruz County Superior Court and that she remains a Bar member in good standing.

hopes to have testify on the Bar's behalf in disciplinary proceedings;[116] past and present Staff Bar Counsel; and anyone who serves or has served on a committee or other body established and constituted by the Supreme Court of Arizona.[117]

3.   The Arizona Bar Abuses Its Credibility with the Public

The Arizona Judicial Department publicly maintains that the State Bar of Arizona disciplines members for the public's protection: "The purpose of attorney discipline is to protect

---

[116]   In the hearing, discussed *supra*, wherein attorney Nina L. Caples gave perjured testimony for the Bar, Staff Bar Counsel Craig D. Henley also initially planned to call as a Bar witness attorney Leslie G. Spira, who had lately been terminated from a position as a Deputy County Attorney for Santa Cruz County, Arizona. *See* Ch. 6 "Attorney D" *and* n. 234 and accompanying text *infra*. Henley scuttled his plan when defense counsel informed Henley that Spira would be cross-examined before the hearing panel apropos of having come to the attention of Oro Valley, Arizona, law enforcement in a July 9, 2011, incident, which news reports suggested had occurred while Spira was intoxicated. Spira was charged with providing false information to police, impersonating a public servant, and other criminal offenses. Her matter, case no. M-1045-CR-201100305, was then pending in Oro Valley, Arizona, Municipal Court. Although the Bar decided it would be impolitic to put Spira on the stand, it evidently wanted to reciprocate for her willingness to serve. The Bar had previously investigated (but not disciplined) Spira for practicing law while on inactive member status. This time, acting on a complaint by a member of the public about the Oro Valley incident, the Bar again investigated Spira (Bar disciplinary File No. 07-0266). Eventually, the Bar sanctioned Spira—but it treated her to an essentially meaningless sanction, a reprimand. Thus the Bar forbore from formal disciplinary proceedings, and the PDJ ordered the Bar's mildest sanction, despite finding that Spira had engaged in illegal conduct. *See* www.azaacpr.org, webpage "Inquisitional Discipline" [3] [c] [iii]. At the time of this writing, Spira has no listing on the Arizona State Bar's "Find a Lawyer" website; while the Illinois Supreme Court Attorney Registration website "Find a Lawyer" Function (concurrently, Spira was a bar member in Illinois as well as in Arizona) lists her as "retired."

[117]   Regarding State Bar of Arizona "Pet Lawyers," *see* www.azaacpr.org, webpage "Inquisitional Discipline" [3].

the public ... ."[118] But if the true objective were the public's benefit, as opposed to the Judicial Department's benefit, it is hard to explain why the Arizona Supreme Court, the Bar, and Bar officials are untruthful with the public about lawyer discipline.

Supposedly, in 2012, the Bar removed its "Member Assistance Program" from actively managing the "therapy" of members and introduced in its place a national corporate player called "CorpCare." "CorpCare" is discussed further in Ch. 5 *infra*.

According to minutes of an August 1, 2014, State Bar of Arizona Board of Governors meeting, the Bar's Lawyer Assistance Programs Director Roberta Tepper told the Board the following about changes in the way in which disciplinary "therapy" was being imposed on Bar members.

> MAP was and still is administratively housed within the Lawyer Assistance Programs (LAP) of the State Bar. ... In October 2012, the assessment/therapeutic portion of MAP was outsourced to an employee assistance provider, CorpCare, on a contract basis for both voluntary and mandatory services. On February 1, 2014, the mandatory service portion of the CorpCare contract was discontinued. ... Members involved in discipline could use the service, **but were no longer ordered to do so**. ... CEO John Phelps decided not to renew the contract and discontinued funding.   [emphasis added]

The preceding is not from a private document but a published report.[119] Therefore, it reflects what the Bar wants not only members of the Board of Governors to think, but also, presumably, what it wants the public to think. The Bar wants the public (including federal authorities) to think that there is no longer any forced mental therapy requirement in attorney

[118]   Arizona Judicial Branch, "Attorney Discipline," *available at*: http://www.azcourts.gov/attorneydiscipline/Home.aspx.
[119]   "Meeting of the Board of Governors of the State Bar of Arizona August 1, 2014," p. 3452, *available at*: http://www.azbar.org/media/869045/080114_bog_meeting_minutes _v1.pdf.

discipline, and that the Presiding Disciplinary Judge would not order an unwilling Bar member to submit to "therapy."

But whether or not the Bar has continued in any sort of contract with "CorpCare," it has certainly continued imposing "therapy" on unwilling members, and its Presiding Disciplinary Judge is certainly continuing to issue orders to that effect.

After the Board of Governors meeting, on September 10, 2014, in a disciplinary case PDJ-2014-9044, State Bar of Arizona Presiding Disciplinary Judge William J. O'Neil issued a "Final Judgment and Order" that reveals the Bar's lack of candor about disciplinary policy.

According to the "Final Judgment and Order," the Bar member is being punished for not complying timely with a previous order to submit to a mental "evaluation" through the Bar's "Member Assistance Program" and for questioning the legitimacy of a "CorpCare" evaluation that, in the member's opinion, reflected coaching by Staff Bar Counsel. O'Neil orders the respondent member to comply with a program outlined in an attached document prepared by Staff Bar Counsel. The following is taken verbatim from the attached document. The document states that there was no issue of any client suffering a financial loss. ("Restitution is not an issue in this matter.")

> Respondent shall make and attend appointments with a health care professional for ongoing mental health counseling for anxiety, depression and substance abuse once a week for the duration of these terms. ... Respondent shall authorize and direct provider or any successor treating health care professional ... to provide a written progress report to the compliance monitor every ninety (90) days ... All medical [sic] except plain aspirin, acetaminophen or ibuprofen must be prescribed by a treating health care professional. Any over-the-counter medications other than those listed above must be specifically approved in advance by the treating health care professional. ... Respondent shall not ingest the following substances: a. Alcohol or foodstuffs or beverages or toiletries containing alcohol, including Nyquil [sic] or Purell type products; b. Foodstuffs containing poppy seeds; c. Foodstuffs containing hemp products; d. Herbal or health preparations

containing derivatives of controlled substances. ...
Respondent shall participate in random biological
fluid testing ... .

This is an obvious instance of Staff Bar Counsel and the
Presiding Disciplinary Judge trying to practice medicine. (On
unauthorized practice of medicine and Arizona law, see n. 57
supra.) Arizona public records associate with this respondent
no substance-related encounter with law enforcement.
Therefore, how would either Bar Counsel or the PDJ know that
an individual who had undergone no unbiased mental
assessment (no mental assessment other than by a Bar-
contracted entity, i.e. an organization in a retainer relationship
to the Bar) needs either "mental health counseling" or
treatment for "substance abuse?"

These medically unqualified people reveal themselves to
be not only disingenuous, and not only medically ignorant, but
downright dangerous. What is "plain aspirin?" Does the Bar
expect the respondent to avoid the flavored chewable variety?
Moreover, a qualified medical practitioner, if ordering a patient
to avoid a certain nighttime cold and flu medicine, would know
how the medicine's name is *spelled.*

The real reason the Bar went into such detail (and the
citation above is hardly representative, for the medical
directions in this document go on for pages and pages) was not
to show that the Presiding Disciplinary Judge and Staff Bar
Counsel are asinine and overbearing, of course. Rather, the
real reason for the detailed fake medical talk in this document
was to thoroughly, and very publicly, shame and embarrass the
respondent.

If nothing else in the PDJ-2014-9044 document
demonstrates how fraudulent the Bar's disciplinary practices
are, the following statement, which also appears in the above-
cited document, p. 11, proves it so:

For purposes of this agreement, the parties agree that
there was no actual harm to the profession.

Lest it be thought that in Arizona, for a lawyer to be
disciplined under such circumstances is odd, let it be said,
first, that there is nothing unique about the Bar imposing
heightened discipline on an attorney who has balked at one of

the Bar's and/or the PDJ's unlawful orders to submit to forced mental therapy through the "Member Assistance Program." For instance, in a case PDJ-2012-9094/Bar disciplinary File No. 11-2964, an attorney who had been sentenced to probation with MAP, and who then balked at the MAP requirement, was subjected to additional proceedings and slapped with a worse sentence of six months' and a day's suspension.[120]

Second, there is nothing unique about the State Bar of Arizona disciplining a lawyer where there is neither an issue of client harm nor harm to the legal profession. In one instance, PDJ-2012-9022/Bar disciplinary File No. 11-0688, a lawyer was suspended because a former landlord brought a civil suit against the lawyer on an allegation that the lawyer owed rent. At issue in that matter was not professional conduct, but the lawyer's personal business. A State Bar of Arizona report of the matter concedes, "The 30-day suspension was based on matters unrelated to the practice of law."[121]

Any Arizona lawyer is at risk of discipline merely because someone with whom the lawyer has had some personal business or interaction—or, perhaps, merely observes that the lawyer imbibed too much at a party—decides to contact the Bar. There is no financial incentive for the Bar to forbear.

Moreover, the Arizona Bar, aware that its disciplinary apparatus operates in a legally questionable manner, abuses the public's confidence in its integrity by denying that it is unlawfully forcing unwilling members into "therapy."

ii.   The Players External to the Bar

Certain organizations external to the State Bar of Arizona have an interest, express or implied, in the way

---

[120]   "PDJ-2012-9094 Report and Order Imposing Sanctions" is *available at*: http://www.azcourts.gov/LinkClick.aspx?fileticket= mWdsr2Z_Y90%3d&tabid=8924&portalid=101&mid=20052. The Bar standardly adds a day to a six month suspension because any suspension of six months or less does not require the sanctioned attorney to petition for reinstatement.
[121]   *See* www.azaacpr.org, webpage "Inquisitional Discipline" [4] [xiii], citing *Arizona Attorney*, July/August 2012, p. 64, *available at*: http://www.myazbar.org/AZAttorney/PDF_Articles/0712LawyerReg. pdf.

Arizona lawyer discipline is practiced.   The following are several such players.

a.   The American Bar Association

In respect of mental illness and presumptions of mental illness among lawyers, the ABA has encouraged state bars to engage in illegal conduct.

For U.S. lawyers, membership in the ABA is optional, but the organization influences how state bars operate. The ABA has sponsored the formulation of model rules on lawyer and judicial ethics that various state bars, including the State Bar of Arizona, use as a model for their own ethics rules.[122] The ABA also publishes Model Rules for Lawyer Disciplinary Enforcement, a collection of suggested rules for "discipline and disability proceedings."[123]

Some of these rules are objectionable and controversial. For instance, one model rule, ABA Model Code of Judicial Conduct Canon 2 R. 2.15, demands that judges report to the disciplinary section of the state bar any lawyer who the judge has seen fit to cite or penalize for some errant behavior in his or her court. The ABA has urged judges to adopt this practice, whether or not their state's version of the Code of Judicial Conduct follows the model rule.[124]

This model rule perverts the proper function of judges, turning them into stool pigeons for the state bar. The rule undermines the principal obligation of judges, that of fairness and impartiality in proceedings. A judge has the obligation to allow each side to present its case—a diminishing possibility when a lawyer has to worry continually that the judge may

---

[122]   *See* http://www.americanbar.org/groups/professional_res ponsibility/publications/model_rules_of_professional_conduct.html.
[123]   *See* American Bar Association "Standards for Imposing Lawyer Sanctions," *available at*:
http://www.americanbar.org/content/dam/aba/administrative/profe ssional_responsibility/corrected_standards_sanctions_may2012_wfo otnotes.authcheckdam.pdf.
[124]   *Id.*, Preface (A) "Background."

make an adverse report to the bar.[125] Judges have more than ample powers to maintain decorum in their courtrooms without rules tilting the power imbalance even more against attorneys, especially since in most states, judges, for good, bad, or no reason, rightly or frivolously, are free to penalize attorneys, while the attorney is precluded by the state's procedural rules from challenging a judge's sanction.[126]

State bars, of course, like the ABA's idea of judges being forced to act as their private police, because it makes it easier for them to raise revenues from lawyer discipline. And judges have no reason to dislike imposing sanctions on lawyers because to do so pecuniarily benefits the court. Thousands of examples could be cited of judges capriciously or wrongfully ordering sanctions, such as an incident when a judge, incensed

---

[125]   *See* Gerald F. Hess, "Rule 11 Practice in Federal and State Court: An Empirical, Comparative Study," 75 MARQUETTE LAW REV. 313 (1992), *available at*: http://scholarship.law.marquette.edu/cgi /viewcontent.cgi?article=1680&context=mulr.

[126]   The usual basis for a court-ordered sanction against an attorney is a rule of civil procedure called Rule 11. The Arizona version of this rule is *available at*: https://govt.westlaw.com/azrules/Document/ NCA759720717411DAA16E8D4AC7636430?viewType=FullText&orig inationContext=documenttoc&transitionType=CategoryPageItem&co ntextData=(sc.Default). It was a R. 11 sanction that the judge imposed on the attorney discussed in nn. 36 and 111 *supra*. Arizona's version of R. 11 does not include any recourse for sanctioned attorneys. A very few states' versions of this rule accord the sanctioned attorney a limited degree of recourse. For instance, in Arkansas and Utah, a judge contemplating imposing a R. 11 sanction on an attorney is required to first provide an opportunity for the attorney to show cause why the sanction is inappropriate. And in Delaware, the sanctioned attorney is automatically entitled to a hearing. *See, respectively,* https://courts.arkansas.gov/rules-and-administrative-orders/court-rules/rule-11-certification-parties-and-attorneys-frivolous; https://www.utcourts.gov/resources/rules/urcp/urcp011. html *and* Edward M. McNally, "Delaware Supreme Court Settles Attorney Sanctions Rules," *Delaware Business Litigation Report*, November 7, 2012, *available at*: http://www.delawarebusinesslitigation.com/2012/11/articles/case-summaries/delaware-supreme-court-settles-attorney-sanction-rules/.

over a cell phone ringing in the courtroom, sanctioned forty-six individuals.[127]

The point is that the ABA is not an association for lawyers but an association for bar associations. Were it concerned about advocating for lawyers, instead of encouraging judges to turn disciplinary enforcers, the ABA would advocate for all states to adopt version of R. 11 similar to those in Arkansas, Utah, or optimally, Delaware (*see* n. 126 *supra*).

The ABA has also promulgated a model rule on conditional admission. It was adopted by the ABA House of Delegates as recently as 2009, well after the passage of the Americans with Disabilities Act in 2001, as well as after the Act was amended in 2008.[128] A proposed version of the model rule from 2008 includes this preamble:[129]

> 1. Conditional Admission. An applicant who currently satisfies all essential eligibility requirements for admission to practice law, including fitness requirements, and who possesses the requisite good moral character required for admission, may be conditionally admitted to the practice of law if the applicant demonstrates recent rehabilitation from chemical dependency or successful treatment for mental or other illness, or from any other condition this Court deems appropriate, that has resulted in conduct or behavior that would otherwise have rendered the applicant currently unfit to practice law, and the conduct or

---

[127]   E. Leo Milonas and Frederick A. Brodie, "The Serious Business of Appealing a Sanctions Order," NY LAW J., August 26, 2013, *available at*: https://www.pillsburylaw.com/siteFiles/ Publications/Article20130826TheSeriousBusinessofAppealingaSanctionsOrder.pdf.

[128]   *See* American Bar Association, "Conditional Admission: Past, Present and Future," *available at*: http://www.americanbar. org/calendar/2014/05/40th-aba-national-conference-on-professional-responsibility/conferencematerials/session2.html.

[129]   *See* American Bar Association, "Model Rule on Conditional Admission to Practice Law February 2008," *available at*: http://www.americanbar.org/content/dam/aba/migrated/legalservic es/downloads/colap/ABAModelRule_ConditionalAdmission_Feb2008 .authcheckdam.pdf.

behavior, if it should recur, would impair the applicant's current ability to practice law or pose a threat to the public.

In 2014, the U.S. Department of Justice imposed a consent agreement on a state bar after an advocacy association complained of the bar's willful violation of the Americans with Disabilities Act. The organization argued that the bar was unlawfully imposing conditions on the admission of certain applicants only because of their past mental health diagnoses and/or treatment histories, although the applicants were otherwise qualified for admission—a violation of the ADA's protections. The DOJ action will be discussed in Ch. 4 *infra*. For now, the point is that the wording of the ABA Model Rule conflicts with the Justice Department's interpretation of federal law. It is an unlawful model rule.

One would think that logically, a national organization such as the American Bar Association, which is supposed to concern itself with justice, would have immediately withdrawn its model rule on conditional admission as soon as it became aware of the 2014 consent agreement. As of the time of this writing, however, the ABA has not withdrawn the rule. At its 2014 national conference, it has hosted a panel on conditional admission;[130] its journal has published a few articles about the

---

[130]   *See* n. 128 *supra and see* Elizabeth J. Cohen, "Many States Embrace Conditional Admission but Panelists Point Out Difficulties in Process," American Bar Association, June 2, 2014, *available at*: http://www.nobc.org/docs/news/Many-States-Embrace-Conditional-Admission.pdf.

consent agreement;[131] yet the ABA continues to operate a "Commission on Lawyer Assistance Programs" whose functions, it says, include to "support all bar associations ... in developing and maintaining methods of providing effective solutions for recovery."[132]

The ABA gives the impression of being an organization that, where federal law is concerned, just doesn't get it.

b.   The National Conference of Bar Examiners

This organization, among its other activities, is an outsourcing entity with which a state bar may contract to conduct its applicant character and fitness evaluations.[133] It thus has its own pecuniary interest in state bars' flagging candidates as unfit for unconditional admission. The U.S. Department of Justice has recently scrutinized this organization for Americans with Disabilities Act noncompliance. This is further discussed in Ch. 4 iii *infra*.

---

[131]   *E.g.,* Martha Neil, "DOJ Says Bar Officials Violate ADA by Asking Applicants Too Much about Their Mental Health," ABA J., February 12, 2014, *available at*:
http://www.abajournal.com/news/article/doj_says_bar_officials_viol ated_ada_by_asking_applicants_too_much_about_the/; Anna Stolley Persky, "State Bars May Probe Applicants' Behaviors, But Not Mental Health Status, Says DOJ," ABA J., June 1, 2014, *available at*:
http://www.abajournal.com/magazine/article/state_bars_may_probe _applicants_behavior_but_not_mental_health_status/; Martha Neil, "Louisiana Supreme Court Settles ADA probe by DOJ Over Mental-Health Queries on Bar Application," ABA J., August 18, 2014, *available at*: http://www.abajournal.com/news/article/ louisiana_settles_ada_probe_by_feds_over_mental-health_questions_on_bar_app; Martha Neil, "Report: DOJ Is Investigating Mental-Health Screening of Bar Applicants by Florida's Top Court," ABA J., March 26, 2015, *available at*:
http://www.abajournal.com/news/article/report_doj_is_investigatin g_mental_health_screening_of_bar_applicants_by_fl/.
[132]   *See* http://www.americanbar.org/groups/lawyer_assistance. html.
[133]   *See* http://www.ncbex.org/about/.

c.   Justices of the Supreme Court of Arizona

For the Arizona Bar's misconduct to have taken place over many years presupposes collusion by the Justices of the Supreme Court of Arizona, of which the Bar is legally defined as a satellite (*see* Ch. 1 *supra*). The wrongful act of former Chief Justice Rebecca White Berch, in reinstating an individual who was ineligible under the Supreme Court's own rules for Bar reinstatement, has been discussed in Ch. 2 i *infra*.

In lawyer admissions and discipline, the Justices have condoned an apparatus that disrespects federal law, state law, and the US Constitution. For instance, the Justices have turned a blind eye to the Bar taking on the role of medical provider by hiring a "therapist" as a member of its paid employee staff, in violation of state law and administrative rules; to the Bar's using this "therapist" in attorney admissions and discipline in violation of federal law (the ADA); and to the Bar's selecting as its employee-"therapist" an individual with a criminal (felony) record, Howard Murray "Hal" Nevitt (whose other distinguished credentials for Bar employment are further discussed in Ch. 5 *infra*).

A lawyer who was admitted conditionally in 2006, prior to agreeing to submit to forced mental treatment, consulted with former Arizona Supreme Court Chief Justice Stanley G. Feldman. Feldman had served on the Supreme Court for 21 years, including five years (1992-96) as Chief Justice. When the lawyer, having no prior mental history, questioned the wisdom of participating in her own libeling as a condition of joining the Bar, Feldman sent back a terse email advising her to do what the Bar required and get admitted posthaste.

Feldman's email is reproduced in Appendix 6-3 (*and see* Ch. 6 "Attorney D") *infra*). It evinces the refusal of Arizona Supreme Court Justices to take responsibility for overseeing an immoral and illegal admissions and disciplinary apparatus. After Feldman left off serving as Chief Justice in 1996, the Supreme Court of Arizona has been headed by several successor Chief Justices, none of whom have done anything to redress State Bar of Arizona lawyer discipline and admissions abuses.[134]

d.   Arizona Center on Disability Law

The lawyer whose conditional admission to the Arizona Bar was described two paragraphs *supra* (and whose Bar admission history is discussed more extensively in Ch. 6 "Attorney D" *infra*) contacted not only former Chief Justice Feldman to express misgivings about the conditions that the Bar was imposing on her admission, but also contacted the Arizona Center on Disability Law. Her issue was scrutinized by then staff-lawyer Jose de Jesus V. Rico ("J.J. Rico").

Rico himself is a licensed Arizona attorney. At the time of this writing, Rico is the organization's Executive Director.

The ACDL states that its mission is to provide protection and advocacy for persons with disabilities. A nonprofit, it receives funding from foundations and government grants.[135] The ACDL has pursued cases in court against governmental bodies that, it alleges, have failed to comply with the ADA.

When the Arizona lawyer, then an applicant for admission, and with no prior mental or substance abuse history, contacted the ACDL about the Bar's unlawful imposition of mental "treatment" as a condition for her licensure, she met with J.J. Rico. Initially, Rico seemed to think her issue had merit.

However, on June 13, 2006, Rico emailed saying that ACDL was refusing her matter. The lawyer had informed Rico that, while she would make a show of agreeing to conditional admission, she would not voluntarily cooperate by telling truthful things about herself to the "therapist" who the "Member Assistance Program" assigned for her to see during the first year of her bar membership. She invented fictitious parents, a fictitious place of upbringing, a fictitious educational history, fictitious marriages and divorces, fictitious employers

---

[134]   The recent Supreme Court of Arizona Chief Justices have been Stanley G. Feldman 1992-1997; Thomas A. Zlaket 1997-2002; Charles E. Jones 2002-2005; Ruth V. McGregor 2005-2009; Rebecca White Berch 2009-2014; W. Scott Bales 2014 to the time of this writing. At the time of this writing, it is speculated that Justice Berch may retire from the Court by or in 2016.

[135]   *See* http://www.acdl.com/history.html.

and bosses, etc., and for an entire year, she fed the "therapist" on these stories. She reasoned that the Bar had already made clear it would not keep confidential the fact of her conditional admission. Accordingly, there was no reason to believe it would keep confidential anything she told a "therapist"—whose "therapy" notes, under a bogus document the Bar required her to sign called a "Therapeutic Contract," automatically became State Bar—and thus, the government's—property.[136] She vowed to reveal nothing truthful about herself that she did not want to see printed on the front page of *The New York Times*.

In response, Rico refused ACDL's assistance on the stated ground that the victim would not cooperate by exposing herself to the probing of a government-supervised "therapist." Rico's email is reproduced in Appendix 6-4 *infra*.

Rico's grounds for refusing ACDL's assistance seem pretextual. It is nonsensical that, while conceding that the Bar was imposing an illegal condition on her admission by forcing her into "therapy," Rico nevertheless insisted that the lawyer cooperate by spilling her guts. Subsequent events have proven the correctness of this applicant's apprehensions. Arizona Attorneys Against Corrupt Professional Regulation has received reports from other Arizona lawyers forced into disciplinary "therapy," stating that the Bar's "Member Assistance Program" Director, Howard Murray "Hal" Nevitt, having undertaken personally to act as their "therapist," has conducted himself inappropriately. Correspondence from several of these individuals appears in Ch. 6 *infra*. It discloses that Nevitt, inquiring about their social contacts, has berated Caucasian lawyers for having friends of the Black race, and has interfered in some individuals' marriages by demanding either that they submit their spouses to his "therapy," or that they abandon their marriages and leave their spouses, or both.[137]

The lawyer who contacted Rico had very good justification to withhold her private thoughts, her social

---

[136]   The MAP "Therapeutic Contract" has been described in n. 54 and accompanying text *supra*. The Bar requires any "therapist" approved to "treat" a member to share with the Bar everything (s)he learns in the course of "therapy." On this point, the text of this document (*see* n. 54 for the cite) speaks for itself.

[137]   *See* www.azaacpr.org, webpage "SBA 'Member Assistance Program'" [1] paragraph 4 *and* [5] [b] paragraph 9. *See also* Ch. 6 "Attorney B," "Attorney C" *infra*.

contacts' identities, the essence of her personhood—to defend everything that Americans cherish as their privacy rights—from the Bar. This is further discussed in Ch. 6 "Attorney D" *infra*.

It makes no sense that Rico should have cared what the lawyer said to or concealed from a Bar-assigned "therapist." He was supposed to concern himself with the Bar's victimizing lawyers with illegal directives in violation of the ADA. It seems likely that Rico's true reason for refusing ACDL action was that he feared that, by fomenting legal action against the State Bar of Arizona, he would be risking his own Arizona Bar license.

e.   The Arizona Legislature

In 2013, an Arizona legislator, Representative John Allen, introduced a bill HB2480 in the Arizona Legislature. Its purport was to abolish mandatory membership in the State Bar of Arizona. The bill would have made it a direct responsibility of the Supreme Court of Arizona to license and discipline attorneys.[138] Reportedly, a motive for introducing the bill was to address a constitutional issue to the effect that mandatory Bar membership amounts to a tax on practicing a profession.[139] The bill did not pass.

To some readers, it may seem strange to contemplate a lawyers' bar not supervised by the state's supreme court. However, in several states, rather than the state judiciary, it is the legislature that regulates the attorneys' bar. Examples are

---

[138]   The text of HB2480 is *available at*: http://www.azleg.gov/legtext/51leg/1r/bills/hb2480p.pdf.

[139]   *See* Gary Grado, "Bill Would Ban Mandatory Membership in State Bar, But Support Lacking," *Arizona Capitol Times*, February 25, 2013, *available at*: http://roselawgroupreporter.com/2013/02/bills-would-ban-mandatory-membership-in-state-bar-but-support-lacking/. According to another source, the bill was prompted by legislative concern over "excessive discipline." *See* "Rep. Allen Proposes HB2480 to Eliminate Mandatory Bar Association," *American Post-Gazette*, March 10, 2013, *available at*: http://sonoranalliance.com/2013/03/10/rep-allen-proposes-hb2480-to-eliminate-mandatory-bar-association/. *See also* www.azaacpr.org, webpage "SBA 'Member Assistance Program'" [7] paragraph 10.

New York and North Carolina.[140]   Compared to the way that the Arizona Judicial Department has condoned corruption in the state bar, changing the Arizona system to a bar directly controlled by the state legislature might be the only way to restore some integrity. This was not, however, the objective of HB2480.

That said, had Rep. Allen's bill passed, while it would have put the Supreme Court directly on the hook for lawyer admissions and discipline, it still may have brought some measure of transparency and accountability to these functions. This is because, unlike the State Bar of Arizona (*see* this chapter, i a *supra*), the Supreme Court is taxpayer-funded— and, depending as it does on the state legislature's allocations to carry on its activities, in its lawyer admissions and discipline functions, the Court would have become answerable to the electorate.

To the Supreme Court of Arizona, this would have been a loss. Concealment and obfuscation in lawyer admissions and discipline is one thing the Court has achieved by instituting the Bar. Another thing the Court has done is gain for itself a satellite body over which the legislature has zero control thanks to an inexhaustible funding source: obligatory membership. The Bar acts as a hatchet man for the Court. HB2480 would have done away with the Bar by killing its funding source.

In 2015, several state legislators re-introduced essentially the same bill under the rubric HB2629.[141] On March

---

[140]   *See* www.azaacpr.org, webpage "State Bar of Arizona: About" [1] paragraph 2. In Oregon, initially, the Bar was established by the legislature, but has since become an appendage of the judiciary.

[141]   See "Nine Legislators Sponsor HB2629 to Reform the Arizona State Bar and Make it Voluntary," *The Stream*, February 10, 2015, *available at*:   http://www.icarizona.com/2015/02/nine-legislators-sponsor-hb2629-to.html.   *See also* two pieces that, by their own terms, were "provided [by an attorney] anonymously out of fear of retaliation by the state bar": "An Attorney Explains Why We Need HB2629 to Eliminate the Mandatory State Bar Association," *The Stream*, March 5, 2015, *available at*: http://www.icarizona.com/2015/03/an-attorney-explains-why-we-need-hb2629.html *and* "Refuting Myths: HB2629 to Eliminate the Mandatory State Bar Does Not Violate the Arizona Constitution," *The Stream*, March 6, 2015, *available at*: http://www.icarizona.com/2015/03/refuting-myths-hb2629-to-eliminate.html.

11, 2015, the bill failed to pass in the House of Representatives.[142] However, in the 2013 and 2015 failures of successive bills intended to abolish the State Bar, one sees a trend that suggests eventual re-introduction and passage. When HB2480 became a bill in 2013, Rep. Allen, who introduced it, did so alone; while in 2015, nine representatives joined together to introduce HB2629, either as sponsors or cosponsors.[143]

iii.   Arizona Bar Disciplinary Corruption's Costs

In Arizona, there are two points at which an individual can come under the scrutiny of the Bar's disciplinary apparatus. The first is when applying for Bar admission. Applicants are scrutinized in the offices of the Supreme Court of Arizona. Admission is conditioned on two factors. One is a showing of the requisite legal knowledge, usually demonstrated by passing the bar exam (administered by the Admissions Unit of the Certification and Licensing Committee of the Supreme Court of Arizona).

The other factor is screening by a group called the Committee on Character and Fitness. The Supreme Court appoints its approximately sixteen members. (Concerning the Committee's composition and current membership, *see* "Attorney Admissions," *cited in* n. 144 *infra*.)

This arrangement figures in the incestuous pattern (observed in this chapter, i a *supra*) whereby over and over, the same people's names recur as members of the State Bar's Board of Governors, as sometime officials of the State Bar, or as previous disciplinary counsel of the State Bar, such as disciplinary hearing officers or probable cause panelists ... and as members of committees, commissions, and task forces, such as the Committee on Character and Fitness. The Committee's members are largely lawyers, although the Court also appoints two non-lawyers who, again, are people well known to the

---

[142]   *See* n. 74 *supra*.

[143]   The nine HB2629 cosponsors are Arizona State Reps. John Allen, Mark Finchem, Anthony Kern, Jay Lawrence, Darin Mitchell, Warren Petersen, Kelly Townsend, and State Sens. Judy Burges and Kelli Ward. *Compare*
https://legiscan.com/AZ/sponsors/HB2480/2013 *and*
https://legiscan.com/AZ/sponsors/HB2629/2015.

Court and the Bar. Medical qualifications are not a factor in member selection; none of the Committee's current members has suitable medical qualifications to diagnose or evaluate mental or substance abuse impairment.

Membership applicants are required to submit a portion of the Bar application called the Character and Fitness portion. The Committee meets to examine this portion. It solicits detailed information about past residences, identities of neighbors in the vicinity of one's past residences, employment (even if temporary and/or part-time), contacts with the justice system and/or participation in legal action, and much more. Final-year law students at Arizona's two university law programs, the University of Arizona and Arizona State University, are counseled to expect to spend almost as much time preparing this application as studying for the bar exam.

The members of the Committee examine all Character and Fitness applications, then flag some applicants as lacking suitable character.[144] Since Howard Murray "Hal" Nevitt became "Member Assistance Program" Director in 2004, the post-flagging procedure has been as follows. Applicants receive

---

[144] One past President of the State Bar of Arizona, and (at the time of this writing) current Chair of the Committee on Character and Fitness (*see* "Attorney Admissions," *available at*: http://www.azcourts.gov/cld/AttorneyAdmissions.aspx), Phoenix lawyer Edward F. Novak, reportedly, has estimated that between 1999 and 2014, the Committee flagged some 214 individuals. *See* Cohen, "Many States," *cited in* n. 130 *supra.* Novak was at an ABA conference when he made this estimate, apparently speaking off the cuff. Whatever its accuracy, this figure would not take into account the hundreds (perhaps thousands) of admitted lawyers on whom the Arizona Bar has imposed forced mental treatment through its lawyer discipline apparatus (further discussed in this chapter *infra*). There is no way for the public to know how many individuals the Arizona Bar has consigned to its "Member Assistance Program" because the Bar does not make the information publicly available. The Bar has disclosed (*see* n. 58 *supra*) that in 2011, it subjected 483 members to formal disciplinary investigation and that the outcomes can be organized into several categories of sanctions; and it has disclosed (see n. 74 *supra*) that in 2013, it subjected 792 members to formal disciplinary investigation and that the outcomes, again, can be organized into several categories of sanctions; but among these categories, the Bar has not disclosed how many of the lawyers were sanctioned with forced mental intervention.

from the Committee a letter advising that their admission will be subject to additional scrutiny by the Bar's "Member Assistance Program" (MAP). The letter provides a phone number at the State Bar of Arizona and instructs the applicant to phone to make an appointment with the Director. The Committee gives the applicant no reason, ever, of the Committee's rationale for the flagging. The applicant is not entitled to a hearing. (This is discussed in n. 51 and accompanying text *supra*.) An applicant who admits to having been treated at any time for mental or substance abuse problems automatically gets flagged, but prior mental or substance treatment is not a factor in the background of many flagged applicants.

When the applicant phones for the appointment, the applicant receives forms requiring a signed consent enrolling him or her in the MAP Director's private "therapy" practice as a "patient." These forms, an accompanying letter from Nevitt advises, must be filled out, signed, and submitted *before* the "evaluation." Nevitt also demands an advance "evaluation" fee, to be paid to the Bar, of several hundred dollars.

The victim is then obliged to meet unsupervised with the Bar's "MAP" Director, Howard Murray "Hal" Nevitt, at the Bar's premises. No third person is present; the meeting occurs behind closed doors.

The meeting is an occasion for the applicant to be humiliated by Nevitt asking questions about many matters having no conceivable relationship to fitness to practice law, including questions about sexual orientation, sexual habits, sexual partners, and sexual preferences. One applicant complained to a state authority that at such a meeting, Nevitt sexually assaulted her; *see infra.*

After the "evaluation" meeting, Nevitt sends the victim a letter, curiously, stating no diagnosis. The letter, rather, directs him or her to visit a psychiatrist or psychologist, who must be approved in advance by Nevitt, for the purpose of *procuring* a diagnosis. Nevitt also sends the victim a copy of a document called a "Therapeutic Contract." By signing it, the victim gives away his or her privilege of confidentiality regarding anything (s)he tells the psychiatrist or psychologist; everything that becomes part of the "therapy" record can be shared with the Bar. In addition, the "Therapeutic Contract" forces the individual to agree to see a "therapist" of Nevitt's choice (or if the victim has the misfortune to have a Phoenix-area address, the victim usually has to agree to accept *Nevitt* as the "therapist"), typically for twelve to twenty-four months, and to pay fees to MAP for "supervising" the "therapy." By signing the "Therapeutic Contract," the victim agrees to "therapy" before there is even any mental illness diagnosis.

A more detailed summary of how this forced-mental-treatment scheme works (including the text of a standard "Therapeutic Contract") is available online.[145]

The other point at which an Arizona lawyer may be forced into disciplinary mental treatment is after admission, upon the Bar's bringing some disciplinary charge against the member. The State Bar of Arizona has a cadre of Staff Bar Counsel alluded to in this chapter, i a *supra*. When one of these anticipates making a charge (or in the Bar's terminology, bringing a "complaint" against) a Bar member, the counsel need not act upon anyone's adverse report, but can initiate the process *sua sponte*—and may, but need not inform the member of the source of the allegations, even if indeed, someone has contacted the Bar to raise them.

In the letter, Staff Bar Counsel may state what alleged acts or omissions on the member's part occasion the investigation. Oftentimes, however—in violation of due process—Staff Bar Counsel does not even bother to list the factual basis of the allegations. Such a communication provides to the recipient no idea what he or she is accused of doing or not doing. *See* Ch. 6, "Lawyer D" *infra* for an example.

Usually, although not necessarily (e.g., not, typically, in cases of interim suspension), even if withholding the factual basis for the allegations, the letter will cite one or more of the lawyer ethics rules in the Rules of the Supreme Court of Arizona R. 42 "Arizona Rules of Professional Conduct," and may also allude to other rules. A common example is R. 41 "Duties and Obligations of Members," among whose provisions is a requirement that an attorney abstain from "engaging in unprofessional conduct" (R. 41 [g])—a term that the rule does not define, but which makes a dandy pretext for a Bar charge.

After the target responds (the Bar allows a minimum time, a few days, for a response), Staff Bar Counsel submits the matter to a committee appointed by the Chief Justice of the

---

[145]   *See* www.azaacpr.org, webpage "SBA 'Member Assistance Program'" [5] [b], [9]. *See also* nn. 54, 85 *supra*.

Supreme Court of Arizona, the "Probable Cause Committee," composed (per Rules of the Supreme Court of Arizona R. 50 "Attorney Discipline Probable Cause Committee") of three "public members" and half-dozen lawyers; all individuals trusted by the Supreme Court. This Committee meets in secret at monthly intervals. Its purpose is to provide an imprimatur of legitimacy to whatever Staff Bar Counsel wants to do. After the Committee considers the matter, the Bar may or may not proceed further. If it does proceed, the matter becomes what the Bar calls a "complaint."[146]

Rules of the Supreme Court of Arizona R. 57 "Special Discipline Proceedings" authorizes Staff Bar Counsel to resolve charges without a hearing ("discipline by consent," aka "informal proceedings" or, in plain English, a plea agreement). In that case, Staff Bar Counsel gets the Presiding Disciplinary Judge to sign an order of whatever sanction the Bar gets the attorney to agree to. The PDJ's order may include requiring the charged attorney to undergo "mental treatment" under the supervision of MAP, even if (as is typical) the Bar presents no evidence that the attorney has a mental or substance problem, *and* even if the attorney, in responding to the Bar's allegations, has not put his or her own mental status at issue by attributing some undesirable conduct to a mental or substance problem.

If Staff Bar Counsel does not offer a plea deal (and this is entirely up to the counsel's discretion), or offers one and the respondent attorney resists the pressure to plead out, then the matter, prior to 2010, would have been reviewed by a lawyer who some supervisory official in the Bar would assign to the case as a hearing panelist. Since 2010, however, the matter is assigned to an official who is employed and paid by the Bar, called the Presiding Disciplinary Judge. At the time of this writing, one individual has occupied this office, William J. O'Neil, as discussed in this chapter, i a *supra.*

If there is no plea agreement, the matter becomes "formal," pursuant to Rules of the Supreme Court of Arizona,

---

[146] Regarding the composition and functions of the "Probable Cause Committee" *see* https://www.azcourts.gov/attorneydiscipline/ AttorneyDisciplineProbableCauseCommittee.aspx *and* https://www.azcourts.gov/Portals/36/ADPCC/Rule%2050.pdf. Concerning the practices of Staff Bar Counsel in charging Arizona Bar members with disciplinary infractions, *see* www.azaacpr.org, webpage "Inquisitional Discipline" [1].

Rs. 47 "General Procedural Matters" and 58 "Formal Proceedings," and the PDJ convenes a hearing.[147] The PDJ secures the presence of one lawyer panelist and one non-lawyer panelist who join him on the decision-making panel.

Following the hearing, if the proceedings are formal, or following receipt of the report of Staff Bar Counsel if the proceedings are informal ("discipline by consent"), the PDJ takes a decision, usually identical to whatever the Bar has recommended, and issues a formal order of discipline. As stated *supra*, this order may include a period of "Member Assistance Program" (MAP) forced mental intervention.

In ordering discipline, although he generally follows the Bar's recommendations, the Presiding Disciplinary Judge acts upon his own discretion. To order "Member Assistance Program" intervention, the PDJ does not require the Bar to present any evidence that the disciplined member has a mental or substance problem. In fact, it is far from unusual that the Bar has presented no such evidence prior to the PDJ's imposition of this sanction.

Nor is it necessary that the disciplined attorney have put his or her own mental status at issue by presenting a mind science professional's report to impute some misconduct to forces beyond the attorney's control. In the majority of cases, it is entirely at the PDJ's whim that he decides to adjudicate a Bar member as mentally ill and in need of "Member Assistance Program" intervention and issues a disciplinary order accordingly. More details are available online.[148]

An attorney who objects, e.g. on the obvious grounds that PDJ O'Neil does not have the professional credentials to assign an attorney a diagnosis of mental illness (and thus the PDJ, in violation of Arizona statutory and administrative law, is practicing medicine without authorization), is subject to discipline, up to and including disbarment, for disobeying a

---

[147]   Thus the disciplinary process differs for applicants and members; a Bar member, when a matter is not resolved by consent, is entitled to a hearing, whereas a Bar applicant who is forced into mental intervention through the "Member Assistance Program" under an order of conditional admission is not entitled to a hearing. This has been pointed out in Chs. 1 and 3 (*see* n. 51 and accompanying text) *supra*.

[148]   *See* www.azaacpr.org, webpage "SBA 'Member Assistance Program'" [5] [a].

judicial order. Some examples are presented in this chapter, i c 3 *supra.*

A number of individuals parasitically benefit from the State Bar of Arizona forcing Bar applicants into "mental treatment." One class of these consists of lawyers who agree to take on the role of "practice monitor" or "therapy monitor" when, unlawfully, the Bar subjects an applicant to conditional admission and the applicant consents to see a "therapist" for a period, typically for one to two years, after Bar admission. Although these "monitor" lawyers are not usually monetarily compensated, generally they are able to claim Continuing Legal Education credit and, thus, are able to meet the Bar's annual Continuing Legal Education requirement while minimizing the cost of buying CLE instructional materials or paying to attend Bar-sponsored CLE events.

Most lawyers who agree to participate in these activities are trying to curry the Bar's favor. However, being lawyers, they are able to acquaint themselves with the requirements of the Americans With Disabilities Act and therefore, they have no excuse for colluding in the Bar's illegal conduct. Some examples of Arizona attorneys who, in this way, have collaborated in the Bar's unlawful treatment of fellow attorneys are David P. Braun of Casa Grande, Arizona, and Eric E. Button of Tucson.

Aside from lawyers who curry the Bar's favor as "monitors" of other lawyers, some employees of the two public Arizona law schools at Tucson (University of Arizona James E. Rogers College of Law) and Tempe (Arizona State University Sandra Day O'Connor College of Law) have curried favor with the Arizona Judicial Department by reporting to members of the Committee on Character and Fitness and to the Bar, identifying law students they contemplate to be future potential fodder for MAP. For instance, in the mid-2000's, among the former's law students, it was notorious that the Committee and the Bar were receiving reports singling out individual students from the two administrators of the Career Services office, as well as from some faculty members.[149]

---

[149]   Although both administrators just alluded to were Bar members, staff, administration and faculty of Arizona's public law colleges need not belong to the Bar. This is because, assuming they confine their professional activities to their school duties, such activities are not considered practice of law.

Another class of parasitic beneficiaries of the Bar's illegal mental treatment policy includes various persons who hold themselves out as experts in "forensic psychiatry" or "forensic psychology." Several Phoenix-area mind science practitioners have listed themselves with the Arizona Bar as available to testify or act as expert witnesses against Bar applicants or lawyers. Examples are psychologist Erin Nelson, Ph.D., of Scottsdale, Arizona; Emergency Medicine physician and "Addiction Medicine" practitioner Michel A. Sucher, M.D., also of Scottsdale;[150] and psychiatrist Elizabeth Kohlhepp, M.D., again of Scottsdale.

Also to be mentioned are "master's-level therapists," psychologists, and psychiatrists who agree to participate in Bar-mandated "therapy." They impose fees for their professional services on Bar members forced into "treatment" under the "Member Assistance Program."

Some of these practitioners prosper as well thanks to the legal system. They are available as court-appointed treatment consultants for individuals on whom a court of law imposes an order of mental intervention.[151] However, absent the scenario in which a defendant comes under a court order, when an individual is made to suffer economically or put in fear of economic hardship as inducement to submit to "therapy" that he or she would otherwise not voluntarily undergo, there is both a legal and an ethical issue.

Some employers, as a condition of letting an employee keep his or her job, target particular employees and demand that they participate in their own libeling, requiring them to submit to mental intervention as a condition of employment. There are mind science practitioners who make a good living from this. An example is a two-man firm of which one partner is the aforesaid Michel A. Sucher and the other is David G. Greenberg, M.D., who like Sucher, is not trained as a

---

[150]   See http://www.greenbergandsucher.com/bios.html.   Dr. Sucher's role in the career of the Arizona Bar's "Member Assistance Program" Director Howard Murray "Hal" Nevitt is discussed in Ch. 5 i, ii *infra.*

[151]   On court-ordered mental intervention, *see* Ch. 4 i *infra.* For a study of harm to the justice system by mind science practitioners who earn their livelihood by offering questionable courtroom expert witness testimony, see Margaret A. Hagen, Ph.D., WHORES OF THE COURT, ReganBooks (1997).

psychiatrist, but has a "certification" in Addiction Medicine. Their Scottsdale, Arizona, firm, Greenberg & Sucher, P.C.,[152] holds itself out as available to oblige employers when they want to force some employee into "therapy."

As stated *supra*, this implicates two issues. The legal issue (the ethical issue will be taken up momentarily) is that, when an employer is making mental treatment a condition of the employee's job, Title I of the Americans with Disabilities Act comes into play. Title I is the employment title of the ADA. It limits the impunity of employers to stigmatize employees who may have, or who the employer treats as having, a disability, whether mental or physical. The present work takes the position that mind science practitioners who, like Greenberg and Sucher, advertise their well-compensated services by way of holding themselves out as prospective collaborators in forcing individuals into therapy who, absent economic need or other non-court-ordered coercion, would otherwise not undertake it, are probably engaging in activity prohibited under the ADA.

That said, it is the position of the present work that a worse type of whoring[153] is evinced by the aforementioned social workers ("master's-level therapists"), psychologists, and psychiatrists who agree to participate in the forced "therapy" of Arizona Bar applicants and members. An applicant may be ordered to undergo the ministrations of the Bar's "Member Assistance Program" to join the Bar, or the Presiding Disciplinary Judge may order a member to undergo "MAP;" the process is described *supra*. In either case, if the victim resides in Maricopa County, MAP Director Howard Murray "Hal" Nevitt may select himself (and in that case, he demands monetary charges from the victim) to provide the "therapy." If he does not provide it, then he gets to approve which "therapist" other than himself provides it. In either case, the victim has to sign an agreement that anything he or she tells the therapist can be reported to government officials.

Under these conditions, it would be only a lawyer who truly is out of his or her mind who would say anything in "therapy" that he or she would not readily tell government

---

152   *See* n. 150 *supra*.
153   For arguments that mind science professionals seek out opportunities to offer testimony as a form of well-compensated academic whoring, *see* Hagen, WHORES, n. 151 *supra*.

agents.[154] For his or her part, the cooperating "therapist" signs a document agreeing to make reports on the "therapy" sessions to the government (the Bar).

The ethical issue, then, is this: although "therapists" who take on these Bar-related jobs for hire are not lawyers, they are responsible for upholding such ethics as may be ascribed to the mind science professions. (This is further discussed in Ch. 4 *infra*.) They should be aware that their professional prerogatives are constrained by the Arizona Constitution's guarantee of an individual right of privacy against governmental intrusion, and by the Americans with Disabilities Act, which makes it an actionable offense to collaborate in the stigmatizing of an individual who is otherwise qualified for professional licensure.

A court-ordered treatment regimen would be an exception; a therapist can impose himself or herself on an unwilling criminal under the terms of a judgment and conviction. But mental treatment imposed by a professional licensing body on a shamed and frightened individual, threatened with loss of livelihood, is not an exception to the protections of the Arizona Constitution and the ADA. (This is discussed further in Ch. 4 *infra*.)

The position of the Arizona Bar victim is especially miserable not only because, in most cases, the individual cannot readily afford the multiple costs of MAP. Typically, he or she is of limited financial means, does not work for a large law firm, and may be carrying massive educational debt for his or her legal training. In addition to that, the Bar victim is usually intimidated and afraid to appear oppositional because the Bar can, if it chooses, defame the victim.

As can be inferred from disciplinary case citations in footnotes herein, the Bar often publishes its version of disciplinary cases online, in its magazine *Arizona Attorney*, and in press releases. This occurs pursuant to one of the Rules of the Supreme Court of Arizona, R. 49 (a) (2) (C) "Bar Counsel." There is no even contest in the battle for reputation because the individual can never command a publicity apparatus as powerful as that available to the Arizona Bar. Members and applicants capitulate and are afraid to defend themselves because they are aware that the Bar can assumes the privilege,

---

[154] *See* this chapter, ii d *supra and see* Ch. 6 "Attorney D" *infra*.

if it so chooses, to triumphantly announce far and wide that it has found another rotten lawyer from whom it is pleased to protect the public.

Therapists who participate in the Arizona Bar's forced mental treatment scheme are initially approached by the stigmatized applicant or lawyer with an account of the "treatment" regimen that the Bar is demanding. On first hearing, any listener, even one who is no expert in the ADA, can tell that the entire setup smells odd and unusual. Those therapists who, notwithstanding, accept victims' money for participating in Bar-ordered discipline are unethical. They should know better than to enrich themselves in furtherance of the Bar's violations of federal law, state law, the Arizona Constitution, and the US Constitution, and they should be professionally disciplined for participating in these violations.

With the above preliminaries, one may consider what costs are borne by a lawyer who starts out a legal career being flagged for conditional admission under the "Member Assistance Program." The first costs to be considered are the less important—the dollar costs.

Once the lawyer submits to MAP, that fact is cited as an aggravating factor in each subsequent disciplinary proceeding. Moreover, each subsequent disciplinary proceeding cites as aggravating factors all previous disciplinary orders, including an initial conditional admission. The imposition of sanctions in a Bar disciplinary order tends to read like a recital of the familiar "Old MacDonald Had a Farm" nursery song.

Suppose an Arizona lawyer were disciplined over the entire course of his or her legal career. Such cases have occurred; see Ch. 6 "Attorney D" *infra*. Suppose in the mid-2000's, a lawyer applying for Bar membership was flagged and subjected to MAP, and the MAP was then used as a ground for a subsequent disciplinary charge resulting in probation, and the MAP and the probation were then used as a ground for a subsequent disciplinary charge resulting in suspension, and the MAP and the probation and the suspension were then used as a ground for a subsequent disciplinary charge resulting in extended suspension, and the MAP and the probation and the suspensions were then used as a ground for a subsequent disciplinary charge resulting in disbarment, and suppose if only one of these proceedings was a formal proceeding and the others were resolved by consent—then over a legal career spanning about a half-dozen years, the individual might have such monetary costs as the following.

For the initial admission conditional to MAP, if the "supervision" of the member's "therapy" is for the minimum period of twelve months, and is not extended, then the member is out $350 for Nevitt's "evaluation" fee. Also, as long as the member is subject to MAP, (s)he pays at least $50 per month to the Bar for "supervision," totaling $600 for the year. (Separately, (s)he may pay anywhere from $240 to $2400 for one year's monthly or biweekly private services of either Nevitt or some other "therapist.")

For the probation and for the next two proceedings resulting in suspension, and for the disbarment, the member is charged fees per the official schedule (*see* n. 107 *supra*). The member is out some $1200 for each order of discipline for the two of the three matters resolved by consent, for a total of $2400; as well as the Bar fee of $4000 for the one matter which results in formal proceedings (a hearing). As a result of the hearing, the member may also pay up to an additional several hundred or several thousands of dollars in PDJ "costs." The $4000 fee for a formal matter (the matter adjudicated in a hearing) becomes a $6000 fee for an appellate hearing if the member appeals to the Arizona Supreme Court. Lastly, there is a fee—at a minimum $1200, or in many instances, higher—for the privilege of disbarment if the member consents to disbarment; a larger fee if the lawyer does not consent and insists on proceedings. The grand total for Bar-imposed fees and costs may be $15,000, $16,000, or higher.

As this shows, if the Bar pursues some one attorney in proceeding after proceeding, all the way to disbarment, the Bar gains far, far *more* in exactions than it can make off that lawyer over 25+ years of membership, assuming an annual member fee of about $500.

In addition, discipline implies other dollar costs. For withdrawal from its contract by any professional liability insurer the lawyer has engaged, the lawyer loses several thousand dollars in already-paid premiums.

For years of subjection to MAP, the lawyer may be out many thousands of dollars for "therapy."

For paying defense counsel for representation in the one

probation matter, the two suspension matters, and the disbarment, the lawyer may be out $100,000 or more.[155]

For loss of years of earning capacity due to barrage after barrage of suspensions and other sanctions, the lawyer may suffer to the tune of a half-million dollars.

All this for seeking a license to practice a profession. But that is not all.

The most weighty costs to attorneys subjected to Bar discipline are the social costs. As noted *supra*, the Arizona Bar gleefully publishes its version of its disciplinary cases online, in its magazine *Arizona Attorney*, and in press releases.

One disbarred member, long after her disbarment, discovered that in the online public file of the disbarment, the Bar, in a perverted gesture combining contempt, viciousness, and creepiness, had published her home address, unredacted, on the front page of the record. Until she discovered this, she was at a loss to fathom numerous anonymous hate calls to her home phone (not a private number) alluding to the disbarment, as well as visits to her door from belligerent strangers. The Arizona Bar appears to intentionally do this to encourage public harassment of former members.

In Ch. 6 "Attorney D" *infra* is recounted the history of one attorney whose legal career followed, more or less, the disciplinary path outlined *supra*. In the entire course of this lawyer's Arizona Bar membership, not one client ever complained to the Bar. Nor, before joining the Bar, had this individual had a history of substance or mental issues. Yet the Bar, after admitting this lawyer conditionally, kept bringing charge after disciplinary charge, culminating in disbarment.

---

[155]   A very few Arizona attorneys have commented publicly about the pecuniary costs they have borne owing to Bar discipline. *See* Heath Dooley, "Another Conservative Attorney Targeted by State Bar's Disciplinary Judge O'Neil" [letter to editor], *American Post-Gazette*, March 13, 2013, *available at*: http://sonoranalliance.com/2013/03/13/another-conservative-attorney-targeted-by-state-bars-disciplinary-judge-oneil/; "Disbarred Deputy Attorney under Andrew Thomas Exposes Corruption of AZ State Bar," *American Post-Gazette*, March 30, 2014, *available at*: http://sonoranalliance.com/2014/03/30/lisa-aubuchon-speaks-out-the-other-side-the-bar-and-media-dont-want-you-to-know/; *and* "Rachel Alexander Legal Defense Fund," n.d., *available at*: http://www.rachelalexanderlegaldefensefund.com/.

According to this lawyer, the social costs of discipline were far more devastating than the monetary exactions. For instance:

Immediately on the Bar's publication of news of the disbarment, this lawyer says that a brokerage firm sent a letter demanding that the lawyer close all accounts and go elsewhere for financial services, stating that the lawyer's disbarment had come to its attention through the press. The firm appeared to assume that if the client had any assets to invest, the client must have come by them through unlawful means.

The lawyer had been active in a religious congregation, performing music at some services, but the congregation's authorities withdrew all arrangements for such participation and communicated that the lawyer's further association with the congregation would not be welcome.

The lawyer, of course, also came to be excluded from all friendly association with former law colleagues.

The lawyer entered into legal proceedings against a contractor who violated a contract for services. The contractor demanded to be paid for undone contracted work. In addition, he had committed destructive acts on the lawyer's property. The contractor's lawyer recited in pleadings and at trial the fact of the opponent's disbarment as evidence of "poor character," hoping to influence the finder of fact. (However, the judge said the Bar history was irrelevant and refused to consider it.)

The lawyer complained to the Arizona Department of Human Rights and the Arizona Attorney General against a local business where she had gone for photocopying services, whose employee had called her such names as "cunt" when she asked for assistance. The business owner's defense was that the complainant was a disbarred attorney.

The lawyer owned some rental property. A tenant violated his lease and was threatening and abusive, even attempting at one point to run down the lawyer with his motor vehicle. The victim obtained an Injunction Against Harassment. The perpetrator was able to persuade an Arizona municipal court judge to quash the protective order, in part, by informing the judge that the victim was a disbarred lawyer. The abusive ex-tenant then continued to harass the victim. The abuse did not cease until the victim hired and paid for counsel to warn the ex-tenant in writing to limit his future contacts to serving process, if he thought he had a case to pursue. (The abuser shut up at that point.)

In sum, when the Arizona Bar disciplines a lawyer—and it disciplines Arizona lawyers more than any other state bar disciplines its lawyers—the Bar publicizes the discipline and publicity gets the public involved. As a result, every miscreant in society feels entitled to defecate on the disciplined lawyer. The miscreant will plead justification for his own wrongful behavior based on the fact that the individual has an Arizona Bar disciplinary record.

The Bar acts badly, and its bad acts engender more bad acts. The public may have the perception that the stigmatized lawyers alone are harmed, but the public is wrong. Shaming justice leads to more shaming justice, affecting everybody.

The fact that the Arizona Judicial Department's policies encourage worse, not improved, conditions of justice is the most obnoxious implication, not of the fact that it disciplines members, but of the fact that officials of the Arizona Judicial Department, including the Bar, have impunity to use, and routinely do use, illegal, unfair and corrupt disciplinary methods.

4.   Minting Money from Madness

The breathtaking circularity of the process had a kind of poetic tightness. Not everybody was accused, after all, so there must be some reason why you were. By denying that there is any reason whatsoever for you to be accused, you are implying, by virtue of a surprisingly small logical leap, that mere chance picked you out, which in turn implies that the Devil might not really be at work ... or, God forbid, even exist. Therefore the investigation itself is either mistaken or a fraud.   ... [T]here was often a despairing pity mixed with "Well, they must have done something." Few of us can easily surrender our belief that society must somehow make sense. The thought that the state has lost its mind and is punishing so many innocent people is intolerable.

Arthur Miller, "Why I Wrote THE CRUCIBLE," *The New Yorker*, October 21, 1996, pp. 158ff.

This chapter first discusses the track record of mind science—the arts practiced by psychiatrists, psychologists, and "master's-level therapists" (social workers), all of whom rely on state licensing to ply their trades—and the knee-jerk reliance of courts on mind science providers, a phenomenon that might be termed the judiciary-therapeutic complex.

Second, this chapter discusses protections against stigmatizing and discriminating against individuals with labels of mental illness, actual or presumed, under the Americans with Disabilities Act and related federal legislation, such as the Rehabilitation Act.

Third, the chapter discusses recent U.S. Department of Justice efforts to limit the impunity of state bar organizations to violate the Act's protections for license applicants.

Thereafter, the chapter discusses obstacles to reform.

Finally, the chapter discusses prospects of reform in bar licensing, focusing on licensing in Arizona.

i.   Mind Science and the Judiciary-Therapeutic Complex

Since approximately 1989, there has been a proliferation of a model of justice based on special tribunals called drug courts and mental health courts. Judges sentence defendants to supervised treatment in addition to, or in lieu of, incarceration.[156]

This creates an extremely lucrative business for providers, since they can induce the courts and extrajudicial branches of government to turn over public monies to grow their services for the incarcerated.[157] They can also offer outpatient services for individuals sentenced to treatment in lieu of incarceration.

Outsourcing justice in this fashion has become so uncontroversial that there seems to be little discussion about whether forensic mind science has benefited anyone or anything other than the cash flows of the practitioners. Judges sentence people to mental interventions as a matter of course.

Yet thanks to the media, the public is all too aware that so-called mind science has not averted such disasters as the intentional murder of air travelers,[158] shootings of unarmed students and faculty in university classrooms,[159] or even the

---

[156]   Derek Denckla and Greg Berman, "Rethinking the Revolving Door: A Look at Mental Illness in the Courts," Center for Court Innovation (2001), *available at*:
http://www.courtinnovation.org/pdf/mental_health.pdf.   *See also* "Mental Health Court," n.d., *available at*:
http://en.wikipedia.org/wiki/Mental_health_court.
[157]   *See, e.g.* the website advertising the University of Connecticut Health Center's "Correctional Managed Health Care" program, *available at*: http://cmhc.uchc.edu/programs_services/.
[158]   March 24, 2015, Germanwings Airlines flight 9525 deliberate crash by mentally ill, suicidal copilot Andreas Lubitz *for which see, inter alia*,   http://www.cnn.com/2015/03/26/europe/france-germanwings-plane-crash-main/; October 31, 1999, EgyptAir Flight 990 deliberate crash by copilot Gameel al-Batouti, *for which see, inter alia*, www.theatlantic.com/magazine/archive/2001/11/the-crash-of-egyptair-990/302332/.
[159]   April 16, 2007, Virginia Tech mass shooting by suicidal-homicidal, legal U.S. resident student Seung-Hui Cho, *for which see, inter alia*,   http://www.cnn.com/2013/10/31/us/virginia-tech-shootings-fast-facts/.

permanent disabling of a Congresswoman from Arizona.[160] It seems a kind of mass social irrationality—the triumph of hope over experience—to assume nevertheless that such problems are somehow addressed by a system whereby a civil authority with no expertise in mind science assumes that it has done something productive by sentencing an ever-growing proportion of the population to the ministrations of mind science practitioners.

If a commercial product, such as a mouthwash, had a track record similar to that of mind science, some federal consumer protection agency would ensure that it came off the market. Mind science practitioners can't even tell reliably when their clients are lying.[161] Yet the courts continue to assume that consigning defendants to "therapy" is a good idea, despite the well-publicized failure of mind science to address social problems or protect the public from harm, and despite the fact that, widely, experts acknowledge that mind science is not scientific.[162] It would, after all, be difficult to imagine another branch of health care that is more controversial than that which is here being discussed under the rubric of "mind science" (the theories underlying the services of psychiatrists, psychologists and "master's-level therapists.") One can hardly think of a branch of medicine that has inspired a website

---

[160]   January 8, 2011, mass shooting resulting in wounding or killing of several individuals, including U.S. Rep. Gabrielle Giffords (D-Arizona) who was left permanently disabled, by mentally ill, suspended community college student Jared Lee Loughner, *for which see, inter alia,* "2011 Tucson Shooting," *available at*: http://en.wikipedia.org/wiki/2011_Tucson_shooting.

[161]   *See, e.g.,* Tori DeAngelis, "An Elephant in the Office," American Psychological Association, 39 MONITOR ON PSYCHOLOGY 33 (2008), *available at*: http://www.apa.org/monitor/jan08/elephant.aspx *and* Gordon Shippey, "My Client, the Liar," Counselling Resource, n.d., *available at*: http://counsellingresource.com/features/2011/01/04/my-client-the-liar/. Mind science practitioners also lie to clients. *See, e.g.* "Do Psychologists Lie to Their Patients?" *Quora,* n.d., *available at*: http://www.quora.com/Do-psychologists-lie-to-their-patients.

[162]   A number of writers have termed mind science a pseudoscience. *See, e.g.* "Anti-psychiatry," *available at*: http://en.wikipedia.org/wiki/Anti-psychiatry. *See also* Stuart A. Kirk *et al.,* MAD SCIENCE: PSYCHIATRIC COERCION, DIAGNOSIS, AND DRUGS, Transaction Publishers (2013).

protesting its legitimacy, such as "Anti-Nephrology" or "Anti-Dermatology." Yet there is a host of websites critical of mind science, including one called "Anti-Psychiatry."[163]

Mind science practitioners have shown great aptitude for creating work for themselves. Critics of mind science point out that over the past five decades, the prevalence of individuals conforming to the diagnostic criteria for some disorder from the premiere mind science diagnostic manual, the DSM,[164] has increased exponentially. By 2003, it was found that 46% of American adults met the manual's criteria for at least one mental illness.[165] Simultaneously, the U.S. prison population has been on an exponential upswing. One source estimates that as the world's leader in incarceration, the U.S. currently has 2.2 million prisoners.[166] The growth in the prison population has created a plethora of lucrative opportunities for practitioners of forensic mind science.

Aside from the issues of privacy implicated by the trend of labeling ever more individuals as sick souls incapable of self-management and therefore, undeserving of being listened to, one of the most serious consequences of the psychiatrization of American society is the increasing tendency

---

[163]   An organization called the Anti-Psychiatry Coalition has taken an activist role in opposing, and warning the public about, the proliferation of social control by the misuse of mind science. *See, e.g.* Lawrence Stevens, J.D., "Psychiatric Stigma Follows You Everywhere You Go for the Rest of Your Life" (2002 Update), *available at*: http://www.antipsychiatry.org/stigma.htm.

[164]   American Psychiatric Association, DIAGNOSTIC AND STATISTICAL MANUAL OF MENTAL DISORDERS (DSM) (2013), first published 1952, is in a fifth edition (DSM-V) at the time of this writing.

[165]   Bruce Levine, Ph.D., "Why the Rise of Mental Illness? Pathologizing Normal, Adverse Drug Effects, and a Peculiar Rebellion," *Mad In America,* July 31, 2013, *available at*: http://www.madinamerica.com/2013/07/why-the-dramatic-rise-of-mental-illness-diseasing-normal-behaviors-drug-adverse-effects-and-a-peculiar-rebellion/, citing article by former NEW ENGLAND JOURNAL OF MEDICINE editor-in-chief Marcia Angell, M.D., "The Epidemic of Mental Illness: Why?" NEW YORK REVIEW OF BOOKS, June 23, 2011, *available at*: http://www.nybooks.com/articles/archives/2011/jun/23/epidemic-mental-illness-why/?page=1.

[166]   The Sentencing Project, webpage "Incarceration," n.d., *available at*: http://www.sentencingproject.org/template/page.cfm?id=107.

of government, including professional licensing bodies, to combat dissent by invoking mind science to discredit their opponents. For instance, according to journalist Glenn Greenwald, to persuade the public that only marginalized groups have anything to fear from the government's covert domestic mass surveillance that Edward Snowden exposed, the government conformed itself to the observation that "demonizing the personality of anyone who challenges political power has been a long-standing tactic" to excuse questionable official acts. Thus, in 2013, commentaries appeared critical of the personalities and mental status not only of Edward Snowden, but also of journalists who reported about Snowden, including Greenwald himself.[167]

The Arizona Bar may be overusing forced mental "therapy" against disaffected or prospectively disaffected members out of similar motives. As mentioned in Ch. 3 ii a *supra*, the U.S. Department of Justice lately became serious about enforcing the penalty provisions of the Americans with Disabilities Act against certain state bars that, by libeling some applicants as mentally ill, arrogated to themselves the privilege of imposing extraordinary, humiliating, and discriminatory conditions on those applicants' admission and licensing (treating them as second-class licensees); yet Arizona's Bar has continued, even in 2015, subjecting applicants to conditional admissions with forced mental "therapy" (see n. 52 and accompanying text and Ch. 3 i c 3 *supra*). The fact that, in the face of a threat of federal action, it has been worth it to the Arizona Bar to continue to do this suggests that this Bar has a very powerful interest in discrediting potential dissenters.

ii.   The Americans with Disabilities Act

The Americans with Disabilities Act (ADA), 42 U.S.C. § 12101 *et seq.* (Pub. L. 101-336), was enacted in 1990 in order to extend to disabled Americans the protections of the Civil Rights Act of 1964 (Pub. L. 88-352, 78 Stat. 241): "Congress recognized that physical and mental disabilities in no way diminish a person's right to fully participate in all aspects of society, but that people with physical or mental disabilities are frequently precluded from doing so because of prejudice,

---

[167]   Greenwald, NO PLACE, p. 226. *See also* pp. 200 and 222-230.

antiquated attitudes, or the failure to remove societal and institutional barriers."[168] Although the original ADA provided for a private right of action (and a small number of aggrieved applicants did successfully file actions against state bars),[169]

---

[168] Congress adopted this language when amending the ADA in 2008. *See* "Findings and Purposes of Pub. L. 110-325," *available at:* http://www.gpo.gov/fdsys/pkg/USCODE-2010-title42/pdf/USCODE-2010-title42-chap126-sec12102.pdf. *See also* Thom K. Cope, "The ABCs of the ADAAA: What Employers Need to Know about Recent Changes to the Americans with Disabilities Act," n.d., *available at:* http://www.mcrazlaw.com/the-abcs-of-the-adaaa-what-employers-need-to-know-about-recent-changes-to-the-americans-with-disabilities-act/.

[169] *See* the United States' amicus brief in a 1994 case *Clark v. Virginia Board of Bar Examiners*, no. CA-94-211A (E.D. Va. 1994), *available at:* http://www.ada.gov/briefs/clark2br.doc. The plaintiff obtained a judgment that she could be admitted to a state bar despite failing to answer a screening question about her past mental history. The court ruled that the Virginia Bar had violated the ADA by attempting to collect mental history information to screen out applicants without a specific showing that the applicant would pose a threat to the public if admitted. *See also* another United States amicus brief in a similar suit brought successfully by a Bar applicant, likewise filed in 1994, in Florida, *Ellen S. v. Florida Bd. of Bar Examiners*, 859 F.Supp. 1489, no. 94-0429-CIV (S.D. Fla. 1994), *available at:* http://www.google.com/url?sa=t&rct=j&q=&esrc=s&source=web&cd=2&ved=0CCUQFjAB&url=http%3A%2F%2Fwww.ada.gov%2Fbriefs%2Fellensbr.doc&ei=QrVOVfjhLoKooQSv8oDgCA&usg=AFQjCNE_zdwe6gs7fMz-NuCSV3Ep0EarHQ&bvm=bv.92885102,d.cGU *and* http://www.leagle.com/decision/19942348859FSupp1489_12 134.xml/ELLEN%20S.%20v.%20FLORIDA%20BD.%20OF%20BAR%20 EXAMINERS. *See also* Lauren E. Chanatry, "Professional Licensing Issues: Title II of the ADA Applied to State and Local Professional Licensing," Southeast Center on the Americans with Disabilities Act (2007), *available at:* http://www.adasoutheast.org/ada/publications /legal/professional_licensing_disability_ADA_TitleII.txt; Stephanie Denzel, "Second-Class Licensure: The Use of Conditional Admission Programs for Bar Applicants with Mental Health and Substance Abuse Histories," 43 CONN. L. REV. 891 (2011), *available at:* http://papers.ssrn.com/sol3/papers.cfm?abstract_id=1566572; *and* Phyllis Coleman and Ronald A. Shellow, "Ask about Conduct, Not Mental Illness: A Proposal for Bar Examiners and Medical Boards to Comply with the ADA and Constitution," 20 J. OF LEGISLATION 147 (1994), *available at:* http://scholarship.law.nd.edu/cgi/viewcontent. cgi?article=1243&context=jleg.

large organizations both public and private were soon successfully defending cases brought by individuals seeking to vindicate their rights under the ADA. The obstacle for plaintiffs was largely in the way the original Act defined disability, making it easy for defendant organizations to mount a defense by denying that their opponent was disabled, or that the opponent was sufficiently disabled to come under the ADA's protections.[170] The ADA was then fairly toothless.

Although more than some ten years after the ADA's passage, the U.S. Department of Justice began to examine various bar associations' conditional admissions practices, whereby candidates were flagged for special conditions on admission or, in some instances, denied admission, because of a history of mental or substance issues, the DOJ was powerless at that time to do much more than suggest that screening questions about personal history on the bar application not get too detailed.

The State Bar of Arizona, for instance, was the respondent to an applicant's ADA complaint in the mid 1990's. However, the DOJ's only action was to instruct the Arizona Bar to slightly edit the wording of the questions about mental and substance history in the Character and Fitness portion of the membership application so as to "focus on behavior rather than status." The DOJ concluded that there was no evidence that the Arizona Bar had engaged in unlawful discrimination by actually using information it had gathered to delay or deny admission. The DOJ did not then raise issues with the legality of conditional admissions as such.[171]

Congress decided to address the limitations of the original ADA to bring its wording better into alignment with its

---

[170]   See Congress' rationale for amending the ADA, with cites to early ADA lawsuits, in "Findings and Purposes," n. 168 supra.

[171]   November 7, 1994, DOJ Coordination and Review Section, Civil Rights Division, Acting Chief Merrily A. Friedlander letter to Stephen C. Villarreal, Chairman, Committee on Character and Fitness, State Bar of Arizona, available at: http://www.justice.gov/crt/foia/readingroom/frequent_requests/ad a_lof/lof038.txt or
https://www.google.com/url?sa=t&rct=j&q=&esrc=s&source=web&cd =1&ved=0CB4QFjAA&url=http%3A%2F%2Fwww.justice.gov%2Fcrt%2Ff oia%2Freadingroom%2Ffrequent_requests%2Fada_lof%2Flof038.txt&e i=vAFNVbLFN9jioAScpoH4Cw&usg=AFQjCNFwA_0RIKlPfI1YeTT4nC H8gq_cEA&bvm=bv.92765956,d.cGU).

original purpose. In 2008, Congress passed the ADA Amendments Act of 2008 (Pub. L. 110-325). The amended version took effect on January 1, 2009.[172] The amendment improved the definitional language under which, formerly, it had been difficult for plaintiffs to establish that they were disabled per the Act. It also added protections for individuals who did not come under the Act's definitions of actual disability (those definitions include a litmus test of incapacity to participate in certain "major life activities") but who could show that that discrimination had occurred on a *presumption* of the individual's disability ("regarded as disabled").[173] The discussion *infra* will expand on the significance of this.

For the moment, it may be emphasized that, under the amended ADA, persons regarded as disabled are entitled to the same protections and remedies as persons actually disabled. This aspect of the amended Act has important implications for the questionable conduct in which the Supreme Court of Arizona's Committee on Character and Fitness, as well as the State Bar of Arizona's Presiding Disciplinary Judge, have been engaging in consigning applicants and members, including many lacking a treatment history, to mental intervention as a condition of practicing law. This, too, is discussed *infra*.

The ADA, as amended, defines a "qualified individual," in the simplest terms for purposes of the present discussion, as one who, with or without reasonable modifications, meets essential eligibility requirements for participation in programs provided by a public entity.[174] Further, the ADA, as amended, defines a "disability" in broad terms, as any "impairment" limiting major life activities, whether physical or mental. And it extends "disability" classification to individuals "regarded as disabled" as follows:

> An individual meets the requirement of "being regarded as having such an impairment" if the individual establishes that he or she has been subjected to an action prohibited under this chapter because of an actual or perceived physical or mental

---

[172]   *See* Cope, "The ABCs," n. 168 *supra*.   *See also* https://www.law.cornell.edu/uscode/text/42/12102.
[173]   *See* Cope, "The ABCs," n. 168 *supra*.
[174]   ADA, as amended 2008, Title II § 12131 (2), *available at*: http://www.ada.gov/pubs/adastatute08.htm#12114a.

impairment whether or not the impairment limits or is perceived to limit a major life activity.[175]

The ADA, as amended, is implemented through regulations. The ADA's Title II is a body of rules relating to action by governmental entities. According to the Title II regulations of the ADA, as amended:

A public entity may not administer a licensing or certification program in a manner that subjects qualified individuals with disabilities to discrimination on the basis of disability, nor may a public entity establish requirements for the programs or activities of licensees or certified entities that subject qualified individuals with disabilities to discrimination on the basis of disability.[176]

According to one authoritative source explaining the rules in fairly non-technical terms:

... [P]ublic entities cannot discriminate against a "qualified individual with a disability" with respect to licensing or certifications. A person is a "qualified individual with a disability" if s/he can meet the essential eligibility requirements for receiving the license or certification. What requirements are considered essential will vary for each particular case. For example, a state could not refuse to issue a license to practice law to someone only because s/he has a diagnosis of mental illness. The denial, however, would be appropriate if the person's illness

---

[175]   *Id.* § 12102 (1), (3) (A).

[176]   U.S. Department of Justice, *Americans with Disabilities Act Title II Regulations*, 28 CFR Pt. 35, § 35.130 "General prohibitions against discrimination" (6), September 15, 2010, p. 34, *available at*: http://www.ada.gov/regs2010/titleII_2010/titleII_2010_regulations.pdf. Concerning Title II and nonprofessional and professional licensing, *see also The Americans with Disabilities Act Title II Technical Assistance Manual* § II-3.7200, n.d., *available at*: www.ada.gov/taman2.html#II-3.7000.

was uncontrolled and s/he would be unable to competently practice law ... .[177]

The preceding discussion leads to a conclusion that the ADA prohibits professional licensing bodies, including state bar associations, from using information about an otherwise qualified applicant's mental or substance history to restrict the individual from obtaining a license to practice the profession unless—and the burden of evidence is on the licensor, not the applicant—the bar association, or other licensing body, can articulate reasonable grounds for treating the applicant as prospectively incompetent to meet his or her professional obligations.

What is more, because of Title II's "regarded as disabled" provision, individuals are entitled to the above protections against intrusions, special conditions, and/or other forms of discrimination in obtaining a professional license, even if they have no actual mental condition, but have been treated as such by a licensing body in making decisions discriminatory to that individual.

iii.   The U.S. Department of Justice

The Judge David L. Bazelon Center for Mental Health Law is a Washington-based, privately funded mental health law project founded in 1972 that has taken a special interest in ADA Title II issues.[178] In 2009, Bazelon joined with other mental health advocacy organizations in sending a letter to the Tennessee Supreme Court advising, as to an amended conditional admissions policy that the Court was then contemplating, that the policy would violate Title II of the ADA, as amended, "by holding attorney licensure applicants with disabilities to a higher standard than licensure applicants

---

[177]   Jodi Hanna and Christine Curley, *Americans with Disabilities Act: Title II—Government Programs and Services*, n.d., p. 321, *available at:* http://www.disabilityrightswi.org/wp-content/uploads/2008/09/ada-title-2.PDF. It should be noted that there is an active substance abuse exception, i.e. the ADA explicitly excludes from its protections a individual actively engaged in substance abuse at the time a governmental privilege, such a professional license, is refused.

[178]   *See* http://www.bazelon.org/Who-We-Are/History.aspx.

without disabilities," and noting, further: "The justification for the conditions is the possibility that 'the conduct or behavior, *if it should recur,* would impair the applicant's current ability to practice law or pose a threat to the public.' The ADA does not permit the Board of Law Examiners to subject a person to differential treatment based on the mere possibility that disability-related conduct *might* recur."[179]

In January, 2011, the Bazelon Center filed the first of two complaints against the Louisiana Bar with the U.S. Department of Justice on behalf of an applicant with a prior mental health diagnosis subjected to conditional admission without "any evidence or medical opinion that her condition was likely to interfere with her practice of law. Our client was required, among other things, to submit for a period of five years to regular 'check-ins' by a court-appointed monitor and have a psychiatrist submit quarterly reports to Louisiana's Office of Disciplinary Counsel. Further, her monitor may make inquiries of her employer or supervising attorney concerning her work." Bazelon complained that the conditions imposed on admission of such applicants were "stigmatizing and intrusive" and violate Title II of the ADA as well as the federal Rehabilitation Act § 504. It added:

> Less than a full license to practice, conditional admissions have been justified as a means of expanding opportunities for practicing law for people with mental illnesses. In practice, however, conditional admissions have become a vehicle for imposing onerous and discriminatory conditions on people with mental illnesses who seek admission to the Bar.[180]

According to Bazelon, the DOJ responded to its complaint by opening cases DJ No. 204-32M-60, 204-32-88, and 204-32-89 to investigate the conditional admissions policies in Louisiana. On February 5, 2014, the DOJ issued a letter

---

[179] For the text of the March 9, 2009, letter, *see* http://www.bazelon.org/LinkClick.aspx?fileticket= wHTBtorxaw0%3d&tabid=602.

[180] Bazelon Center, "Louisiana Bar Conditional Admissions," *available at:* http://www.bazelon.org/In-Court/Current-Litigation/Louisiana-Bar-Conditional-Admissions.aspx.

addressed to the Louisiana Supreme Court, the Louisiana Supreme Court Committee on Bar Admissions, and the Louisiana Attorney Disciplinary Board. The letter described the particulars of Louisiana Bar conditional admissions, summarized the protective provisions of the ADA, as amended, and concluded that the conditional admissions policies violate federal law: "The letter informs Louisiana that it must refrain from using questions about diagnosis or treatment unless the applicant raises his or her mental health conditions to explain past concerning conduct. ... Louisiana must evaluable all pending applications without considering the applicant's responses to mental health questions. Furthermore, it asks the state to identify individuals [previously] subject to unlawful conditional admissions and admit them unconditionally to the Bar."[181]

The letter instructed Louisiana to take a variety of specific remedial measures, including making regular reports to the DOJ for the succeeding five years and offering compensatory monetary damages to individuals who, in violation of the ADA, were discriminated against in the bar admissions process.[182]

The issuance of the February, 2014, DOJ letter to Louisiana was followed by a formal settlement agreement. The Louisiana Bar admissions apparatus agreed to a number of conditions. Among these was an obligation to pay a settlement of $200,000 to each of a number of "affected bar applicants

---

[181]   Bazelon Center, "U.S. Justice Dept. Finds States Violate ADA if Inquire [sic] into Mental Health Condition or Treatment when Assessing Fitness to Practice Law," *available at*: http://www.bazelon.org/News-Publications/Press-Releases/2-10-14-LA-State-Bar.aspx. Via a link on that webpage, one can access the February 5, 2014, DOJ letter to Louisiana, *or see* http://www.bazelon.org/LinkClick.aspx?fileticket=7fvtHYXZawM%3d &tabid=698 *or* http://www.ada.gov/louisiana-bar-lof.pdf. For other pertinent cites, *see* nn 4, 131 *supra*.
[182]   February 5, 2014, DOJ letter to Louisiana, pp. 31ff., *cited in* n. 181 *supra*.

and attorneys."[183]

When announcing this settlement agreement, the DOJ revealed that it was also raising ADA issues with the bar admissions programs in Vermont and Connecticut and with the National Conference of Bar Examiners.[184] The last of these, the National Conference, has been discussed in Ch. 3 ii b *supra*.

In addition, the DOJ has announced a formal investigation of Florida Bar conditional admissions.[185]

iv.   Mine is Bigger and Different than Yours

In Arizona, what are the chances of reform? With the oversized bureaucracy, as well as vast financial interests at stake, there is no likelihood the State Bar of Arizona disciplinary apparatus will reform *sua sponte*. There is simply no practical incentive to desist or to reform from within. How and whether change may occur depends on the comparative size of the capital available to opposing entities—and which side could financially outlast the other in a confrontation.

The obstacles to reform also include an indifference, or an ideological complacency, borne of willingness to accept the line promoted by the State Bar of Arizona. Why is it wrong, some readers may reason, if the Arizona Bar happens to

---

[183]   *See* Department of Justice Office of Public Affairs, "Department of Justice Reaches Agreement with the Louisiana Supreme Court to Protect Bar Candidates with Disabilities" [press release], August 15, 2014, *available at*: http://www.justice.gov/opa/pr/department-justice-reaches-agreement-louisiana-supreme-court-protect-bar-candidates. *See also* "Bazelon Center's Complaints Result in Agreement Ending Discrimination Against Bar Applicants Based on Mental Health Conditions," *available at*: http://www.bazelon.org/News-Publications/Press-Releases/8-15-14-LA-Bar-Applicant-Complaints-Settlement.aspx. For the cite to the text of the agreement, *see* n. 4 *supra*.
[184]   Department of Justice Office of Public Affairs, "Department of Justice Reaches Agreement," n. 183 *supra*.
[185]   *See* Martha Neil, "Report," n. 131 *supra*. *See also* Julie Kay, "Justice Department Investigates Florida Supreme Court on Bar Mental Health Screening," *Daily Business Review*, March 26, 2015, *available at*: http://www.dailybusinessreview.com/id=1202721703206/Justice-Department-Investigates-Florida-Supreme-Court-on-Bar-Mental-Health-Screening.

investigate many members, even if happens to do so more than the bar in any other state, and has a correspondingly large bureaucracy devoted to that purpose, and larger member impositions to enable it to pursue that purpose? If there are disciplinary excesses from time to time, leaving aside the issue of the federal and state constitutions and laws, isn't that the price people may expect to pay if they are caught doing something the authorities think is wrong? Isn't it the same in the criminal justice system?   Law enforcement might sometimes apprehend the wrong people; people are sometimes wrongfully accused; they may feel manipulated into a plea bargain; sentences may be harsh; isn't that the price everyone pays for living in a civil society? Is it a big deal if, like the justice system, the State Bar of Arizona does some controversial things too?

But in answer, Arizona Bar discipline differs from criminal justice. It differs from any kind of justice, and it differs in a multitude of ways, so that the individual who applies to join the Arizona Bar to pursue a career practicing law can anticipate much less protection of his or her civil rights than a criminal.

Many of these differences are implicit from the discussion of the policies, rules and procedures of conditional admission and attorney discipline in Ch. 3 *supra.*

Here are some of the differences:

1.   Under the US Constitution, in the criminal justice system, people of limited means enjoy the benefit of counsel, if necessary at public expense, in proceedings for serious crimes entailing large financial and personal penalties upon conviction.   An Arizona Bar member, by contrast, may be unable to hire defense counsel to defend a formal disciplinary proceedings, since the costs of professional defense can amount to tens of thousands of dollars.

2.   Under the US Constitution, an individual accused of a crime has a right to confront accusers; whereas the State Bar of Arizona may bring allegations *sua sponte* against members without disclosing who has complained, or if anyone has complained, and without enumerating what alleged actions or omissions of the attorney are at issue; and likewise, may subject applicants to conditional admission without ever answering applicants' questions about the evidentiary grounds.

3.   In a criminal case, the prosecution customarily introduces expert evidence that a defendant's mental imperfections are related to the defendant's involvement in crime prior to the judge's sentencing the defendant to some form of mental intervention; whereas in Bar disciplinary proceedings, the Presiding Disciplinary Judge, at his whim, routinely sentences members to the ministrations of the Bar's "Member Assistance Program" (coerced mental therapy) without there having been *any* evidence introduced at the disciplinary hearing that the member has a mental or substance problem *and* without the member putting his own mental status at issue in defending the charge by ascribing some undesired conduct to a mental or substance problem. And in lawyer admissions, the same thing happens when the medically unqualified Arizona Supreme Court Committee on Character and Fitness flags applicants as requiring mental "treatment," also through the Bar's MAP program, as a precondition to obtaining a law license.

4.   In courts of law, while the tribunal may order a defendant to undergo mental treatment, there is no pecuniary benefit to the court in so doing; whereas the Arizona Bar recasts perceived defects in "character" as mental illness *and* receives financial benefit in so doing.

5.   While restitution and some types of administrative costs may be ordered, no judge in a criminal case imposes costs on a defendant for the judge's time and trouble in attending the hearing, since that would be an obvious conflict of interest; whereas, as alluded to in n. 84, Ch. 3 i c 2, and Ch. 3 iii *supra*, and as shown in Ch. 6 "Attorney D" and Appendix 6-13 *infra*, in Arizona Bar disciplinary proceedings, the Presiding Disciplinary Judge, although he is salaried, is free to impose his own "costs" on the disciplined attorney, just because he showed up for the hearing—and he does not have to justify so doing.

6.   The criminal justice system does not recognize a class of "untouchable" members of society; all are presumed equal under the law. On the other hand, the Arizona Bar virtually never pursues discipline against certain classes of lawyers, including members who happen to also be judges, members of large law firms, lawyers who the Supreme Court of Arizona chooses as members of the various committees,

administrative bodies and tribunals it establishes and constitutes, and present and former Staff Bar Counsel.

7.   Courts of law (even if more in a token fashion than by positive action) recognize that the objectives of justice include some component of offender rehabilitation; whereas the stated purpose of Arizona Bar discipline is never to rehabilitate the member.

8.   There are lawyer ethics rules that constrain the prerogative of criminal prosecutors to abuse the right of a defendant to a fair trial. For instance, in criminal proceedings, E.R. 3.8 "Special Responsibilities of a Prosecutor" imposes on a prosecutor a duty to avoid prosecuting charges not supported by probable cause; a duty to ensure that the defendant is aware of the right to counsel and has had a reasonable opportunity to obtain counsel; and even a duty to disclose all evidence known to the prosecutor that mitigates against the State's case and in favor of the defendant's innocence. Furthermore, all lawyers have a duty in proceedings to be truthful with the tribunal (ER 3.3 "Candor Toward the Tribunal") and fair to opposing parties (ER 3.4 "Fairness to Opposing Party and Counsel"). In turn, this entails a duty to correct any fact the attorney has introduced in a proceeding that the attorney subsequently discovers to be false. In Arizona Bar disciplinary proceedings, on the other hand, Staff Bar Counsel and everybody else connected with the Bar's side of the case, including witnesses favorable to the Bar, even when such witnesses are lawyers, have free rein to cheat in proceedings. This is due to statutory immunity accorded to the Bar, its employees and its friends, from any liability for unfair process such as suborning or committing perjury, packing the adjudicatory panel with one's cronies (in the instance of the PDJ), and everything else that the Arizona Bar routinely does in derogation of the rights that a respondent Bar member would enjoy if (s)he were a defendant in a criminal court.

9.   Courts, even in the Southern states of the U.S., no longer impose indefinitely renewable punishments; yet in Arizona Bar disciplinary cases, the PDJ commonly issues orders allowing the Bar to automatically renew, at its discretion, the PDJ's term of sanction against a member. As well, it is a standard part of an order of conditional admission that the Director of the "Member Assistance Program" may indefinitely renew or extend the initial period of the sanction.

10.   And in Arizona Bar discipline, it being the objective to personally and financially ruin the target, inability to pay Bar impositions is a ground for burdening the impecunious with new sanctions; whereas in the courts of the land, sanctions of the "debtor's prisons" type went out along with the stocks, pillory, and whipping post in the public square.

11.   Courts of law may sentence defendants to mental treatment; but a court of law, unlike the Arizona Bar, never employs its own "therapist" to order "treatment," conduct "treatment," nor enrich himself by charging defendants fees for "treatment."

12.   In a criminal proceeding, the accused is entitled to a hearing; whereas for innocently applying to the Arizona Bar for membership, an individual can be libeled by the Supreme Court of Arizona's Committee on Character and Fitness as needing mental intervention without the benefit of *any* hearing, whether or not the applicant then abandons the Bar application or continues to pursue admission to the Bar.

If there ever should occur reform of the corrupt Arizona lawyer discipline apparatus, it is very unlikely to arise from any individual's suit or any class action suit against the Arizona Bar. This is in part due to the financial imbalance noted *supra*. The Arizona Bar's assets as of calendar year 2013 are in excess of $11million (*see* n. 48 *supra*). No plaintiff suing over his or her own harms, or group of similarly situated plaintiffs, could financially outlast the Bar.

What is more, there is a "Who will bell the cat?" issue. Unfairly sanctioned lawyers are unwilling to risk more severe sanctions by publicly opposing the Bar. This is borne out by correspondence to Arizona Attorneys Against Professional Regulation, received through the "contact" form on the AZAACPR website.[186] Correspondence has emanated from Bar members reciting instances of corrupt disciplinary practices whereby they have suffered grievous harms, while cautiously asking the anonymous recipients not to divulge their identities. Then too, no lawyer licensed in Arizona is eager to risk his or license by filing a direct suit against the Bar. Even though, with assistance of Arizona-licensed counsel, one may sue the MAP

---

[186]   *See* n. 11 *supra*.

Director individually (*see* Ch. 5 *infra*) and although an Arizona-licensed attorney has sued the Justices of the Supreme Court of Arizona individually (*see* n. 62 *supra*), and even though by the Supreme Court rule establishing it, the Arizona Bar may be sued, as noted in n. 13 *supra*, no Arizona lawyer in private practice and no Arizona law firm sues the Arizona Bar.

Only reform from without is possible—and only at the hands of someone or something bigger than the Bar.

v.   Discussion

It will be recalled from discussion in this chapter *supra* and in Ch. 3 ii e *supra* that, in recent years, the State Bar of Arizona has faced an existential threat from two quarters: the Arizona Legislature, which from time to time entertains bills to abolish the Arizona Bar; and the U.S. Department of Justice, which has exacted penalties against the Louisiana Bar admissions apparatus over unlawful conditional admissions, and which has investigated or is investigating several other state bars.

Arizona Attorneys Against Corrupt Professional Regulation has complained about corrupt Arizona Bar discipline both to Arizona legislators and to the U.S. Department of Justice. None of the addressees have responded to AZAACPR's communications as of the time of this writing. AZAACPR has also received reports from Arizona lawyers that they have individually complained to the DOJ. This is documented in Ch. 6 *infra*. At the time of this writing, the DOJ has not responded by investigating the Arizona Bar.

Heretofore, the DOJ has confined its attentions to a handful of Eastern U.S. states and has not turned its attention to Western state bar organizations. This may be merely because of geographical convenience. Or it could reflect the activities of state bar lobbyists. The State Bar of Arizona is not the only Western U.S. state that employs lobbyists.[187] And some lobbyists that the Arizona Bar employs do not restrict their influence to Phoenix, but work for a corporation with a national presence, including a Washington, D.C., branch office, as discussed in Ch. 3 i a *supra.*

It is, alternatively, possible that the DOJ is picking off lighter fruit before it goes after tougher cases. In the settlement agreement between the DOJ and Louisiana, one of the terms to which the latter consented was to compensate certain "Affected Individuals," persons discriminated against in the Bar admissions process, $200,000 each, and not to retaliate against any of these "Affected Individuals." The DOJ specified that there were seven of these "Affected Individuals."[188]

Arizona would be a much more complex case for the DOJ because a far greater number of individuals could claim to have suffered discrimination in violation of the ADA. The victims include not only numerous attorneys who disclosed a history of mental or substance treatment in their Bar applications, but also attorneys who had no such prior history and were nevertheless unlawfully "regarded as disabled" with mental problems, either in the admissions process or in lawyer discipline. They, like the numerous applicants who disclosed an actual mental history, were inveigled into the Bar's "Member Assistance Program"—and the number can only be estimated, but there could possibly be many hundreds of such individuals. This differs from the situation that the DOJ addressed in Louisiana where, apparently, every person deemed an "affected individual" had stated on a Bar application that he or she had been in mental or substance therapy. There is also a question of how far the DOJ would have to go beyond the ADA in investigating the Arizona lawyer

---

[187]   The California Bar also employs a lobbyist (and, as in the case of the Arizona Bar, this fact has aroused public criticism). *See* http://archive.calbar.ca.gov/calbar/2cbj/97dec/97dec-19.htm.   In 2015, pressured by continual criticism, the California Bar began offering members a discount on their dues should they not wish to support the Bar's lobbying agenda. *See* "Information about your 2015 membership fees," *available at*:
http://www.calbar.ca.gov/Portals/0/documents/reports/2014_State mentofExpendituresofMembershipDues2013_R.pdf.
[188]   *See* paragraph 22 of the settlement agreement, *cited in* n. 4 *supra.*

admissions and discipline apparatus' civil rights violations. By unlawful process and unlawful disciplinary orders, the Presiding Disciplinary Judge, who is a Bar employee, and the Bar have deprived lawyers not only of their disability rights under the ADA, but also of their US Constitution Fourteenth Amendment Rights, plus the privacy guarantees of the Arizona Constitution.

In addition, Arizona is a special case because its Bar has employed a "therapist," Howard Murray "Hal" Nevitt. The extent of the ensuing wrongfulness is elaborated on in Ch. 5 *infra*; for the moment, it suffices to state that this "therapist" has enriched himself through a blatant conflict of interest—by recommending, as part of his official duties, that numerous Bar applicants, and numerous already admitted Bar members, undergo "Member Assistance Program" intervention; and by then making himself these members' paid "therapist," plus forcing many such individuals to become patients of his private company. Will the DOJ want to take on lawyer admission and disciplinary corruption on such an outsized scale as has been going on in Arizona?

There is an even chance that instigating reform will become the sole task of the Arizona Legislature. To be sure, the attentions of the DOJ and the legislature need not be mutually exclusive.

Another federal entity that might suitably investigate the State Bar of Arizona is the Internal Revenue Service (IRS). There are two likely grounds. As noted two paragraphs *supra*, the Bar has colluded with its hired "therapist," Howard Murray "Hal" Nevitt, in a racket whereby the latter has been signing up Bar members as private patients of his own for-profit business, which is located away from the Bar's premises. Appendix 6-6 *infra* shows how, consigned to the MAP program, a Bar applicant was maneuvered into additionally agreeing to be a patient of Nevitt's private company—and had to sign a contract to that effect. Another instance of the same thing—a MAP victim forced into agreeing to the "services" of Nevitt's private company—is documented in the Arizona Board of Behavioral Health Examiners Findings of Fact in AZBBHE File No. 2011-0063, discussed in Ch. 5 ii *infra*.

The Arizona Bar is constituted as a nonprofit organization exempted from federal income tax under the

Internal Revenue Code § 5 (c) (6).[189] As a § 501 (c) (6) nonprofit, the Bar can and should be investigated by the IRS for surreptitious transfer of its assets—assets that are supposed to be dedicated to not-for-profit purposes—to one of its employees, to support *his* for-profit enterprise.   For racketeering and violation of the IRC, the IRS should investigate not only the Bar, but also Nevitt.

Secondly, the Bar employs lobbyists, as was discussed in this chapter *supra* and in Ch. 3 i a *supra*. The Internal Revenue Code places significant restrictions on lobbying by § 501 (c) (6) entities. It requires that such lobbying be limited and relate strictly to the organization's tax-exempt purpose.[190] The IRS can and should investigate the State Bar of Arizona for likely violations of the IRC's restriction on lobbying.

That said, it is conceivable that ultimately, the Bar will continue its corrupt lawyer discipline practices unopposed because no entity will take on the Arizona Judicial Department. But for the moment, it is worth considering how the legislature might act.

Given that the Arizona Bar lobbies elected officials, at the time of this writing, the Arizona Legislature has shown remarkable independence of purpose in having twice considered bills to abolish the State Bar of Arizona. Suppose the legislature did abolish the Bar. Then its work would only be beginning, since there would be numerous claimants seeking redress.

What the legislature might do then is establish a Legislative State Bar Truth and Justice Commission. Individuals appointed by the legislature and/or the state governor to resolve grievances against the Bar and the Arizona Judicial Department could staff the Commission. Serving on the Commission would be restricted to individuals with no prior approval ("old boy" or "old girl") status with the State Bar of Arizona or the Supreme Court of Arizona. The members, in

---

[189] *See* State Bar of Arizona, "Financial Statements," *available at*: http://www.azbar.org/AboutUs/FinancialStatements. *See also* Rules of the Supreme Court of Arizona R. 32 (a), *cited in* Ch. 1 *supra*.

[190] *See* Jonn Francis Reilly and Barbara A. Braig Allen, "Political Campaign and Lobbying Activities of IRC 501(c)(4), (c)(5), and (c)(6) Organizations," 2003, *available at*: http://www.irs.gov/pub/irs-tege/eotopicl03.pdf.

other words, should be individuals whose participation could not be jocularly attributed to their being "Bar-flies."

Included among the Commission's tasks might be the following:

1. Hold public hearings and take testimony from aggrieved lawyers and Arizona Bar applicants.
2. Assume control of the assets of the State Bar of Arizona, holding them strictly in trust for the costs of the Commission's operations and for reparations to aggrieved Bar members and applicants.
3. Require the Supreme Court, on penalty of being held in contempt of the legislature, to turn over to the Commission all documents submitted to, generated by, or associated with the Committee on Character and Fitness, in order to make such documentation available for perusal by any affected applicant upon the applicant's showing that he or she was flagged with conditions on his or her admission.
4. Require, as well, the erstwhile State Bar of Arizona, all members of the Bar's Member Assistance Committee (MAC),[191] and Howard Murray "Hal" Nevitt, on penalty of being held in contempt of the legislature, to turn over to the Commission all files and documents in their possession pertaining to the conditional admission, mental "evaluation," or mental "treatment" of Bar applicants, in order to make such documentation available for perusal by any affected applicant, upon the applicant's showing that he or she was flagged with conditions on his or her admission.
5. In addition, require the erstwhile State Bar of Arizona to turn over all its disciplinary and personnel files.
6. In the case of every Bar applicant who did not put his or her own mental status at issue (by ascribing some undesired conduct to a mental or substance problem) in applying for Bar admission, and whose admission was made conditional on MAP intervention notwithstanding, upon such an aggrieved

---

[191]   For a list of the Member Assistance Committee's members and activities in 2013-14, *see* April 26, 2014, "Committee Wrap-Up Report," *available at*: http://www.azbar.org/media/445663/ member_assistance_committee_wrap_up_report_2013-2014.pdf. The report shows that, like the Supreme Court Committee on Character and Fitness, this State Bar committee has no medically qualified members.

individual's application, the Commission may pay monetary reparations out of the assets taken over from the State Bar of Arizona and/or from other suitable sources, such as penalties exacted from those who unjustly enriched themselves or who colluded in such misconduct against the aggrieved individual.

7.   In the case of every Bar member who did not put his or her own mental status at issue (by ascribing some undesired conduct to a mental or substance problem) in applying for Bar admission, and whose admission was made conditional on MAP intervention, since the Bar has routinely treated a history of conditional admission as an aggravating factor for subsequent disciplinary proceedings, the Commission may ask the legislature to pass a private bill vacating all subsequent disciplinary orders issued against the member and, if appropriate, reinstating that individual to the practice of law in Arizona; and, moreover, the Commission may ask the legislature, in passing a private bill, to also provide for monetary restitution to the member, upon the member's documenting his or her financial harms due to disciplinary orders imposed subsequent to the conditional admission.

8.   In the case of every Bar member who can show, by a preponderance of evidence, that he or she was disciplined unfairly, e.g. by a disciplinary panel one of whose members was a personal confederate of the Presiding Disciplinary Judge, or by a showing that Staff Bar Counsel willfully introduced false, misleading or perjured charges or evidence at a disciplinary hearing, or made false allegations, or by any other unfair condition that prejudiced the outcome in the disciplinary process, the Commission may ask the legislature to pass a private bill vacating the order of discipline and providing for monetary reparations to the member upon his or her documenting costs of fines, fees and expenses of disciplinary defense; and if there remain no other disciplinary orders pertaining to that member, the private bill may also, if appropriate, reinstate that individual to the practice of law in Arizona. In addition, since the Bar has automatically treated every prior discipline as an aggravating factor in all subsequent discipline, if a member can make a showing of unfair discipline in one disciplinary matter, the Commission may ask the legislature to pass a private bill vacating that and all subsequent orders of discipline against the member.

9.   Subpoena the Arizona Board of Behavioral Health Examiners' Executive Director Tobi Zavala and erstwhile Executive Director Debra Rinaudo, and its attorney, Marc H. Harris, for investigation of the circumstances of Howard Murray "Hal" Nevitt's licensure; require the Board, on penalty of being held in contempt of the legislature, to turn over all documents in its possession pertaining to the licensure of and complaints against Howard Murray "Hal" Nevitt; and make all such documents, heretofore concealed, available for public inspection.

10.   Subpoena the erstwhile CEO, General Counsel, and Personnel Records Manager of the State Bar of Arizona, on penalty of being held in contempt of the legislature, to turn over for scrutiny all documents pertaining to the association by employment, contract, informal work agreement, etc., with the Bar, of Howard Murray "Hal" Nevitt; and make these documents available for public inspection.

11.   Ask the U.S. Attorney to convene a federal grand jury to consider bringing charges of racketeering again the following: (a) the State Bar of Arizona's erstwhile CEO John F. Phelps, its erstwhile General Counsel John A. Furlong, Howard M. "Hal" Murray Nevitt, and Hon. William J. O'Neil; and (b) the Justices of the Supreme Court of Arizona; the relevant judges and officials or ex-officials of the Probate Department of the Maricopa County Superior Court; Peter and Heather Frenette; and all members of the erstwhile "Committee on Improving Judicial Oversight and Processing of Probate Matters." If the U.S. Attorney will not agree to do so, the Commission on Truth and Justice may ask the legislature to require the Maricopa County Attorney to convene such grand jury or grand juries.

12.   The Commission may consider asking the legislature to order the investigation of any lawyer who has served either Bar applicants or other Bar members as disciplinary defense counsel, upon any client Bar member or Bar applicant's showing, by a preponderance of evidence, that the defense counsel violated an ethical obligation, such as by overcharging, failure to zealously represent the client, etc.

13.   The Commission may ask the legislature to adopt legislation (a) prohibiting all Arizona professional licensing organizations from using the services of lobbyists (this will benefit the legislature itself by helping to protect its public reputation); and (b) altering Rules of the Supreme Court Rs. 46

and 51 so as to abolish the privilege of judges to forgo the approval of the Arizona government in creating and/or filling a judgeship, as well as any privilege of creating a tribunal *de novo*.

14.   The Commission may ask the legislature to adopt legislation modifying Arizona Rules of Civil Procedure R. 11 to make it resemble Delaware's version of R. 11, so as to afford an attorney, when sanctioned by a judge in a court proceeding, an automatic right to appeal the sanction.

5.   The Careers of Howard Murray "Hal" Nevitt, Director of the Arizona Bar's "Member Assistance Program"

...[A] Potemkin court. ... [A] stuffy room presided over by a corrupt judge, policed by unthinking guards, with lawyers who are there just to give the appearance of a real trial, and with no defendant in the cage; a place where lies reign supreme, a place where two and two is still five, white is still black, and up is still down, a place where convictions are certain, and guilt a given.

A place where an innocent man who was murdered by the state, a man whose only crime was loving his country too much, can be made to suffer from beyond the grave.

This is Russia today.

> Bill Browder, RED NOTICE. 2015: Simon & Schuster, p. 370.

... [T]he blacklist was a time of evil and ... no one on either side that survived it was untouched by evil. ... The first thing you did was go out to try to sell your house before anybody discovered—keep it quiet, get as much work as you can before it becomes public ... save every penny, and prepare to become a nobody. ... [Before Congress HUAC:] I think that there is a question of constitutional rights involved here. I believe I have the right to be confronted with any evidence that supports this question. I believe I have a right to see what you have.

> James Dalton Trumbo, 1970 Academy Award acceptance speech and 1947 testimony before Congress (*see* n. 8 *supra*)

Some readers may object that throughout this book, quotation marks have set off the name of the State Bar of Arizona office headed by Howard Murray "Hal" Nevitt, the "Member Assistance Program." The use of quotation marks has been intentional, owing to the term "Assistance," since this program has assisted no one other than those who have mined it for financial gain. Readers may also object to the use of quotation marks herein every time Nevitt is referred to as a "therapist." This usage too is intentional, since as will be shown *infra*, Nevitt, being a convicted felon, has never been qualified for an Arizona therapist license.

It is indisputable that Nevitt has been a salaried employee of the Arizona Bar. Moreover, lately as of the time of this writing, Arizona Attorneys Against Professional Regulation has received information that Nevitt now serves the Bar as a "consultant." Notwithstanding, some readers familiar with the State Bar of Arizona's communications since approximately 2012 may object that they see evidence that Nevitt is no longer directing the "Member Assistance Program."

There is, to be sure, evidence that the "Member Assistance Program" still exists. The Arizona Bar still lists an office with that designation in its "Staff Quick Reference List." However, Nevitt formerly was named as that office's Director, but at the time of this writing, the list omits information as to who is running MAP.[192] The Bar has also removed from the internet, or modified, some of its other official communications that once named Nevitt as MAP Director— although not all of them.[193]

Actually, the Bar does so much purging of its online public communications (such as by eliminating Nevitt's name from its "Staff Quick Reference List") that it might as well post every public communication on Snapchat. This is also true of the online public communications of the Supreme Court of Arizona. One is reminded of the protagonist of George Orwell's 1984, Winston Smith, and his fellow clerks at the Ministry of Truth, busily rewriting and expunging names of "unpersons" from newspapers in order to alter history.

Since 2012, the Bar has disseminated a few documents in which, coyly, hints have been dropped that functions of the "Member Assistance Program" have been outsourced and/or that Nevitt is a "former MAP Director."

For instance, minutes of a recent State Bar of Arizona Board of Governors Meeting speak of a "transition of the administration of the Member Assistance Program ... to

---

[192]   For the cite to the list, *see* n. 70 *supra*.
[193]   For instance, at the time of this writing, the internet carries a brochure produced by the Arizona Bar to welcome new members, naming Nevitt as the "MAP" Director; *see* www.azaacpr.org, webpage "Member Assistance Program" [1] paragraph 19, *citing* http://www.azbar.org/media/438414/new_member.pdf.

CorpCare, a company that was hired to provide behavioral health services to Bar members."[194] As was discussed in Ch. 3 i c 3 *supra*, the Bar contracted with "CorpCare" in 2012. However, in 2014, citing "service issues," the Bar supposedly discontinued its contract with "CorpCare." This raises a question about what service provider has been subsequently foisted on applicants and members ordered into "therapy."

To cite further evidence, in some disciplinary decisions issued since 2012, the Presiding Disciplinary Judge has been referring to Nevitt as MAP Director in the past tense.[195]

The public may be excused if, at this time, it cannot determine whether Nevitt is or is no longer at the Bar. As discussed in Ch. 3 *supra*, the Bar's lack of transparency is impressive. The Bar engages in so much secrecy that, if Nevitt is at the Bar at the present time, the Bar won't affirmatively say so; nor will the Bar issue any public announcement explicitly dissociating Nevitt from the Bar. At the time of this writing, the internet carries no announcement that Nevitt no longer works for the Bar, or alternatively, whether as an independent contractor, employee, or in some other capacity, he does still work for the Bar, and whether he does so in the office of the "Member Assistance Program" or in some other hutch or cranny of the Bar's premises.

The Bar's unwillingness to make an explicit disclosure about Nevitt's current position with or dissociation from the

---

[194] *See* "Meeting of the Board of Governors of the State Bar of Arizona June 18, 2013 Arizona Biltmore Resort – Grand Ballroom Phoenix, AZ," pp. 3396-97, *available at*:
http://www.azbar.org/media/721794/061813_board_minutes_draft_v4_w_motions.pdf.

[195] In an October 15, 2012, "Report and Order Imposing Sanctions" in a disciplinary case PDJ-2012-9094, p. 2 (6), the PDJ refers to Nevitt as a "former MAP director." *See* www.azaacpr.org, webpage "SBA 'Member Assistance Program'" [1] paragraph 19 *and see* http://www.azcourts.gov/LinkClick.aspx?fileticket= mWdsr2Z_Y90%3D&tabid=6472&mid=9452. *See also* a November 28, 2012, "Report and Recommendation" in PDJ-2012-9069, *available at*: http://www.azcourts.gov/LinkClick.aspx?fileticket=wVNL_Kmfndg%3 D&tabid=6730&mid=9816, p. 3 (7) and p. 5, referring to Nevitt as "then-Members [*sic*] Assistance Program Director" and "former Director of the Member Assistance Program." In this matter, as in a number of other disciplinary matters, Nevitt testified as a witness before the PDJ and a disciplinary hearing panel.

Bar is one reason the present work takes the position that, as of the time of this writing (mid-2015), Nevitt is still serving the State Bar of Arizona. In addition, evidence is found in other facts. Consider:

1.   In an email to Arizona Attorneys Against Professional Regulation dated August 1, 2012, reproduced in Appendix 5-1 *infra*, State Bar of Arizona CEO John F. Phelps addresses concerns of Arizona Attorneys Against Corrupt Professional Regulation by defending Nevitt, telling AZAACPR its complaints are unfounded. The email says, in effect, that neither has Nevitt done anything wrong, nor has the Bar misbehaved in utilizing Nevitt's services. Since the Bar's CEO's position—in mid-2012—is that Nevitt has done nothing wrong, why would the Bar discontinue Nevitt's services?

2.   It appears Nevitt is the only licensed "therapist" to have ever worked at the premises of the Arizona Bar (*see* this chapter, i *infra*). As stated *supra*, according to its official announcements, in 2012, the Bar outsourced MAP "therapy" services to a national entity, the corporation "CorpCare." Subsequently, members directed by the Bar to "CorpCare" have emailed AZAACPR stating that, in "evaluation" and/or "therapy" sessions, "CorpCare" "therapists" have admitted that, as to what mental diagnosis to assign and/or what "treatment" to recommend in a given case, the "CorpCare" "therapist" is taking directions from someone at the Arizona Bar. (One such communication to AZAACPR is reproduced in Ch. 6 "Attorney B" *infra*.[196]) If not Nevitt, who would *that* be?

3.   At the time of this writing, online advertisements for Nevitt's "therapy" services state that he directs the State

---

[196]   *See also* www.azaacpr.org, webpage "SBA 'Member Assistance Program'" [1] paragraph 21, stating that in 2014, individuals assigned to MAP were being directed to first phone not "CorpCare," but rather, to dial a certain number at the Bar. Calls to this number seem to have been taken by one Yvette Penar, presumably a clerical worker of the State Bar of Arizona.

Bar of Arizona's "Member Assistance Program."[197]

4.   Before 2012, e.g. in 2011, in some disciplinary matters, the Presiding Disciplinary Judge issued disciplinary orders imposing sanctions extending over several years.   In such a case, the PDJ assigned some role in implementing the disciplinary sanction to Nevitt, specifically in the latter's capacity as MAP Director.   There is no record of the PDJ subsequently modifying the order so as to reassign that role— as one would have expected if anyone else than Nevitt had succeeded him in running the Bar's MAP program.[198]

5.   In 2013, a Bar member (her Bar history is further discussed in Ch. 6 "Attorney D" *infra*), who had been admitted conditional to MAP in 2006—despite no prior mental or substance history—wrote to the State Bar of Arizona requesting all records pertaining to her conditional admission. The relevant part of the correspondence is reproduced in Appendices 5-2, 5-3 and 5-4 *infra*.

As shown in Appendix 5-2 *infra*, the Bar's General Counsel John A. Furlong responded to the records request with a letter dated June 14, 2013, stating that the Bar treats admission documents as confidential under Rules of the Supreme Court of Arizona R. 37 (c) "Miscellaneous Provisions Relating to Admissions," but that, notwithstanding, it was providing records.

R. 37 (c) designates as confidential all records created or amassed, whether by the Bar or by the Supreme Court's Committee on Character and Fitness, pertaining to an applicant's admission.   It is silent, however, about *medical* records created or amassed by the Bar or the Committee.

The Bar member examined the documents that Furlong provided.   As shown in Appendix 5-3 *infra*, on June 21, she wrote back to Furlong, saying that the documents provided were not responsive to her request.   She stated that she wanted to see the documentation comprising the grounds for her being subjected to conditional admission, including both the records of the Committee on Character and Fitness (flagging her as a mental case) that had been transmitted to the Bar, as well as

---

[197]   Various websites could be cited.   *See,   e.g.* http://familypsychassociates.com/therapists.html#Nevitt   (last accessed 7/4/15). *See also* www.azaacpr.org, webpage "SBA 'Member Assistance Program'" [1] paragraphs 18ff.

[198]   *See, e.g.* the 2011 Bar discipline case cited in n. 105 *supra*.

the record made by Howard Murray "Hal" Nevitt when in 2005, on the Bar's premises, he subjected her to a "screening evaluation" resulting in his decreeing that she would have to undergo "Member Assistance Program" intervention to join the Bar—and wherein he, Nevitt, physically molested her. The Bar member also demanded all records created or amassed by Nevitt and/or MAP over the year following her admission, when Nevitt was "supervising" her "therapy," which entailed his obtaining notes from the "therapist" he had assigned to her pursuant to the Bar's "Therapeutic Contract."

Furlong responded with a letter dated June 28, 2013, reproduced in Appendix 5-4 *infra*, wrongfully stating that Supreme Court rules (rules he had cited in his earlier letter) protected the Bar from having to disclose the documents. This is inaccurate. The rules do not intrude on the statutory right of an individual to obtain medical records, including mental "treatment" records.[199] The Bar and its employees are not at liberty to flout the state law requiring providers to honor patients' requests for such records. Even if R. 37 (c), cited in Furlong's June 14, 2013, letter, conflicted with the medical records statute (and the present work takes the position that it does not, because the Bar has exceeded its mandate to oversee Bar admissions by insinuating "therapy"), the statute is state law—not a mere Supreme Court rule. Thus, the statute prevails.

The statute protects a public right, and a Bar applicant or lawyer is a member of the public. Such rights cannot lawfully be abrogated on the excuse that the individual practices law or used to practice law. The inquirer has a statutory right to see the grounds based on which Nevitt decided to make a "therapy" case of her and subject her to a "therapeutic evaluation." Furthermore, what happened *after* she was admitted surely is not covered by R. 37 (c), which concerns only Bar admissions. Accordingly, she has a right to see the records of MAP's purported "supervision" of her "therapy," during which time—a year—she was subjected to Nevitt's repeated follow-up phone calls and letters, in addition to her furnishing required periodic reports to him. And since the Committee of Character and Fitness' determination, and

---

[199]   Pursuant to statute, A.R.S. § 12-2293 (A); *see* n. 57 *supra.*

Nevitt's "evaluation," were causal to this year of so-called "therapy," the member has a right to see those records too.

Contrary to Furlong's assertion, R. 37 (c) does not lawfully shield the Bar from responsibility for furnishing a member, on request, with the member's "therapy" records.

Also, as to the rule's protecting the Committee on Character and Fitness from having to disclose records of its deliberations, that privilege too is questionable. By flagging subjects for mental "evaluation," the Committee has forfeited the protection of R. 37 (c) by exceeding its mandate to evaluate applicants for professional licensure—and it has exceeded its mandate by violating federal law, the ADA, and the state statutory prohibition on practicing medicine without a license.

Furlong's June 14, 2013, letter, reproduced in Appendix 5-2 *infra*, also alludes to Rules of the Supreme Court of Arizona R. 70 (b) "Public Access to Information," which shields from disclosure "work product" of the Bar and its officials. Again, however, the rule does not justify whatever the Bar may have thought it was doing by hiring a "therapist." More to the point, it conflicts with lawyer ethics rules by trying to shield *non-lawyers* who the Bar happens to employ, such as Howard Murray "Hal" Nevitt. Furthermore, the rule enables the Bar (and is intended to enable the Bar) to conceal evidence that could be dispositive in a suit against the Bar on a theory of *respondeat superior* for employee misconduct. This puts the rule into conflict with the Arizona Constitution art. 18 § 6 "Recovery of Damages for Injuries." It accords the state's citizens an inviolable "right of action to recover damages for injuries" (i.e., a right to sue in negligence).[200] Thus R. 70 (b) not only overreaches, but even illicitly empowers the Bar to engage

---

[200] The Arizona Constitution's art. 18 § 6 "Recovery of Damages for Injuries" broadly guarantees the right, in Arizona courts, to bring actions in tort. The Arizona Supreme Court has held that this right extends not only to negligence claims but also to actions in defamation. *See Boswell v. Phoenix Newspapers, Inc.*, 730 P.2d 186, 152 Ariz. 9 (Ariz. 1986) (*en banc*), *available at*: http://law.justia.com/cases/arizona/supreme-court/1986/18159-pr-2.html.

in unconstitutional activity.[201]

In the June 28, 2013, letter, Furlong did not stop at disingenuously invoking rules but also accused this lawyer of being "unprofessional" and said her June 21 letter was an attempt to "threaten" both him and the Bar. This too is untruthful. An examination of her letter, reproduced in Appendix 5-3, shows it contains no threat and no improper language whatsoever. Not only was the accusation ridiculous and untruthful, but Furlong's pantywaist response was also downright ironic. For, years, as General Counsel, it is Furlong who has been advising the Bar on the unlawful racket whereby it had taken financial advantage of this woman; libeled her—including by falsely denouncing her in public as mentally ill; bullied her; practiced "therapy" on her and unlawfully concealed the records thereof from her; and compromised her safety, beginning in 2005 when the Bar dedicated a private room on its premises to making the selfsame Bar applicant physically accessible to Nevitt, under the pretext of a "therapeutic evaluation." (*See* Ch. 6 "Attorney D" *infra.*)

It happens that, at the same time she wrote to the Bar, the lawyer directed the same request to Nevitt. Appendix 5-5. She sent him a letter similar to the one she had addressed to the Bar, using the latest address she had been able to discover online for Nevitt, a Phoenix outfit called "Desert Cove Recovery Center" (*see* www.azaacpr.org, webpage "SBA 'Member Assistance Program'" [1] paragraph 22). Nevitt responded with a letter dated July 9, 2013, using old stationery for his Phoenix private practice "Innovative Workplace Solutions" (which he had already closed before 2013, shifting his practice to an outfit called "Family PsychAssociates;" *see id.* paragraph 20).

Nevitt did not state that he no longer was working for the Bar, although he asserted, "I am no longer an employee of the State Bar of Arizona." He answered the inquirer's request for his records by stating that all records were at the Bar. Nevitt enclosed a letter he purported to have sent to the

---

[201]   Furlong may have been implying that, having unfairly stigmatized this particular lawyer upon her admission with MAP, the Bar, by citing the circumstances of her admission as an "aggravating factor" in every record of subsequent discipline inflicted on her, somehow placed Nevitt's doings under the protection of R. 70 (b) by changing the records from medical in character to something else. This would be circuitous logic at best. *See* Ch. 6 "Lawyer D" *infra.*

"Lawyer Assistance Program" at the Bar for the purpose of "forwarding" the member's request. This and Nevitt's letter to the inquirer are reproduced in Appendix 5-5 *infra*.

The member believes that in the July 9, 2013, letter, Nevitt was disingenuous in asserting that the records she was seeking resided only at the Bar. This is so because, prior to giving the member, then a Bar applicant, an "evaluation," Nevitt obliged her to sign and return a contract for services with his private company, Innovative Workplace Solutions, LLC (on whose stationery Nevitt wrote his July 9, 2013, letter). This is discussed in Ch. 6 "Attorney D," while a copy of that contract appears in Appendix 6-6 *infra*.

Nevitt made this individual his private client, and as such, she is entitled to get her records from him. (Indeed, for years, Nevitt has shifted Bar members' records from the Bar's premises to his own business premises, as is discussed in connection with Arizona Board of Behavioral Health Examiners File No. 2011-0063 in this chapter, ii *infra*.)

The preceding discussion leads to the following point. Even supposing it were so that Nevitt has been 100% dissociated from the Arizona Bar, and the Bar is too coy to make any announcement publicly saying so, it remains a fact that, at the time he did the "therapeutic evaluation" at issue in the aforementioned correspondence, Nevitt certainly was a Bar employee. He was the Bar's "therapist," and any member who was subjected to his ministrations is entitled on request to his or her records, whether Nevitt is still at the Bar, in a shed behind the Bar, or in Outer Mongolia, and irrespective of what title or duties, if any, the Bar currently assigns him.

Moreover, even if at the time of the 2013 correspondence, Nevitt were no longer serving the Bar in any capacity, and all his MAP-related records were at the Bar, there would be no valid ground for the Bar to withhold the records of a former employee's "therapeutic evaluation" of a Bar applicant. The Bar employed Nevitt as a "therapist" in 2005 when it victimized this member. An individual subjected to "therapeutic evaluation" is entitled to the records by state statute. The Bar and Nevitt, in playing their game of "hide the records," were and continue to be conspiring together to violate the member's statutory right to access. There can be no other than a twofold motive: to protect Nevitt, as well as to shield the Bar from *respondeat superior* liability—and the most compelling possible reason the Bar would want to protect Nevitt, as well as itself, is that the Bar has never ended its association with Nevitt.

Too, the Bar is responsible for using unlawful tactics to protect itself from charges of racketeering by concealing evidence, choosing instead to join with Nevitt in playing a shell game[202] over records to which requestors are, by state statute and federal authority, entitled.

Lastly, even if at the time of this writing, Nevitt is in no association whatever with the Bar, the fact remains that for years, he was the Bar's salaried employee. Whatever may be his status with the Bar at the time of this writing, the Bar was and is responsible for hiring a convicted drug-dealer-user/felon, a killer, and an alleged sexual predator—and for covering up what he was doing at the Bar's premises.

Nevitt's background is discussed in the remainder of the present chapter.

i.   Howard Murray "Hal" Nevitt, Disgraced Law Enforcement
        Officer, Killer, and Felon[203]

Nevitt's background, ironically, would have made him unsuited for Arizona Bar admission. The unsuccessful 2004 Arizona Bar member application of James Hamm, an ex-convict once imprisoned for drug crimes and murder—crimes similar to Nevitt's crimes—bears this out.[204]

From 1994 to 2000, lawyer David N. Horowitz was Director of the State Bar of Arizona's "Member Assistance Program." At the time of this writing, he is in private practice of law in Phoenix.[205] From 2000 until 2004, the Director of the "Member Assistance Program" was a non-lawyer with an

---

[202]   The "shell game" is discussed in n. 50 and accompanying text *supra.*

[203]   *See also* azaacpr.org, webpage "SBA 'Member Assistance Program'" [8] and [10] [viii], [ix], outlining Nevitt's career.

[204]   *See id.* [8] paragraph 7.

[205]   *See* http://www.lawyers.com/phoenix/arizona/david-n-horowitz-36453862-a/ *and see* the listing for Horowitz on the State Bar of Arizona's website's "Find a Lawyer" function.

educational background in business administration, Diane M. Ellis.[206]

Meanwhile, as a young man, Nevitt started a career as a police officer for the City of Scottsdale, Arizona. One of his colleagues on the force was Mark Salem.[207]

In 1986, at the age of twenty-nine, terminated from the police force which he had served since 1978, Nevitt entered the facilities of the Arizona Department of Corrections as prisoner no. 058931, convicted in Maricopa County Superior Court case no. CR0000-156528 of two crimes: conspiracy; and possession and sale of a narcotic substance (cocaine), both class 2 felonies. During his imprisonment, Nevitt was disciplined for prohibited conduct, including operating a gambling ring in the prison and improper exchange of money and/or property.[208]

A few months prior to his disgrace and discharge, Nevitt, while on patrol, drew his gun and shot dead a mentally ill, gun-brandishing adult male. The man's parents sued in wrongful death and negligence. The ensuing civil case *Mulhern v. City of Scottsdale* went on appeal and, as an appellate case, has been published.[209] The Arizona Court of Appeals upheld the trial court's ruling that the City of Scottsdale had committed no negligence in retaining Nevitt on active duty at the time of the shooting even through his superiors knew, or should have known, that Nevitt was then engaged in alcohol and drug abuse and drug dealing.

By the time this case came to court, having been convicted separately on the drug charges, Nevitt was already a

---

[206]   *See* www.azaacpr.org, webpage "SBA 'Member Assistance Program'" [10] [ix] *and see* http://www.legalspan.com/catalog2/faculty.asp?UserID=U200111062453918014223%20%20%20&OwnerColor=%2300008C&recID=20030901-927128-85830.

[207]   *See* Salem's LinkedIn profile, *available at*: https://www.linkedin.com/pub/mark-salem/a/5b4/456. Mark Salem has been a defendant in a defamation suit alleging he may have acted badly on behalf of the Bar's Presiding Disciplinary Judge, William J. O'Neil. *See* Ch. 3 i c 1 *supra*. *See also* www.azaacpr.org, webpage "SBA 'Member Assistance Program'" [5] [a] paragraph 7.

[208]   *See*   https://corrections.az.gov/public-resources/inmate-datasearch [enter "Nevitt" as the search term].

[209]   *Mulhern v. City of Scottsdale*, 799 P.2d 15, 165 Ariz. 395 (Ariz. App. 1990), *available at*: http://az.findacase.com/research/wfrmDocViewer.aspx/xq/fac.19900510_0040291.AZ.htm/qx.

guest of the state. On the civilian's killing, Nevitt was never charged. His sentence on the drug charges was for five and a half years, but he was paroled two years ahead of the end of the sentencing period.

A mental evaluation by a Ph.D. psychologist Bruce Kushner, dated March 29, 1986, done preparatory to the court's disposal of Nevitt's case, found that Nevitt had longstanding polysubstance addiction issues as well as anti-social traits. However, the report, while acknowledging the shooting incident, referred to it only superficially, saying the incident had "not been fully explored" because it had not resulted in charges, while the crimes for which Nevitt had been charged took precedence. A copy of the report appears as Appendix 5-6 *infra*.

Appendix 5-7 reproduces a letter from a Dr. Damstra, another mind science professional. The letter, dated May 22, 1986, was procured by Nevitt's counsel, O. Joseph Chornenky, who also passed on this letter to the court to seek leniency in sentencing.

After his prison release, Nevitt earned a master's degree in social work at Arizona State University. He applied for licensing as a "certified substance abuse counselor" and as a "certified baccalaureate social worker." The Arizona Board of Behavioral Health Examiners conferred these licenses on Nevitt on January 1, 1994, and he has been continuously licensed since. However, the original 1994 licenses are now "closed" and "converted." From July 1, 2004, to the time of this writing, the Board has licensed Nevitt as a "Licensed Clinical Social Worker," license no. LCSW-3406, and as a "Licensed Independent Substance Abuse Counselor," license no. LISAC-0837.[210]

The Board has now been licensing Nevitt for over twenty years in violation of Arizona statute. A.R.S. § 32-3275 (A) (6) prohibits the Board's licensure of a person who has engaged in unprofessional conduct. A.R.S. § 32-3251 (15) defines "unprofessional conduct" and cites numerous criteria therefor, including criteria that should have disqualified Nevitt from licensure at the outset. Among these is the fact that he was stripped of his law enforcement authorization (peace officer certification) when in 1986, he was fired for misconduct by the

---

[210]   *See* http://www.azbbhe.us/ProDetail.asp?ProfID=30640.

131

Scottsdale Police Department. For this, licensure is precluded under §32-3251 (15) (ll). In addition, the very first definition of "unprofessional conduct," § 32-3251 (15) (a) addresses, and precludes, the licensure of a convicted felon.[211]

AZBBHE has repeatedly received complaints against Nevitt for unprofessional conduct. It is impossible to say how many complaints in all against Nevitt the Board has received because it publishes no information about complaints it does not formally investigate. Three Nevitt complaints that did result in formal investigation, two of which allege sexual misconduct, are of record. They are discussed in this chapter, ii *infra*.

Each time the Board has investigated a sexual assault allegation against Nevitt, the complaining party has raised the question as to why Nevitt was ever licensed in the first place. The Board has never responded. Arizona Attorneys Against Corrupt Professional Regulation has been contacted by the first individual who instigated an allegation of sexual misconduct against Nevitt that went so far as to be considered at a Board hearing. According to this individual, a Board member said, "Oh, ugh, we cannot get into that," when at the hearing, the complainant raised this question.

Eventually, the Board again investigated Nevitt after another individual alleged sexual misconduct. At the hearing to consider this allegation, the individual's statement was audio-recorded. A transcription appears in this chapter, ii *infra*. As the transcription shows, that individual, too, raised the question of why the Board ever licensed Nevitt—and that individual, too, received no answer.

Arizona Attorneys Against Corrupt Professional Regulation is aware that investigative journalists have unsuccessfully filed Freedom of Information Act (FOIA) requests with the Arizona Board of Behavioral Health Examiners to discover the particulars of Nevitt's licensure. The Board is unlawfully concealing from inquirers the particulars of the unusual circumstances whereby Nevitt, although unqualified for licensure, attained his licenses.

---

[211]   Aside from those criteria cited *supra*, there are other provisions of state statute which Nevitt's licensure violates; no attempt is made here to list all of them exhaustively. However, for a more complete listing, *see* www.azaacpr.org, webpage "SBA 'Member Assistance Program'" [10] [ix] [b].

More details about Board investigations of Nevitt are provided in this chapter *infra*.

In 2003, lawyer Chornenky went to court on Nevitt's behalf again. On August 5, 2003, in Maricopa County Superior Court, under the case number for his client's original criminal case (*see supra*), Chornenky filed an "Application to Set Aside Judgment of Guilt, Dismiss Charges, Restore Civil Rights and Restore Right to Possess Weapons." This document is reproduced in Appendix 5-8 *infra*. Chornenky supplemented his application, which was ultimately successful, with letters of well-wishers writing in support of Nevitt. Several are reproduced in Appendix 5-9 *infra*.

Two of these correspondents deserve special mention because they may have had a personal or pecuniary interest in seeing Nevitt replace Diane M. Ellis as the Director of MAP. Nevitt replaced Ellis in 2004, the year after the Application was filed. One of the correspondents was Ellis herself; *see* Appendix 5-9 *infra*.

Another individual who addressed a letter in support of restoration of Nevitt's "civil rights," also reproduced in Appendix 5-9 *infra*, was the Emergency Medicine-trained M.D. with a certification in Addiction Medicine, Michal Sucher, who was discussed in Ch. 3 iii *supra*. According to one source, about the final year of Ellis' tenure as Director of the Bar's "Member Assistance Program," Sucher's name began to appear in disciplinary orders as "Medical Director" for MAP. And in the period 2006-08, after Nevitt became MAP Director, he and Sucher were referring disciplinary subjects back and forth between one another, respectively as MAP Director and MAP "Medical Director."[212]

Yet another individual who, significantly, contributed a letter supporting Nevitt's cause in court, reproduced in Appendix 5-9 *infra*, is longtime staff attorney for the Arizona Attorney General's Office, as well as the attorney for the Arizona Board of Behavioral Health Examiners, Marc H. Harris. Since 2011, Harris has repeatedly been present at Board hearings where charges against Nevitt have been considered. Harris has advised the Board on these cases, even though he admitted in the supporting letter, dated March 31, 2003, that he had used Nevitt's services on behalf of the Attorney General

---

[212]   *See* www.azaacpr.org, webpage "SBA 'Member Assistance Program" [10] [ix] [a].

as a consultant and has had a personal relationship with Nevitt—and is therefore conflicted.

Harris has misconducted himself by failing to recuse himself from involvement in Nevitt's AZBBHE disciplinary matters.[213]

ii.   Howard Murray "Hal" Nevitt, "Member Assistance Program" Director and Bar Employee

As stated *supra*, in 2004, Nevitt succeeded Diane M. Ellis as Director of the State Bar's "Member Assistance Program." Michal Sucher, M.D., mentioned in this chapter, i *supra*, had been "Medical Director" for MAP under Ellis.   As also mentioned *supra*, between 2006 and 2008, Sucher was named as MAP's "Medical Director" in Bar documents concerning conditional admissions and attorney discipline.   In such documents, generally, Sucher was assigned some role relating to applicants' or members' substance abuse issues and/or remedial measures for same.

In time, however, Sucher's name disappeared from disciplinary and conditional admissions documents as Nevitt, more and more, "expanded the scope of his 'mental health' activities well beyond members and applicants with substance abuse issues" and began to target others, including "hapless lawyers and would-be lawyers who have no prior history of substance abuse or any other mental health issues (especially going after women and minorities in solo law practices ...)."[214]

On November 5, 2010, responding to a female subject's complaint of stalking and sexual assault, the Phoenix Police Department opened a report, DR No. 2010 01588991, naming Howard Murray "Hal" Nevitt as the suspect.   The same non-lawyer female subject would later file an Arizona Board of

---

[213]   For instance, Harris was present at two meetings of committees of the Arizona Board of Behavioral Health Examiners wherein allegations in File No. 2011-0063 (discussed *infra*) were considered, on July 21, 2011, and November 3, 2011.   Harris' name is listed in both meetings' minutes.   *See, respectively,* http://azbbhe.us/sites/default/files/sa_pdfs /sacc%20July%2011%20min.pdf *and* n.   96 *supra. See also* www.azaacpr.org, webpage "SBA 'Member Assistance Program'" [1] paragraph 13.
[214]   *See id.* [10] [ix] [b].

Behavioral Health Examiners complaint and a civil suit against Nevitt.

The police report states that, according to the female subject, for several years she had been doing some casual, part-time clerical work for Nevitt who, she said, she knew to be the Director of the Bar's "Member Assistance Program," as well as a married man. The report states: "On 2-7-10 ... Hal came to her home and forced her to masturbate him. ... Hal walked to the victims [*sic*] bedroom where she followed and [he] pulled down his pants and told her to give him a hand job. She said she told him she didn't want to." The report goes on to state that Nevitt spoke to the police when first contacted by phone about the investigation, but thereafter, handed off all police communications to his lawyer, O. Joseph Chornenky. No criminal proceedings ensued.

In October, 2010, the same female subject filed a complaint, File No. 2011-0063, with the agency responsible for licensing Nevitt, the Arizona Board of Behavioral Health Examiners. According to the complainant, she raised two allegations.

The first was that Nevitt had violated HIPAA privacy rules and AZBBHE patient confidentiality rules. It was alleged that Nevitt had shared with the complainant, who was neither a lawyer nor a Bar employee, but a part-time assistant at his private practice, information about his "services" with respect to a State Bar of Arizona member subjected to MAP, of which Nevitt was the Director.

As stated in n. 213 *supra*, at meetings on July 21 and November 3, 2011, the Board considered this allegation. As an outcome, the Board issued a Consent Agreement dated November 14, 2011. Nevitt, as Respondent, was made to acknowledge the veracity of Findings of Fact, including the following:[215]

...

---

[215] AZBBHE File No. 2011-0063, Consent Agreement, Findings of Fact, pp. 3-5. The complete Consent Agreement is *available at*: http://df7s0hkt8o8r9.cloudfront.net/media/english/pdf/sanctions/ HGPYF625546F380F4904B11152011.pdf. For the cite to the November 3, 2011, AZBBHE Substance Abuse Credentialing Committee Meeting Minutes recording the decision to discipline Nevitt, *see* n. 96 *supra*.

2.   Respondent is the Director of the State Bar's Member Assistance Program ("MAP"), a confidential program for impaired members.

3.   As the Director of MAP, Respondent had access to confidential behavioral health information regarding Bar Members.

4.   Beginning in 01/08, Respondent began documenting communications from third parties including Complainant indicating that a specific attorney ("Attorney") was abusing alcohol.

5.   In response to these communications, Respondent began encouraging Attorney to voluntarily enter MAP to address her alcohol abuse issues, which Attorney initially declined. Eventually, Attorney was mandated to submit to an evaluation for structured monitoring.

6.   After Complainant initiated her concerns about Attorney, Respondent hired Complainant to provide administrative services at his private practice ("IWS")[216] independent of his duties as MAP Director.

7.   In 01/10, Attorney entered MAP and Respondent began monitoring/treating her according to Attorney's MAP program with regard to her alcohol abuse issues.

8.   Respondent ensured that Attorney signed a HIPAA form, which prohibited Respondent from disclosing any information about her without a signed release of information authorization.

9.   Respondent disclosed the following to her [Complainant]: a. Information Respondent received indicating that Attorney was abusing alcohol. b. Actions the State Bar took with regard to its investigation of the allegations against Attorney.

---

[216]   Innovative Workplace Solutions, LLC, a company that Nevitt established and operated for several years. IWS appears to have subsequently morphed into another entity called Family PsychAssociates. According to the Arizona Corporation Commission listing for IWS (File No. L10831765), *available at*: http://ecorp.azcc.gov/Details/Corp?corpId=L10831765 (last accessed 6/28/15), the latest listed street address of IWS is an address identical to that of Family PsychAssociates, *available at*: https://plus.google.com/101682473072710619484/about?gl=us&hl=en. *See* n. 221 and accompanying text *infra*.

10.   Complainant's allegations were supported by audio recordings she made of telephone conversations with Respondent.

11.   Respondent acknowledged that he discussed confidential information about Attorney obtained while in his position as the MAP Director with Complainant without Attorney's written permission to do so. ...

...

13.   The State Bar confidentiality agreement Respondent signed specifically provided that he was prohibited from releasing any confidential information he obtained through his State Bar employment without ... prior written consent ... .

14.   There was no information indicating that Respondent sought or obtained prior written consent from the State Bar before releasing confidential information regarding Attorney to Complainant.

15.   There was nothing about the IWS confidentiality agreement that relieved Respondent of his obligation under the State Bar confidentiality agreement to obtain prior written consent before releasing any confidential information he obtained through his State Bar employment.

Finding of Fact (6) *supra* discloses that the complaint concerned a MAP case about which the complainant learned while working not for the Bar, but for Nevitt's private practice. The significance of this is that it is evidence that Nevitt has made it his routine to take cases of Arizona Bar members on whom MAP has been imposed and transfer the cases to his own private practice (in this instance, "IWS," or Innovative Workplace Solutions, LLC—a private practice that he has operated concurrent with serving the Bar as MAP Director). In other words, Nevitt has been treating the Bar's "mental" cases as his own private patients. Another instance of this is discussed in Ch. 6 "Attorney D" and Appendix 6-6 *infra*.

It is the position of the present work that the Arizona Bar has been aware of and has colluded with Nevitt in this; and that accordingly, the pattern comprises actionable racketeering.

The Board took action with an Order requiring Nevitt to sign the Consent Agreement (which he did, dating his signature

November 11, 2011), to undergo probation, to pay a $1000 civil penalty (which the Board stayed pending compliance with the consent agreement) and costs, and not to engage in clinical activities while subject to the agreement.

Unaccountably, however, the Board suspended the agreement and released Nevitt from all its terms on April 2, 2012.[217]

According to the complainant, the same complaint, AZBBHE File No. 2011-0063, included another allegation against Nevitt, one of sexual misconduct. At its November 3, 2011, meeting, according to the complainant, the Board heard the complainant's evidence about the alleged sexual assault, but the members voted not to pursue the allegation.[218]

Nevitt was also busy in 2011 due to a separate complaint, AZBBHE File No. 2011-0119, filed by a different complainant. The Arizona Board of Behavioral Health Examiners, evidently taking its cue from the State Bar of Arizona, has failed to be transparent about complaints against Nevitt, including this complaint. No information has been provided to the public other than a record that the complaint was dismissed. Arizona Attorneys Against Corrupt Professional Regulation, however, has received information that the complaint was due to a refusal by Nevitt to provide "treatment" records to the complainant, a Bar member subjected to mental "therapy" under MAP. Minutes of the

---

[217]   See April 4, 2012, "Case No. 2011-0063 Release from Consent Agreement and Order," *available at*:
http://azbbhe.us/pdfs/BoardOrder/2011-0063.pdf *and see* n. 210 *supra* for a cite to a summary alluding to this Release and Order. The abrupt suspension of the disciplinary Order begs the question of manipulation, possibly though Nevitt's friend, lawyer Marc H. Harris, perhaps acting for the State Bar of Arizona, which then employed Nevitt as its "therapist" and MAP Director.

[218]   See Ch. 3 i b 2 *supra*. N. 96 *supra* includes a cite to a roll call vote by Board members who attended the November 3, 2011, AZBBHE meeting. The meeting minutes (also cited in n. 96), p. 4, indicate that this particular vote was taken on the allegation that resulted in the Consent Agreement. There is no record in any AZBBHE public document of the File No. 2011-0063 complainant's advancing a sexual misconduct allegation against Nevitt, nor of how the Board disposed of same.

Board's October 6, 2011, meeting indicate that the Board considered and voted to dismiss this complaint.[219]

On January 20, 2012, the same female subject who complained to the Phoenix Police Department and to AZBBHE in File No. 2011-0063 also, through counsel, filed a civil action against Nevitt, Maricopa County Superior Court Case No. CV2012-001509. The Complaint alleged Assault, Battery, and Intentional Infliction of Emotional Distress. Nevitt, named with his marital community and his company Innovative Workplace Solutions, LLC, as Defendant (the Arizona Bar was not a Defendant), was represented by attorneys James L. Blair and N. Todd McKay of the Phoenix law firm Renaud Cook Drury Mesaros, PA.

Arizona Attorneys Against Corrupt Professional Regulation has received information that in this matter, funding for both legal services to Nevitt and for a monetary settlement were furnished by professional liability insurer called Home Assurance/Chartis Insurance Group. However, at the time of this writing, it is unclear who paid the insurance premiums for Nevitt's policy.

An Amended Verified Complaint filed on April 17, 2012, stated that Plaintiff had been working for Defendant and Defendant's company, Innovative Workplace Solutions, LLC, under contract, and that she had also been performing personal duties for Defendant (paragraph 72). Further, it stated that Defendant has falsely made representations to the Plaintiff about "getting Plaintiff a job as his assistant in his capacity as Director of Member Assistance Program [*sic*] of the State Bar of Arizona" (paragraph 65) and had been "telling Plaintiff she could get her 'foot in the door' for a position as Defendant's assistant at the State Bar of Arizona in a position opening up in the near future" (paragraph 67). Allegedly, Nevitt also tried to put himself in a position of trust and confidence with the plaintiff by seeking out details of her life and mental state.

---

[219]   *See* the July 21, 2013, AZBBHE meeting minutes *cited in* n. 213 *supra*, referring to this file number, *and see* "Arizona Board of Behavioral Health Examiners Meeting Minutes October 6, 2011," *available at*: http://azbbhe.us/pdfs/minutes%20agendas/board %20oct%2011%20min.pdf. *See also* www.azaacpr.org, webpage "SBA 'Member Assistance Program'" [6] paragraph 8.

The Amended Verified Complaint also alleged a sexual assault, for which it says the Plaintiff had been compelled to seek medical treatment, as follows:

14.   On January 19, 2010, Defendant went to Plaintiff's home in Maricopa County, Arizona, unannounced.

15.   Defendant took Plaintiff's hand and told her "come with me" and led Plaintiff to Plaintiff's bedroom.

16.   Defendant stated "trust me" and then unzipped his pants.

17.   Defendant pulled Plaintiff toward himself, grabbed her by the hair on the back of her hair [sic], and then shoved Plaintiff onto her bed.

18.   Defendant told Plaintiff he was very stressed out.

19.   Defendant then demanded that Plaintiff masturbate him.

20.   Plaintiff, who was in a state of panic and rapidly escalating fear for her safety, told Defendant she did not want to do that.

21.   Defendant then told Plaintiff, "Trust me, it's okay and nobody will know."

22.   Plaintiff again told Defendant "No", and began to cry hysterically.

23.   Defendant forced Plaintiff to masturbate him while holding the back of her neck with his hand.
...

28.   Plaintiff then got up from the bed, washed her hands, walked to the living room, and sat on the couch shaking and crying, and in a state of shock.

29.   Defendant then came to the living room and tried to sit next to Plaintiff who was sitting on the couch. Plaintiff then got up from the couch and walked toward the front door.

30.   Defendant then stated, "Come over here, I want to hold you and make you feel better."

31.   Plaintiff asked Defendant to leave because she was extremely upset, was crying and fearful of Defendant due to the sexual assault Defendant had

just committed upon Plaintiff in the manner
described above.
32.   Plaintiff was at the front door and demanded
the Defendant to leave.
33.   Defendant then grabbed Plaintiff's hand and
tried to place it on his crotch area while shoving
Plaintiff against the entryway closet door.
...
36.   Defendant then stated, "Feel this. This is what
you do to me."
37.   Plaintiff then became angry pushing
Defendant away from her and again demanded that
Defendant leave.

Because the Plaintiff stated that she could identify
distinctive physical characteristics of Nevitt's genitalia, her
attorney requested, and obtained, a court order requiring
Nevitt to submit to a physical examination by a physician.
Nevitt, presumably on advice of his counsel, never complied
with the order. The case did not go to trial. It ended in a
settlement in mid-2014.

On June 28, 2012, a different complainant sent the
Arizona Board of Behavioral Health Examiners a letter which
eventually became the start of another disciplinary matter,
AZBBHE File No. 2013-0002.[220] The complainant alleged that
Nevitt had sexually assaulted her, a Bar member applicant, on
December 23, 2005, at the State Bar of Arizona's Phoenix
premises, under the pretext of a MAP-related "therapeutic
evaluation."

The complainant told the Board that Nevitt had directed
her in writing to pay in advance for "evaluation" after the
Supreme Court's Committee on Character and Fitness flagged
her as mentally ill, notwithstanding her lack of any prior
mental or substance history. The letter is reproduced in
Appendix 6-7 *infra*. The body of the letter states:

---

[220]   A concise summary of AZBBHE File No. 2013-0002 is
available at: www.azaacpr.org, webpage "SBA 'Member Assistance
Program'" [1] paragraphs 12-13. *See also* Ch. 6 "Attorney D" *and*, for
the text of the complainant's June 28, 2012, letter to AZBBHE, *see*
Appendix 6-7 *infra*.

On the aforementioned date, about 1 or 2 pm, directed by Nevitt in advance as to where and when to appear for the supposed "evaluation," I went to the SBA [State Bar of Arizona] offices at 4201 N. 24th St., Phoenix, 2d floor. Across from the receptionist desk was a small enclosed room. I was instructed to sit inside there and wait. Mr. Nevitt entered and from then on for the next hour, he and I were alone and he kept the door closed. His "evaluation" included detailed questions about my sexual habits: was I homosexual or heterosexual, was I or had I been married, how many times had I been married, when had I first and how recently had I had sexual relations, how frequently on average did I engage in sexual relations, through which orifice(s) and/or with what objects did I engage in sexual acts, and several other sex-related questions.

I do not consider these as questions appropriate to mental health provider's first professional meeting with a subject who has not complained of sexual dysfunction and where the goal is (supposedly) to determine whether that person has the mental stability to engage in the practice of law.

At the conclusion of the "evaluation" I rose from my chair and made for the door, at which point Nevitt stepped between me and the door, blocking my exit. He put out his right hand, fondled the left side of my neck and my left shoulder, and then moved his hand so that the palm made contact on the clothes over my left breast. I immediately took two steps backward, breaking the contact. Nevitt stopped himself and frowned. Evidently he was considering the potential risk, the room containing us being just off SBA's busy main lobby. He stepped away and I rushed out of the room.

Nevitt then retaliated by issuing a letter to the Committee [on Character and Fitness] stating that he considered me as needing mental illness treatment during my "difficult" first year of membership in SBA for the purpose of "relationship dynamics."

142

The Board convened a meeting on December 5, 2013, to consider the allegation (*see* n. 91 and accompanying text *supra*). While counsel, one Faren Akins, appeared for Nevitt—and Nevitt's friend Marc Harris, counsel to the Board, was present—Nevitt did not appear. The Board, in an odd reversal of the expected order of events, first took a vote to dismiss the complaint, then invited the complainant to make a statement. The statement was audio-recorded and a transcript has been made available to Arizona Attorneys Against Corrupt Professional Regulation. The complainant said:

> I'm the complainant in File No. 2013-0002 concerning this Board's licensee Howard "Hal" Murray Nevitt. I complained on June 28, 2012. I received a notice from this Board postmarked July 1, 2013, inviting me to submit additional materials. On July 22, I did submit additional documentation by mail.
>
> The notice I received from this Board states in capital letters boldface: "YOU ARE STRONGLY ENCOURAGED TO ATTEND THE INFORMAL MEETING. IF YOU CHOOSE NOT TO ATTEND, THE CREDENTIALING COMMITTEE MAY PROCEED IN YOUR ABSENCE AND MAKE RECOMMENDATIONS TO THE BOARD DESPITE YOUR FAILURE TO ATTEND THE INFORMAL MEETING."
>
> Because I don't want to see more people victimized, I've taken my courage in my hands and I've come to this meeting. In my mailing of July 22, I noted that Nevitt has had a felony conviction. In 2003, he applied to the Maricopa County Superior Court to set aside his conviction and, in his application, he also asked that his "gun rights" be restored.
>
> I didn't know about any of this when there took place the meeting on December 23, 2005, at the premises of the State Bar of Arizona, where Nevitt was an employee. I'm talking about the meeting at which he fondled me, and as an outcome of which he directed me to get mental therapy, under his supervision, as a condition of joining the Bar. I did not and do not

consider myself the mentally ill party; but even if I had been seeking mental illness treatment, I certainly would not have sought it from a 400-pound ex-convict, a degenerate with a history not only of drug dealing, but also of murdering a civilian under the color of law, as I have described in my July 22 materials.

When it licensed him, what in the world was this Board thinking? When it hired him, what in the world was the State Bar of Arizona thinking? As a five-foot tall, sixty-year-old woman, I have taken my courage in my hands to come to this meeting. Now, I want to ask only that the Board arrange with building security so that I can get away from this place while Nevitt, if he is present, is made to stay in this room until I am safely gone. And other than that earnest request, that's all I have to say.

Around 2011 or 2012, or about the time complaints against him began to proliferate with the Arizona Board of Behavioral Health Examiners, Nevitt stopped publicly identifying himself with his business "Innovative Workplace Solutions, LLC" (although at the time of this writing, it still has an active listing with the Arizona Corporation Commission). He has transitioned his professional activities to another entity at the same Phoenix street address, "Family PsychAssociates." In addition, Nevitt's name has been associated with several other Phoenix-area or Scottsdale-area "therapy" outfits as a consulting "therapist," including one outfit called Desert Cove Recovery Center and another called North Ridge Counseling.[221]

Arizona Attorneys Against Corrupt Professional Regulation is sometimes addressed with non-lawyers' concerns about Nevitt. For instance, in 2014, Arizona Attorneys Against Corrupt Professional Regulation received several emails. The authors stated they were non-lawyers and not under Arizona

---

[221]   *See* www.azaacpr.org, webpage "SBA 'Member Assistance Program'" [1] paragraphs 20, 22. *See also* n. 216 *supra.* At the time of this writing, Nevitt's name, photo and bio appear among the "therapist" listings for Family PsychAssociates, *available at:* http://familypsychassociates.com/therapists.html (last accessed 6/29/15).

Bar "Member Assistance Program" supervision. Both complained that Nevitt had behaved unprofessionally in a group counseling session at the aforementioned North Ridge Counseling. The authors said they had researched Nevitt online and found the AZAACPR website. At the time of this writing, Nevitt continues to be listed as a "program clinical director" at North Ridge Counseling.[222]

To close this chapter, there follows the content of these emails. Names (if provided; many correspondents contact AZAACPR anonymously or use fictitious names) and contact information are redacted.

The following chapter will reproduce communications from aggrieved State Bar of Arizona members.

(1)

Sep 26, 2014

From: ███████████████
To: Bartus Trust

hello,

I,m not sure if you can help me but, I,m enrolled at North Ridge counseling, There is a counselor here, his name is Hal Nevitt, I,m worried about this person as a counselor, yesterday he badgered me for 45 minutes in group meeting. The women in the group were very nervous, one had to leave.

I do not trust anyone at north ridge, thats why I,m contacting AZAACPR.
Should I be concernerd?
My number ██████████

(2)

Sep 26, 2014
From: ████████████
To: Bartus Trust

---

[222]   *See* http://northridgecounseling.com/about/staff/ (last accessed 6/28/15).

I am currently doing outpatient counseling at North Ridge Counseling in Scottsdale. Hal Nevitt is one of the therapists there. This article was brought to my attention following an incident that occurred on 9/25/2014 during our morning group.

I feel unsafe and I am unsure of how to proceed. Can someone please call me? I am in group again with him this morning from 10:00 - 11:15am. My mobile number is ██████████.

Thank you,

██████████

(3)

Sep 27, 2014
From: ██████████
To: Bartus Trust

Hi,

Thank you for the information.

I am not an attorney. I am someone who has been victimized by him while he was leading our group counseling session.

I Googled his name and your website came up. I am completely horrified (although not surprised) by what I read.

Thank you again for helping me.

Sincerely,

██████████

146

6.   In Their Own Words:
State Bar of Arizona Members Speak

A government program with secrecy plus lack of oversight leads to mission creep. And that leads to the move to the indefensible.

Fritz Schwarz, lead counsel to the 1975-1976 Church Committee hearings in Congress.[223]

At the time of this writing, the State Bar of Arizona is phasing in a $60 member dues increase.[224] The State Bar of Arizona has nearly 20,000 members.[225] As mentioned in Ch. 4 *supra*, the U.S. Department of Justice began intensively investigating unlawful state bar admissions practices about 2011. The website of Arizona Attorneys Against Corrupt Professional Discipline launched in 2012. It began educating the public about Arizona Bar corruption, including the excesses committed under the aegis of the Bar's "Member Assistance Program."

Assuming that annually, the Arizona Bar used to take in a king's ransom (it reported about a quarter of a million dollars' annual income) from the "Member Assistance Program," but by its own report, MAP no longer garners such vast revenue,[226] the dues increase will compensate. It will provide additional revenue of $1.2million annually by the time it is fully phased in. This will be more than enough (several times over) to compensate, if indeed there has been any revenue lost.

Although it is the present work's position that the Arizona Bar is not being and has never been transparent about

---

[223]   *Cited by* Bill Moyers, "Another Church Committee?" *Bill Moyers Journal,* October 26, 2007, *available at:* http://www.pbs.org/moyers/journal/blog/2007/10/ another_church_committee_1.html *and cited in: 1971* (documentary film) (Maximum Pictures & Fork Films 2014).
[224]   *See* n. 59 *supra.*
[225]   *See* http://www.martindale.com/Professional_Development/ Bar_Associations/US_State/arizona.aspx.
[226]   *See* n. 48 *supra.*

how much money it takes in from unlawful "therapy"-related impositions, suppose as follows. Even if over the last few years, annual MAP revenue has gone from, say, a million dollars to zero, still, the dues increase will fully compensate. But an alternative way of looking at it is that the victims of MAP excesses have heretofore been subsidizing lower dues for an entire membership that is kept in subjection to the State Bar of Arizona's avarice.

But there is much worse at hand. The fact that the dues increase more than offsets any financial losses the Bar may be experiencing, and enriches the Bar's coffers more than ever before, is ominous for justice in Arizona. The State Bar of Arizona is the moneymaking arm of the Arizona Judicial Department. More money at the disposal of government, plus secrecy and nonaccountability, is not a recipe for self-reform. On the contrary, it means that the corruption of the Arizona Judicial Department and its satellites is about to get worse.

As the it appointed a "Cover-up Committee" about probate matters in 2010 (*see* Ch. 2 ii *supra*), the Supreme Court of Arizona lately says it is constituting a committee to make changes to the Bar. The membership of this committee consists of the usual suspects (some of their names, like those of past Bar Presidents Ed Novak and Amelia Craig Cramer, and Supreme Court of Arizona Justice Rebecca White Berch, appear elsewhere herein, and all the members have the approval and confidence of the Arizona Supreme Court). The committee's stated purpose is to propose changes to the Rules of the Supreme Court of Arizona as regards the functions of the Board of Governors of the State Bar.[227]

---

[227] For a listing of the members of this committee, termed the "Task Force on the Review of the Role and Governance Structure of the State Bar of Arizona," *see* Gary Grado, "State Supreme Court to Look into Potential Changes in State Bar," *Arizona Capitol Times*, July 30, 2014, *available at*: http://azcapitoltimes.com/news/ 2014/07/30/state-supreme-court-to-look-into-potential-changes-in-state-bar/. *See also* Supreme Court of Arizona Administrative Order No. 2014-79 establishing the committee, *available at*: http://www.azcourts.gov/Portals/22/admorder/Orders14/2014-79.pdf; *and* a committee report dated September 1, 2015, *available at*: http://www.azcourts.gov/Portals/74/GOV/REPORT/WebFINALM andGReport%2008312015.pdf.

Thus, in its customary fashion, the Arizona Judicial Department is responding today to critics as it did in 2010—with reassuring public noises suggesting a possibility of improvement and reform. But the fact that the Bar is going after more and more impositions from members shows that the real path will be to anywhere but reform.

As noted *supra*, without placing his or her professional license at risk, no Arizona-licensed lawyer can sue, or take vigorous issue with, the State Bar. Over the several years of its operation, AZAACPR's website has received communications from victimized Bar members and applicants. Most either do not give away much about themselves, or alternatively, ask that their identifying information not be disclosed.

In this chapter, redacted content from their emails is reproduced. In most, only the name and contact information is omitted *infra*; correspondents' names are omitted even if the name provided is an obvious pseudonym. In some instances, to protect the correspondent's identity, other material is also redacted. Redacted material is blacked out or replaced by text in square brackets.

An exception is made in the case of the last lawyer whose story will be shared *infra*. A disbarred attorney who cannot be re-disciplined, she has agreed to disclose her identity and has shared much more detailed information about her experiences with State Bar conditional admissions and discipline than any other correspondent.

Here are the stories of victims of State Bar of Arizona corruption.

Attorney A

Oct 17, 2012
From: ███████████
To: Bartus Trust

I need to talk to someone who can give me candid feedback on the MAP process for a (prospective) conditional admitee.

I am a ██████-licensed attorney in good standing. I took a 2-year contracted job in AZ, for which I took and passed the July 2012 UBE (AZ) exam, with very high marks. But I do have one blemish on my record -- a DUI from my 2L year in law school. Standard, non-aggravated misdemeanor out of ████████. No other substance abuse issues whatsoever.

Today, I got notice from the CCF that I have to undergo a mandatory $1,200 "long" psych evaluation. After that, in an undisclosed amount of time (no ballpark figure was given despite my request), I will be conditionally admitted (no idea as to what kinds of conditions), though a colleague of mine who has gone through this a few years ago tells me that it will most likely be one year with mandatory meetings and random drug/alcohol testing.

Since I am a member of the ████ bar in good standing (yes, they vetted the same issue, which was obviously more recent when I applied to the ████ bar, but I was fully cleared), and my family and partner live in ████, and my current AZ job contract expires in 14 months anyway -- should I just withdraw my bar application and quit my AZ job?

Thank you very much!

Attorney B

Oct 31, 2013
From: ████████████
To: Bartus Trust

I am an AZ attorney who has been dealing with the abuses of the SBA, MAP and Hal Nevitt for well over 5 years. Based on Hal's reccomendation, the Bar even required my non-attorney husband to undergo psychological evaluation as a condition of my admission. Despite the full cooperation of both me and my husband and an evaluation by an outside therapist, Hal actively attempted to get me to leave my marriage for years. I complained that Hal was inappropriate and sexist and requested he leave his door open and not hug/touch me during our mandatory meetings, after which he and other Bar employees became even more aggressive and fabricated allegations against me and required me to comply with additional unnecessary/unfounded psychological treatment. I

150

have submitted a "clean MMPI II", an evaluation by an outside therapist, letters from 2 of my treating physicians and letters/evaluations from 2 physicians chosen by the Bar to no avail. Also, I recently had an "evaluation" through Corp Care, and the evaluator essentially told me the Bar instructs him what to recommend. It makes me wonder whether Hal is still pulling the strings, and if not, who is?

These are just a few small examples of my experiences with the Bar/MAP. It has been an unbelievable and unfounded source of stress and intrusion into my personal and professional lives, and regardless what they do to me, I want to help protect future attorneys/applicants from such abuses. The Bar and MAP are overstepping; yet, they hold all the power over AZ attorney's careers, so no one wants to stand up to them.

I would really like to discuss my experiences with you ASAP. Please call me at ███████████.

████████

Nov 4, 2013
From: ██████████
To: Bartus Trust

I completely understand. I actually would appreciate if you would not post my name on the site should you use my story. I have seriously considered a lawsuit. In response to your questions:

1. I have heard rumors of the issues involving MAP and Hal, so I searched the web for "Arizona State Bar scandal," and your site came up.

2. I know a few people who have had similar issues with the bar, but there is only one attorney who may be willing to participate in a lawsuit. He has considered it himself, but he is still a successful practi

151

Nov 4, 2013
From: ██████████
To: Bartus Trust

Oops. I accidentally sent my email before it was
finished. Sorry.

1. I searched on "Arizona State Bar scandal" online, and your
site came up. 2. I know a few others who have had problems
with the bar, but only one of them may be willing to participate
in a lawsuit. He has talked about it before but is a successful
practicing lawyer, so he may be hesitant. He may, however, be
willing to handle a lawsuit. 3. Yes, please give my contact
information to the ██████ considering a suit.   4. Yes, I would
be willing to participate in a lawsuit. I have thought about it
myself but have been afraid it would make things
worse.   However, I realize the bar is never going to stop
creating issues for me. If I do lose my license trying to
improve the system for others, it would be worth it to me. 5. I
have not lodged complaints with any agency outside the bar
itself.   My attorney and friends advised me against it. I have
spoken about it extensively with attorney and non-attorney
friends, my lawyers, doctors and 2 counselors. ████████████
████████████████████████████████. 6. I would be willing
to speak to ██████████, but I am a little worried that a
number of the details of my story will point the bar directly to
me. If I have already lost my license when a suit is filed, I fear
I will lack credibility. I will discuss it further with my attorney
and maybe just be careful how much I divulge. ████████████
██
██
████████████████████████

Thank you for your email and for the work you are doing with
AZAACPR. Someone needs to let people know the truth and
let attorneys know they are not alone. I look forward to
hearing from someone.

████████████

Nov 6, 2013
From: ███████████
To: Bartus Trust

I will speak to my friends about contacting you. My husband
is willing to be part of a lawsuit, but he is wary of speaking to a
reporter at least prior to that. I can ask him again, but he is
just concerned that something he says or does will affect my
situation with the bar.

███████████

Nov 6, 2013
From: ███████████
To: Bartus Trust

Thank you for your confidentiality and understanding.

Yes, the attorney I spoke of is admitted to practice in federal
court. I will call him to discuss his willingness to handle a
lawsuit(s) and get back to you.

███████████

Nov 20, 2013
From: ███████████
To: Bartus Trust

I was prefer not to have my name or documents published at
least for now. I am still in the midst of the storm with the bar
and fear retaliation. I've been a little worried about how much
to share with you for fear of the bar finding out.

I have been
███████████████████████████████████ and have
not had much free time. I do not have anything documented
about my complaints/request regarding Hal. I know that was
unwise, but he got upset and I was afraid of retaliation when I

153

just talked to him and "my" attorney about it, that I was afraid of the retaliation. I asked him not to touch/hug me and to leave the door open during our meetings, and I discussed it with my attorney who said she addressed it with Hal or bar counsel. I know she spoke to Hal about it, because he brought it up at our next meeting. He said he knew I was "telling people" he was inappropriate toward women and "assured" me I was wrong. I do not believe we emailed about it but will check. Hal ran so extremely hot and cold with me, and I often told people he seemed bipolar. He would be all huggy and almost "tender" with me but other times would yell at me and not allow me to speak. He had me in tears more than once during both meetings at one of his offices or unscheduled calls at home.

As for my husband, I will look for the documentation. I believe it is in either my initial conditional admission agreement or my MAP agreement. If not, it is certainly documented in emails and the therapist's evaluation. I imagine the therapist would surely have proof of it also. It was in ███, but it was a big issue and there was a lot of communication about it.

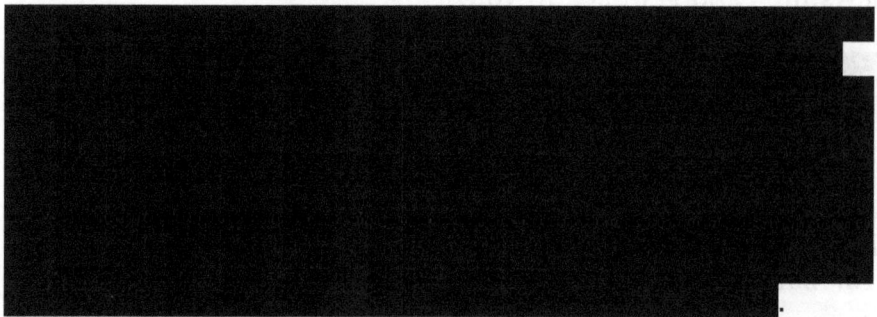

Do you know of a good lawyer for defending against the bar? What do you think of ██████████████ ████████ or ████████?

I have recently found out that [NAME OF STAFF BAR COUNSEL] requested a hearing for my "noncompliance" for not signing the terms they required in time after a CorpCare "evaluation". However, my attorney ████████ told me to get a second evaluation to dispute CorpCare's. He now tells me he told ███ I was doing that but she "wasn't happy with it". He shoild have told me she hadn't agreed to the second eval. Both attorneys I have hired for bar matters have actually worked against me, and I don't know who to trust.

The therapist who did my second evaluation said Hal's behavior toward me was unethical, and I feel awful for not standing up to it at the time. I am so traumatized by this whole process that I am close to voluntarily handing over my license. It is sad after how hard I worked to become a lawyer.

As for the friend I mentioned previously, he just completed a 6-month suspension and doesn't wanted to rock the boat. What they did to him was ridiculous.

Attorney C

Aug 19, 2014
From: ███████
To: Bartus Trust

I am a qualified individual bar applicant with a disability/perceived to have a mental disability by the Arizona State Bar Authority, forced into a Second Class Licensure Program in violation of the ADA. In my case there are countless other instances of the SBA's violation of numerous other laws, including their own S. Ct. Rules. CCF's fishing expedition began in Feb. 2006, and I am still paying a high price for being an accommodated bar applicant.

My encounter with Hal Nevitt/MAP was confusing and unpleasant at best, and led to numerous psychiatric evaluations. And while he did nothing inappropriate, I got a definite "predator" vibe from him; he was very scary, however, as he ran arbitrarily hot and cold - like dealing with someone who is manic - one day affectionate, and the next abusive.

My odyssey to find a competent impartial lawyer proved fruitless, and by the end, I was penniless and forced to forgo due process and the pursuit of justice altogether.

I have submitted a complaint to the DOJ, but have little faith it will ultimately benefit me. it would be great if your group had any resources or ideas to share. I will be happy to share all info with you.

Please call me or email me:

███████████

Aug 19, 2014
From: ███████████
To: Bartus Trust

How do I become a part of your group?

Aug 20, 2014
From: ███████████
To: Bartus Trust

Have you seen this?:

http://campaign.r20.constantcontact.com/render?ca=db7146d
e-4952-4c29-ac85-d60a1c483ca2&c=7cb95fd0-244e-11e4-adfe-
d4ae5275b546&ch=7cbf2c30-244e-11e4-adfe-d4ae5275b546
U.S. Justice Dept. Finds States Violate ADA If Inquire into

Mental Health Condition or Treatment When Assessing Fitness
to Practice Law

███

Aug 24, 2014
From: ███████████
To: Bartus Trust

Hello AZAACPR -- I am glad to hear from you.   I will address
your other email after this one.   I am assuming you will want
to adjust your big picture and focus in on one issue, and that is
SBA's flagrantly arrogant commitment to continue to violate
the ADA, and not just getting Hal's head on a platter (which
would also be pretty special, but I don't know if that is as
within reach as obtaining justice for ADA violations).

Although you did not state one way or the other in your below
email to me, I am also assuming you had not heard of the DOJ
smackdown on the Louisiana SBA till I brought it to your
attention.   Have you read the Settlement yet?   It just came out
-- I will forward Bazelon's notice shortly, and you can pull up
the actual Settlement document yourself.   You should also
read the catalyst for the Settlement -- the DOJ's Feb. 5, 2014
Letter to LA SBA -- and compare it to the outcome of the
Settlement.   The DOJ's actions are incredibly significant, and
show a commitment to pursuing this across US jurisdictions --
the time to make noise is now -- the more AZ people that turn
to the DOJ for help now, the faster AZ will get an ADA wakeup
call smackdown too:

I learned, that in addition to numerous U.S. Circuit Courts
unanimously ruling in favor of Bar Applicants who are
experiencing similar discriminatory practices at the hands of
State Bars as I am, that on May 29-30, at the 40th ABA National
Conference on Professional Responsibility, the ABA and is now
acknowledging and beginning to accept the insidious nature of
Conditional Licensing Programs, and they are now actively
involved in *discussing* the problem (albeit without any
recommendations for remedial measures; and most notably see

how the representative from AZ could care less about the outcome of the DOJ's post-investigation findings).

1. Attached herein is the ABA Conference Report:
2. http://nobc.org/docs/news/Many-States-Embrace-Conditional-Admission.pdf

Speakers addressing the topic admitted that "according to the federal government [the Conditional Licensing Program's Process is] *crusted with some requirements that are illegal.*" [emphasis mine]   This is the first time I have seen - throughout all my research over these long years - any member of the legal community say the words "illegal" or "violation" (other than the unanimous Circuit Court Judges, and the victims in those cases and their attorneys) in conjunction with the Conditional Licensing Programs.

Please keep in mind while reading this Conference Report, that the representative from Arizona was AZ attorney Ed Novak - a CCF Member of the panel at my Formal Hearing who gave me Conditional Licensing for having a history of "mental/emotional instability."   Note that while everyone else at the ABA Conference is somewhat sympathetic to those forced into Conditional Licensing Programs -- and also worried about the DOJ Letter to Louisiana -- Novak is the only one who is not only not in the least bit deterred by the DOJ's investigation, but he further inflates himself and advocates the outrageously illegal position that *all* Bar Applicants who apply for Accommodations on the Bar Exam should *necessarily* be forced into a Second Class Licensure Program.   He rationalizes that by applying for Accommodations they are necessarily admitting that they are not as competent to practice the law as other Bar Applicants who do not need Accommodations, and in this way the public is protected from incompetent handicapped Accommodation-needing attorneys!

This DOJ/LA SBA outcome is huge -- this is bigger than anything I have ever thought possible in all my years (7 years now) of going through this torturous nightmare and abuse at the arbitrarily cruel and law-breaking hands of the SBA, and portends an end to the SBA-sanctioned systemic

158

institutionalization of discrimination that is being perpetrated against those with disabilities across U.S. jurisdictions.

This puts *__all__* Bar Authorities in U.S. jurisdictions on notice that they, too, are operating in violation of the ADA (they just haven't been investigated yet).   It's only a matter of time before more lawsuits will bring a sea change in the way Bar Authorities are getting away with using and abusing Conditional Licensing Programs to illegally discriminate against those Bar Applicants with mental disabilities.

Have you seen the ADA related articles by Stephenie Denzel (CT Law Review) and Professor Jonathan Bauer?   I will attach herein for your convenience.   (Page 126 of Bauer's CT Law Review Article lists over 10 cases -- all unanimously found in favor of the Applicants who brought the lawsuits -- that provided the DOJ with support for the LA investigation.   Indiana has recently added another victory, *see*, ACLU of IN v. IN St. Bd. of Bar Exam'rs. (US St. D. Ct. S.D. IN 2011).)   Ms. Denzel clearly lays out exactly why Conditional Admission Programs, as implemented, are illegal under the ADA.   Of course when I brought Ms. Denzel's argument, I was pinned with inability to respect the law, along with accusations that paranoia and narcissism, due to some mental disorder (that I don't have but got labeled with because I applied for an Accommodated Bar Exam situation due to ███████████
███████.   And, of course, the CCF further opined that if I have all those other features of mental illness, then I must surely have ██████████ or some other crippling mental disorder (and Hal made sure to get much of that in his "Report," albeit with impropriety and by making illegal "diagnoses"; it was clear to me that he was doing what the SBA directed him to do, but it was also clear to me that he was conflicted because he knew I had no mental disorders).

So these are the two key Law Review Articles which are our roadmap to an ADA Title II Federal Court claim, which the DOJ also used during their investigation of LA SBA:

1.
SECOND-CLASS LICENSURE: THE USE OF CONDITIONAL
ADMISSION PROGRAMS FOR BAR APPLICANTS WITH MENTAL
HEALTH AND SUBSTANCE ABUSE HISTORIES
By Stephenie Denzel (CT Law Review):

2.
THE CHARACTER OF THE QUESTIONS AND THE FITNESS OF
THE PROCESS: MENTAL HEALTH, BAR ADMISSIONS AND THE
AMERICANS WITH DISABILITIES ACT
By Jon Bauer:

http://papers.ssrn.com/sol3/papers.cfm?abstract_id=293613

And while all of what the AZ SBA has put me through is clearly
violative of the ADA, they are also very deft in working hard at
sabotaging any case I might attempt to bring against
them.   Their problem is that there are people who will be able
to see through the subterfuge, and identify and punish their
misuse of power and authority.

I have forwarded your page entitled "THE STATE BAR OF
ARIZONA'S 'MEMBER ASSISTANCE PROGRAM' (MAP)" to the
DOJ.   Straight into the hands of an interested DOJ investigator
in the Civil Rights Division, who has already made a comment:
"very interesting!   I will review this" -- I expect the DOJ
investigator will comment further, but I am fearing that she
will be leery of your site because of the lack of publishing and
contact information; you have a great title for your Group, but
you kind of shoot your credibility in the foot when you shroud
yourselves in secrecy and make yourselves unavailable.   I
completely understand why you do that, but I just wanted you
to know what I would think if I were the DOJ investigator; she
really has no way of verifying who you are, and I have no way
to tell her how to contact you for further information if she has
questions for you.   All I can do is tell the investigator that
there are relevant portions of your website that refer to things
that I have experienced, and that they are pretty accurate and
right on point; from there I can only say that I presume that
much of the rest of your accusations against the AZ SBA are
also likely true, though statements like *"Mark Harrison said he
would keep $10,000 for a retainer with or without retention of*

160

services" - and - "*Hal Nevitt weighed 400 pounds*" also displaces your site's credibility and sort of reduces the site to "gossip rag" status (sort of an "*enquiring minds want to know*"-type perspective). I have dealt with Mark Harrison throughout my ordeal, and while he is part of the authoritarian establishment, and is complicit in perpetuating the ADA violations, he does not want to keep your $10,000 -- he is merely advising you that that is his usual retainer fee and you'd better be ready to plunk it down if you want him to represent you. And Nevitt doesn't at all look like he weighs 400 pounds -- it would be more apt to say he looks like he's rather fit for a short guy, albeit still overweight (the missive makes it sound like he looks like Refrigerator Perry, but he does not).

I only tell you these things because I want to be constructive -- I want you to succeed and to be able to help others -- I want you to look credible and respectable, and you really do a good job of that, except for those really inappropriate, obnoxious, and totally unbelievable and unreal statements; it's funny how even two or three little missives can bring down an entire body of fine work!

I will keep you posted. Thanks for writing.

██████████

Aug 24, 2014
From: ████████████
To: Bartus Trust

SBA is clearly the puppetmaster here, and while they are vehemently protecting Hal/MAP/MAC/CorpCare (they keep changing the name) to the best of their ability, because he's got the goods on them, if push ever comes to shove they will throw him under the bus so fast you won't even see skidmarks. SBA has rather ambiguously denied Hal Nevitt's involvement (to me) for a very long time, even though conflicting information can be found all over the Internet. For me, it's been a long time since I've talked to Nevitt because I retained legal counsel, but it does seem -- now and ever since the SBA began denying Nevitt and MAP (and now they are denying "MAC" and

161

"CorpCare") -- as if there is some smokescreen activity and puppeteering going on around here. Penar is my "Compliance Monitor," but she doesn't seem to give a rat's behind about anything, and doesn't even answer the phone when I do my mandated weekly check-in by telephone. It must be sweet getting paid to do nothing when you are charged with "Protection of the Public" from dangerous mental defects like me.

I can say that Hal went to a lot of trouble to create confusion as to who was who and what was what in the SBA ██████████ ██ ██. This conversation between my attorney and Hal Nevitt revealed that the Committee is suspecting I have a mental disorder and that I have been screened out and targeted for the investigation process and conditional licensing because of perceived but erroneous psychiatric reasons (keep in mind that I am ██ years old, and had a troublesome childhood and youth -- but with a pristine work history, & felony-free, & moral turpitude-free Record ████

The CCF used Nevitt to get the ball rolling on the fishing expedition -- their witch hunt -- and I can tell you Nevitt was relentless in his questioning of "my mental illness"; he actually kept referring to *"my mental illness"* during the 4 hour interview. He was very solicitous and acted concerned and worried for me when I kept responding with *"what mental illness?"*; he would then respond back that it was safe to tell the affable Mr. Hal about my frightful battle with bi-polar.....and so on......

I can completely corroborate that the interview with Nevitt was pretty awful for other reasons, too. He asked me if I'd "ever been in a three-way," and if i had ever had "lesbian tendencies." He wanted to know how many men I'd "fucked" and he wanted a number. He wanted to know when the last time I engaged in sexual relations was. I thought there would be no end to his need to know the specifics of my past and present sexual activities, and I wondered why, but was scared to ask.

He wanted to know what races my friends' ███████████████
(when he learned that ████████████████████, who is a
████████████████, is married to a black ████ (he learned this
because ███
███████████████████████████████████, which spawned the
conversation about race).

The whole interview was miserable, and I felt violated the
whole time -- I couldn't believe someone was even asking me all
these sensitive, personal questions. But ████████████ -- the
most dangerously complicit lawyer in the AZ legal community -
- advised me not to refuse to answer anything, and to act very
happy to be there; he even suggested I go into the meeting and
thank Hal for *inviting* me to come, and to send a thank you
note afterwards, too (which, like a moron, I did).

Please be aware that while I earlier told you that it seemed
disingenuous for your website to publish that Hal weighs 400
pounds, that position in no way negates the fact that he is
indeed an imposing figure -- especially to a smaller woman --
short and fit (but overweight) as he is. It is indeed a bit
arresting and disturbing when he shuts the door to his little
office behind him, while you are pushed into a corner way at
the back of the room -- I hated it and felt claustrophobic and a
tiny bit scared to be honest -- and I'm not at all a
claustrophobic or scaredy-cat person.

You will **never** hear SBA use the phrase "Second Class License"
as they know it is another way of saying "illegal" and "violation

of law(s)." They clearly subscribe to the theory that if they repeat the phrase *"a license is a license"* enough times the sheeple (even though those sheeple are trained & seasoned lawyers) will eventually buy into it and not question their omnipotent authority. And until now they've been right, but things are about to change with this new involvement by the DOJ.

[Can one find counsel to sue the Bar?] No. Not in Arizona yet. Everyone's too scared, and the legal community is utterly complicit -- they're all programmed to adhere the old adage *"there's the right thing........and then there's the way things are."* In addition,   the DOJ's LA Investigation & Settlement hasn't reached enough people yet; and neither has news of all the unanimous Federal Cases won in favor of Applicants who have filed ADA claims with the same or similar facts as mine.

If we could somehow team up and create some kind of program to present at the law school level -- get this information out to students in law schools -- across the whole country -- remedial measures and justice would begin to be exacted at the speed of light, instead of this interminable turtle-crawl-to-justice SBAs are forcing with their commitment to corruption and overwhelmingly out of control power trips.   SBA's hatred of minority groups beats out truth, fairness, and honesty all day every day.

I would love to see everyone who was abused by SBA/Nevitt/MAP/MAC/CorpCare come together in a class action lawsuit; I just don't know that you've got enough good evidence (aside from the gal who witnessed identifying features of Nevitt's genitals), and I don't know if you've narrowed down and stated your claim succinctly enough. What you want (aside from general justice for corrupt regulation) is kind of confusing, and also I'm not sure if you've zeroed in on all the right laws/violations. Not that your indictment is not good -- I think(6) it's really good -- otherwise I would not have sent it to the DOJ -- I just think it needs more editing and tailoring and perhaps research. But what do I know? don't listen to me if you don't want to -- I'm just a lowly victim accused of having psychiatric defects in possession of a grubby second class license!

[No Arizona-licensed attorney will file a class action:] BINGO.

Even if you did find a lawyer who would agree to help you --
and that will be tough, but you will find one – ███ -- they will
nevertheless work hard to sabotage your case, throw you under
the bus, and then squeeze all of the money they can out of you
while they're looking you straight in the eye and
sympathetically telling you they're doing everything they can to
help you.   That is how I lost almost a hundred thousand
dollars to a local attorney who promised to take my case to
Federal Court, but then when we had exhausted all state issues
and were ready to file in Federal Court, he withdrew, with the
insinuation that, what was I going to do? complain to the Bar
and thus expose myself as emotionally and mentally unstable?
because my attorney won't sue the SBA in Federal Court?
Ha!   So off he went into the sunset with the only money I had,
and I'm sitting her without a crumb in my cupboard; I'm lucky I
have a roof over my head and the utility bill paid..... between
the SBA's insatiable demands for IMEs and dragging my
licensing ordeal out for 7 years, and the lawyer's insatiable
desire for legal fees, I am left broken, and broke.....and
completely deprived of a livelihood....in _any_ field, because of
the Terms & Conditions and the numerous instances of
deprivation of confidentiality.

{Complain to AZBBHE about Nevitt?] No.   I have no real,
helpful evidence to do anything like that; plus, it's not a cause
that immediately benefits me.   In addition, they will say that
without any good hard evidence it makes me look like a crazy
woman and bolsters their case against me and will give them
even more ammunition to discriminate against me even further
(and believe me, they can impose further discrimination and
punishment on me -- just because they've given me this crappy
second class license, does not mean that all I have to do is do
my time).

But once the terms and conditions of the DOJ's Settlement with
LA becomes law in all the land, then the rest will be easier to
chip away at anyway (much like the history of discrimination
against communists/blacks/Jews/women in general/etc. But
for now, the best thing to do is to find a cause of action -- a

narrowly tailored issue (like SBA perpetrates Title II ADA violations) -- and stick with it, and try to come up with helpful ways to get the information about what SBAs are doing, disseminated out to interested parties. My thought is to find a team of people in-the-know who want to get together and develop a program to present to law schools, to arm people who are going to be likely targets with information -- and to prepare themselves through appropriate action -- to protect themselves before they ever even apply to sit for the Bar Exam, and especially before they submit their Character & Fitness Applications.

[Willing to speak with journalists?] Right now: yes.

Later: no.

I currently have a line in the water, and don't want to do anything to jeopardize that. But, yes, someday I will definitely want to get with your journalists; I can't wait to tell others what is going on in the hopes that others can protect and arm themselves against the corrupt and insatiable hunger for power of the AZ SBA.

[File a police complaint?] No. I have zip zero nada hard evidence; I sure wish I would have gone into that meeting with a digital recorder and demanded to record the session, but I didn't. ██████████ told me not to, and condescendingly informed me it made me look paranoid to even think of it when I asked him if I should.

I hope the DOJ investigator reads the link to your page I submitted. Could I see what it is that you submitted to the DOJ? When did you submit your complaint?

███████

I'm not sure if Mr. Levine was one of the *__hundreds__* of attorneys I contacted for help; I'd have to go through boxes and boxes of documents to be able to say one way or the other.

[May it be assumed you corresponding under a pseudonym?] Since you have opted not to share your identities with me, and

166

since you will not communicate by phone or in person with me, I'll keep the status quo.

██████

Thank you,

████████████

Aug 24, 2014
From: ██████████
To: Bartus Trust]

██████

As of today the DOJ is interested in my case. _**NOW**_ is the time for these other people who were wrongly "branded by Nevitt as needing mental therapy" to step up. NOW is the time for _**them**_ to contact the DOJ. I have already forwarded your page to them, and they think it's interesting, so telling them, again, what you state in your above section of your email to me, won't do anybody much good. What will be good is if these lawyers and bar applicants go to the DOJ's site and follows the simple instructions:

http://www.ada.gov/fact_on_complaint.htm

Just file the short bare bones complaint form and then put in a call to the U.S. Department of Justice Disability Rights Section of the Civil Rights Division -- I dug around on the Bazelon documents and found the names of three attorneys, and left messages for them all. And they called me back. That's how I did it, and your people can too. If there are truly a bunch of bar applicants and/or lawyers out there in AZ that have experienced this type of discrimination, then this is their time; after the DOJ's investigation of LA, all other jurisdictions are on notice that they're coming for them too, so wake up and step up -- bring it if you've got it!

But be careful that whoever is bringing a charge doesn't get lost in the forest for the trees; pick an issue (mental disability/ADA Title Ii violation is apparently the hot topic right now) and stick to it. Other complaint-issues may or may not come into play later (for example, so far, no one's interested in my deprivation of due process issue so I'm not addressing it) I would advise to just drop it unless and until someone shows an interest.

Having said all that, I don't have a lot of faith that the DOJ will want my case because the AZ SBA was much smarter than LA's SBA. LA's SBA was blatantly drafting their documents stating "We recommend Conditional Admission for Applicant X due to their diagnosis of bi-polar disorder" and other such on-its-face violative text. They were stupid. AZ is not -- AZ works knows exactly what they are doing (using the Conditional Licensing Program as a tool to punish/retaliate/discriminate) and they work very hard to draft their documents using untruths, half truths, misinformation and flat out bold faced lies. They utilize circuitous writing trickery and creative writing by deception and deceit. It might be a cold day in hell when they get caught, but I think that eventually they will. Maybe just not with my case, because they worked the system well in drafting all my documents and my case is really sticky and unpleasant to slog through (it must've been a joy to go through the LA documents and see all the textbook violations -- like grease on a pig).

Let's hold off -- I still think you guys should get organized and get your people to inundate the DOJ with your ADA complaints. Let's get Arizona on the DOJ's radar!

█████

And, if you think mentioning my name will help you, I would think again. If the DOJ ultimately decides that my case is crap, then you will not be affiliated with crap. Plus, I'd rather you didn't.

█████

Attorney D

Attorney D, who has agreed to be identified, is Miriam H. Klaiman. She attended law school later in life than is typical, having previously earned a Ph.D. at the University of Chicago in Linguistics and an M.D. at the University of Minnesota Medical School. Before embarking on the study of medicine, she had done field research in India and had published numerous scholarly articles and books, including a 1991 book *Grammatical Voice* published by Cambridge University Press.

Klaiman entered medical school at the age of forty. She completed the M.D. degree in the usual four years, spending several months during her undergraduate training as a medical volunteer in India. She then undertook postgraduate (residency) training.

In 1998, during her very first week in a one-year general medicine residency located halfway across the country from her home, calamity struck; Klaiman's husband died of a sudden but treatable disease. Worse, and essentially signaling the impending end of Klaiman's medical career, the death occurred owing to another doctor's negligence—failure to timely treat. The doctor diagnosed correctly but made no treatment arrangements, leaving the patient to suffer untreated until the situation was irremediable.

Klaiman engaged counsel. Her attorney brought suit against several defendants, including the treating physician and the hospital where he had privileges, to which her husband had been admitted. The case did not proceed to trial but, eventually, concluded in a settlement.

While awaiting settlement of the litigation and of the estate, Klaiman continued, for financial reasons, to work as a medical resident. However, repeatedly confronting conditions in hospital medicine similar to the conditions that had occasioned her husband's death from negligence, she became unable to observe the reticence expected under that code of medical professional conduct colloquially known as "the Brotherhood of Silence." She saw in-house patients die of medical negligence. She saw hospitals withhold from survivors information about the circumstances of in-house deaths.

Klaiman once broke the usual protocol against criticizing another doctor by advising a family they might consider suing the medical director of the nursing home where

169

their father resided, and where he had been allowed to go without effective treatment. He had suffered from constipation for so long that he burst his intestines. Klaiman worked on his case when he was admitted to intensive care suffering from peritonitis.

Senior doctors noticed Klaiman's outspokenness and came to see her as a potential liability to have around their wards. Klaiman also became eager to leave hospital medicine because she was afraid that, given hospitals' unyielding procedural protocols and the culture of the medical profession, it would be only a matter of time before she would have on her own conscience the death of a patient. Klaiman says she sleeps well because, to the best of her knowledge, she got out of medicine before she ever had a hand in any such outcome.

Eventually, a residency refused to renew Klaiman's annual contract after she complained about interference in her care of patients by another resident, a man who seemed incapable of practicing medicine without subjecting others on the wards to his obscene conception of sexual humor. In several instances, his interference caused delays in the processing of medical orders. He had also been sending Klaiman obscene emails. The director of Klaiman's program said he thought the male resident had done nothing wrong. About this time, her other litigation concluded and the formalities of her husband's estate were completed.

Klaiman found counsel; the counsel negotiated a pre-litigation formality by obtaining a "Right to Sue" letter from the U.S. Equal Employment Opportunity Commission; and Klaiman sued for sexual harassment and retaliation.

The defendant medical residency and its sponsoring university hospital organization, unsurprisingly, prevailed in the litigation. In the U.S., women have traditionally had a right to sue, but have rarely won sexual harassment lawsuits.

As she embarked on the litigation, Klaiman's situation was distressing. The residency director expected Klaiman to continue to treat patients for the remaining six months of her contract even though, dishonestly, he asserted in a letter notifying her of the non-renewal that her knowledge of medicine was inadequate. If that were true, why would this man allow her to work unsupervised on the wards for an additional six months? He also expected Klaiman to continue to endure the gruesome conditions typical of U.S. residencies—

conditions that amount to a form of slavery. Klaiman was and had been working about 120 hours a week at so meager a salary that her hourly compensation calculated out at less than minimum wage. Worst of all was the disrespect and continued sexual harassment, Klaiman still being a relatively new widow.

Eventually, as a law student, Klaiman would publish a law journal article about the slave-like conditions of hospital residency training.[228] This article became one of two published articles Klaiman authored during law school for which she received a second prize in a national law student writing competition.

In the early 2000's, Klaiman left medicine for good and applied to law school. She was accepted by and offered a full tuition scholarship at the University of Arizona. She graduated *magna cum laude* in the customary three years. Immediately, Klaiman took the mid-2005 Arizona Bar exam, passed it, and applied for admission.

What ensued is alluded to in Ch. 3 (*see* nn. 49-50 and accompanying text) *supra*. Klaiman received a letter dated November 28, 2005, from the Supreme Court of Arizona's Committee on Character and Fitness, directing her to have an "evaluation" at the hands of "Member Assistance Program" Director Nevitt. *See* Appendix 6-1 *infra*. Klaiman sent back a letter dated December 6, 2005, asking the Committee on what ground she was being flagged. Appendix 6-2. She addressed the letter to administrator Carolyn de Looper. De Looper never answered this letter.[229]

Klaiman then approached several attorneys. Each reported back that he informally asked around and could suggest some conjectures as to the Committee's reasons, but no explanation was ever forthcoming from the Committee; nor were any of the said attorneys willing to put into writing what, if anything, they had gleaned by asking around.

What occurred next is described in Ch. 3 ii c *supra*. At the University of Arizona, Klaiman had taken a class on

---

[228]   M.H. Klaiman, "Bonded Labor Characteristics of U.S. Postgraduate Medical Training," 39 HEALTH LAW 373 (2006).

[229]   Carolyn de Looper has, for many years, worked alternatingly for the Supreme Court Committee on Character and Fitness and for the State Bar of Arizona. At the time of this writing, she is listed under "Membership Administration and Services" on the Arizona Bar's "Staff Quick Reference List." *See* n. 70 *supra*.

Arizona constitutional law taught by former Arizona Supreme Court Chief Justice Stanley G. Feldman. After retiring from public service, he had gone into private practice in Tucson. Klaiman contacted Feldman at his law firm, asking for advice what to do, only to receive back from him an email dated March 15, 2006, essentially saying that she should keep quiet and do whatever she was told to do in order to get into the Bar. Appendix 6-3.

As described in Ch. 3 ii d *supra*, Klaiman also contacted the Arizona Center on Disability Law. It refused to get involved. Appendix 6-4.

Howard Murray "Hal" Nevitt, Director of the Bar's "Member Assistance Program," sent Klaiman a letter dated December 9, 2005, demanding $350 in advance for an "evaluation" he scheduled for December 23, 2005. Appendix 6-5. At the same time, Nevitt also required Klaiman to sign and return an "informed consent" form for his own private practice, Innovative Workplace Solutions, LLC—showing that he anticipated making a "patient" of Klaiman no matter what findings the "evaluation" would yield. Appendix 6-6.

It being the case, however, that Klaiman resided many miles from Phoenix, in Tucson, she was spared ever having to meet again with Nevitt in person after the "evaluation." Nevitt was in the habit of requiring MAP targets like her, Bar members located far from his base of operations in Phoenix, to find local "therapists" for their further "treatment."

Years later, on June 28, 2012, expecting to be disbarred, Klaiman described the goings-on at the December 23, 2005, "evaluation" in a letter of complaint addressed to Nevitt's licensor, the Arizona Board of Behavioral Health Examiners. Appendix 6-7. Klaiman reported Nevitt for sexual assault. The incident has been alluded to in Ch. 3 i b 1. Her complaint is cited in Ch. 5 ii *supra*. As is also discussed there, the Board declined to discipline Nevitt. And, in retaliation, the Bar did, pretextually, disbar Klaiman three months later. This is described *infra*.

Klaiman was admitted in 2006 after the Supreme Court of Arizona affirmed Nevitt's recommendation of conditional admission subject to the ministrations of the Bar's "Member Assistance Program." This occurred as follows: Klaiman received notice from de Looper dated January 30, 2006, advising that the Court would rule on the MAP recommendation. Appendix 6-8. Klaiman phoned de Looper at the Supreme Court to ask if she could attend and/or address the court. De Looper told her no. The Court issued its rubber-stamp ruling on April 21, 2006. Appendix 6-9. Thus Klaiman's conditional admission became final without her ever getting or ever being offered a hearing.

Klaiman was admitted after paying the Bar hundreds of dollars in fees for second-class membership (membership subject to conditions), as well as after signing a "Therapeutic Contract" similar to that reproduced for public perusal elsewhere.[230] But curiously, as an outcome of his December 23 "evaluation," Nevitt did not formulate any diagnosis of Klaiman's purported mental illness. This is seen in a memo Nevitt addressed to the Committee on Character and Fitness, dated January 9, 2006. Appendix 6-10. Nevitt never provided Klaiman with any information about the outcome of his "evaluation" and he never stated a diagnosis. Klaiman had no previous mental or substance history.

This is to say that, without any actual diagnosis, Klaiman was presumed to be, and was made to sign a document admitting herself to be, mentally ill. To practice law, the Bar required her to lie and to sign a libel against herself. She was ordered to see a psychologist or psychiatrist as soon as admitted to the Bar, but didn't know what she was supposed to ask to be "treated" for.

By the terms of this travesty of a "Therapeutic Contract," Klaiman was forced to have twelve meetings over a year's time to see (and pay) therapists. Klaiman regarded them as unethical detritus of their so-called profession. When she presented, not only did she not know what mental illness the Bar thought she had, but they did not know a diagnosis for her either. Yet they signed a document furnished to them by the Bar, agreeing to share anything they might learn about her. Per terms of the "Therapeutic Contract," Klaiman was required to consent to that. Klaiman understood that, as a cost to her of obtaining a law license, the Bar was delegating her case to people who in turn, in the guise of "therapy," were agreeing to rat her out to the government.

Accordingly, Klaiman regarded the "therapy" as a sham intended to enrich the Bar as well as provide it with personal

---

[230]   *See* n. 54 *supra*.

information for it to use to her disadvantage. Therefore, in "therapy," Klaiman took care to tell nothing truthful about herself. She lied about her social history, her educational history, her sexual and marital history, her ongoing employment, her friends, what books she read and what movies she saw, and so on. She made up a fictitious life history, wrote it down, memorized it, and re-studied it before each and every "therapy" session. Before each session, she would also make up some fictitious difficult situation she had faced and resolved since the last session. And at no time did any therapist suggest to Klaiman that the account she gave of herself was not believed.

As the Bar required, Klaiman filled out quarterly reports and mailed them to Nevitt, not only accounting for her monthly "therapy" sessions, but also about her meetings with "practice monitors" with whom Nevitt assigned her to meet periodically. In her view, these people, Arizona Bar members, were even more unethical than the therapists. These lawyers wanted to curry favor with the Bar and get free Continuing Legal Education credits in exchange. They most of all, being lawyers, should have known better than to collude in the Bar's unlawful "therapy" scheme.

Klaiman was also victimized repeatedly, and unlawfully (under the ADA as well as under the Arizona Constitution's guarantee of individual privacy), by the Bar's publicizing the fact of her being forced into mental "therapy" as a condition of getting a professional license. The Bar publicly declared that her conditional admission was an aggravating factor every time, after 2006, it slapped Klaiman with a new disciplinary order.

Such orders were designed to keep Klaiman perpetually shelling out fines and penalties to enrich the Bar. Each new disciplinary order was a public, never a confidential, document.[231]

After her admission, in 2007, Klaiman filed a Cochise County, Arizona, small claims case *in pro per* (on her own behalf) for unpaid wages. She filed suit against another lawyer in whose office she had worked for about ten weeks. The lawyer, Nina Lou Caples of Sierra Vista, Arizona, filed no answer. Notwithstanding, Caples transferred the matter out of small claims, engaged counsel (a party to a case in small claims cannot be represented by counsel), and proceeded to litigate in justice court. Ultimately, Caples sought both judgment in her favor as well as well as attorney's fees.

After the judge refused to award any money to either side, on September 17, 2008, Caples initiated a Bar complaint against Klaiman, Bar disciplinary File No. 08-1652. Caples complained to the Bar that she had spent some tens of thousands of dollars on the lawsuit. The putative fees were racked up defending a suit that had started in small claims and in which less than a thousand dollars' unpaid wages damages were at issue.

Caples filed her complaint in several submissions over a period of months. It eventually amounted to over a hundred pages of allegations and exhibits. Almost nothing Caples complained of had any bearing on the court proceedings in the small claims matter, much of it being a litany about the period Klaiman had worked for Caples more than two years earlier, with some of the allegations both unsupported and so

---

[231]   *See, e.g.* PDJ-2011-9060, SBA file no. 10-0329, "Report and Order Imposing Sanctions," pp. 2 (2), 16, *cited in* www.azaacpr.org, webpage "SBA 'Member Assistance Program'" [5] [a] paragraph 2. This document is public pursuant to Rules of the Supreme Court of Arizona R. 70 "Public Access to Information." By R 70 (g), the only way of concealing the contents of Bar discipline documents is to obtain an order requiring Bar to seal all or parts of such documents. Such an order has to be obtained from a Bar official—lately, from the Presiding Disciplinary Judge. However, by R. 70 (a) (1), (5) and (6), a protective order cannot issue to conceal the fact of forced mental therapy imposed either as a result of discipline or conditional admission. The Arizona Judicial Department has foisted this ruse on Bar members in order to unlawfully defeat their right to the protections of the ADA as well as the privacy provisions of the Arizona Constitution.

outlandish and/or babyish that the Bar never addressed many of them.

Caples, for her part, never addressed the allegation that she owed Klaiman unpaid wages. However, in tacit confession of her dishonesty, after the conclusion of the court case and during the pendency of her Bar complaint, Caples issued and sent to Klaiman two checks for the unpaid wages. Klaiman says she has kept the two checks uncashed.

The Bar never held Caples to account for misuse of process (attempting to turn a small claims complaint into a personal financial windfall), over-litigating, and frivolously litigating. Although Klaiman's suit was far from the first instance in which the Bar received information that Caples has abused court process,[232] and although previously, the Bar has investigated Caples, it has never disciplined Caples. This is presumably because it is handy for the Bar that Caples is willing to bear false witness in Bar investigations and proceedings (*see infra*)—investigations and proceedings that enable the Bar to levy impositions on other lawyers.

In pursuing File No. 08-1652, the Bar committed two serious acts of procedural unfairness. First, Staff Bar Counsel Stephen P. Little was so impatient to slap Klaiman with a sanction that he got a disciplinary order issued while withholding from Klaiman an opportunity to see, let alone respond to, Caples' allegations. Klaiman had notified Little in writing that, judging by the page numbering and non-sequiturs in Caples' material that Little had photocopied and sent her, the material was incomplete. Despite this notice, Little obtained an "Order of Probation, MAP and Costs" against Klaiman.

Klaiman appealed. She also asked that the disciplinary matter be dismissed due to procedural unfairness since, as she pointed out, Staff Bar Counsel's misconduct had resulted in irremediable prejudice to her.

Although Little did not succeed in forcing through the kangaroo order, he did succeed in prejudicing his superiors who evaluated the appeal. They decided not to close the file—

---

[232]   For abusing a garnishment order, Caples was investigated in Bar disciplinary File No. 06-1393. Likewise, Caples misused court process and litigated frivolously in suing a former client in Pima Superior Court case no. M-1041-CR-99270634. The Bar was informed of this but did not investigate. *See* Appendix 7-1 *infra*.

presumably because they could not charge fees for a case that did not result in an order of discipline—and, in a September 29, 2009 order, the Bar put Klaiman on disciplinary probation. The Bar charged her "costs" of $1250.

A second, and much more serious procedural lapse of Staff Bar Counsel was his failure to inform Klaiman at any time of the factual basis for the Bar's allegations. The proceedings were thus flawed at their basis.

In criminal court, a defendant gets an arraignment. In this matter, however, and no doubt far from uniquely, Staff Bar Counsel concealed its chargesheet. Whether out of laziness, incompetence, venality or greed, Little never provided Klaiman with information as to what acts or omissions of hers allegedly were at issue. Little provided Klaiman only with the raw dozens and dozens of pages sent in by Caples—and that too, only partially.

Little put Klaiman in the position of struggling to figure out, for instance, whether Caples' adolescent allegation that in the office, Klaiman had given off "body odor," implicated the Bar's catchall ethical rule against "engaging in unprofessional conduct" (Rules of the Supreme Court of Arizona R. 41 [g]).[233]

The Bar both charged and convicted Klaiman without providing her with notice of what she had supposedly done wrong. It acted much after the fashion of the Committee on Character and Fitness when it convicted Klaiman of "mental illness" while refusing to disclose its grounds.

In admissions and discipline, Arizona Bar members are not infrequently denied due process in this fashion. When this occurs, the Bar member never knew what hit him or her.

File No. 08-1652 became the first of a series of Bar disciplinary cases against Klaiman relying on perjured testimony, unfair procedure, and intentionally concealed or falsified allegations.

In PDJ-2011-9060/Bar disciplinary File No. 10-0329, the Bar charged Klaiman with filing and pursuing frivolous

---

[233] At the time of Caples' complaint, an earlier version of R. 41 (g) was in effect, enjoining members "to abstain from all offensive personality." Even more so than the version of R. 41 (g) in effect at the time of this writing, the earlier "offensive personality" version, in its vagueness, obviously was a pretext for the Bar to impose discipline at its whim.

litigation after opposing counsel arranged for the Bar to charge Klaiman to that effect.

The Bar pursued the complaint out of favoritism toward opposing counsel Georgia A. Staton of the large and influential Phoenix law firm Jones, Skelton & Hochuli, PLC. The collusion between Staton and the Bar has been alluded to in Ch. 3 i b 1 *supra*.

Klaiman was then litigating a case CV-2008-0630 in Santa Cruz County, Arizona, Superior Court arising from theft and publication of one former assistant county attorney's confidential employee file documents by another assistant county attorney, Leslie G. Spira (*see* n. 116 *supra*). The Santa Cruz County Attorney, Spira's employer, eventually terminated Spira. It did so without publicly divulging the grounds,[234] but not before the County and the County Attorney defended the case. The County obtained representation through its insurer, the Arizona Counties Insurance Pool. This is an administrative entity in Phoenix whose functions include assigning and compensating lawyers to defend Arizona counties in court actions. This Pool had an employee, one Cindy Byrne, who had been assigning Staton in many such cases. Byrne assigned Staton to defend Santa Cruz County in Klaiman's case.

Bar disciplinary File No. 10-0329 against Klaiman arose when Staton persuaded Byrne to send the Bar a complaint saying that she was aggrieved by Klaiman pursuing litigation that, she said, Staton had assured her was frivolous.

Byrne wrote twice to the Bar denouncing Klaiman and was upfront in admitting that she was writing at the instigation of opposing counsel Staton.[235] The Bar acceded to Staton's

---

[234] *See* www.azaacpr.org, webpage "Inquisitional Discipline" [3] [c] [iii], *citing* Austin Counts, "Former Attorney Charged with Impersonation," *Santa Cruz Valley Sun*, July 28, 2011, *available at*: http://www.nogalesinternational.com/scv_sun/news/former-attorney-charged-with-impersonation/article_67c706d9-449f-55d0-937e-da282a12885f.html.

[235] Within a few months of her second letter to the Bar, Byrne was no longer employed by the Arizona Counties Insurance Pool. Arizona Attorneys Against Corrupt Professional Regulation understands that Byrne's actions came to the notice of her superiors, who may have correctly perceived that she was putting her employer in a conflict of interest, inasmuch as ACIP's function is not to try to influence the outcome of court cases against Arizona counties, but to assist them with obtaining counsel for their defense.

effort to influence the outcome of the litigation. It initiated disciplinary action against Klaiman during the pendency of the lawsuit, thus revealing—not for the first time—the Bar's willingness to interfere in the administration of justice.[236]

Investigating Klaiman was not the only way the Bar, colluding with Staton, sought to influence the litigation. It also provided Staton with the free use of the Bar's Phoenix premises as the site for a deposition of the Bar's disciplinary records clerk. The notice of deposition appears in Appendix 6-11.

This incident has been alluded to in Ch. 3 i b 1 *supra*. Bar officials—CEO John F. Phelps and General Counsel John A. Furlong—misused the Bar's premises by turning them over for a private firm's deposition in a matter in which the Bar had no interest. The two officials did this to show favoritism to Staton and her law firm. By this maneuver, Staton and the Bar obliged Klaiman to sit through a recitation of detailed facts of her history of discipline, such as the forced mental "treatment" imposed at the time of her Bar admission under the Bar's "Member Assistance Program." The history had no bearing on the ongoing litigation; the deposition record was neither filed in nor considered by the Santa Cruz County Superior Court. The Bar's and Staton's purpose was not to discover information to be used in litigation. The purpose, rather, was to embarrass Klaiman for the objective of intimidating her from further litigation against Santa Cruz County and the County Attorney.

The Bar also took no action when, during the litigation, for the sheer purpose of harassing Klaiman, lawyer Staton violated the Arizona "false liens" statute by unlawfully recording a lien on Klaiman's *home*. This is alluded to in n. 93 *supra*. The lien remained of record for months. Staton refused to withdraw it until Klaiman obtained an order of the Santa Cruz County Superior Court requiring Staton to record its release. Meanwhile, Klaiman filed a Bar complaint against Staton, Bar disciplinary File No. 09-2078. Beyond assigning the matter a file number, the Bar did nothing; it declined to investigate, let alone discipline, Staton for engaging in criminal activity.

Indeed, despite multiple complaints, including one from the La Paz County Attorney (mentioned in n. 93 *supra*), the Bar has never disciplined Staton, who serves one of the large,

---

[236] *See* the discussion of the Bar's interference in probate litigation filed by attorney Grant Goodman, Ch. 2 ii *supra*.

influential Phoenix law firms that the Bar treats with favoritism.[237]

Staff Bar Counsel Craig D. Henley pursued the complaint instigated by counsel Staton (through her pal Byrne) and set it for a hearing before a panel headed by Presiding Disciplinary Judge William J. O'Neil. This panel was one of the several kangaroo panels on which the "public member" panelist, supposedly present to help the judge achieve an impartial ruling, was a business crony of Judge O'Neil's, Robert M. Gallo. (*See* Ch. 3 i c 1 *supra.*)

It should be noted that the Bar chose the venue for the hearing without consulting Klaiman; the significance of this will be clarified *infra.*

Henley intended to call the lawyer who had occasioned the Santa Cruz County lawsuit by stealing confidential documents, Leslie G. Spira, as a witness for the Bar, but reconsidered after Klaiman's disciplinary defense counsel informed him about Spira's pending criminal proceedings. (*See* nn. 116 and 234 *supra.*)

Henley did, however, call Staton. She testified that Klaiman pursued the litigation even though Staton had told Klaiman that she, Staton, the party opponent's counsel, considered it frivolous. Since Staton had not been called as an expert witness on trial procedure, is not clear why an opinion on the merits of litigation by the counsel for the party opponent was of any interest to the tribunal.

Henley then called to the stand Caples, who had no first-hand knowledge of the Santa Cruz County litigation. The PDJ nevertheless allowed Caples to testify as a "character witness" based on Klaiman's former employment some six years earlier in Caples' office, and based on Klaiman's suit against Caples for unpaid wages.

What ensued is alluded to in n. 112 and the accompanying text *supra.* On the stand, Caples perjured herself by testifying that a certain client (here called "Mr. Sesile") had complained about Klaiman's services. Subsequently, an affidavit was obtained from "Mr. Sesile" (with whom Klaiman had remained in occasional friendly contact all the years since leaving Caples' employ). It refuted Caples' testimony.

---

[237]   For more particulars about unethical conduct by Staton, *see* www.azaacpr.org, webpage "Inquisitional Discipline" [3] [c] [i].

Klaiman's counsel furnished the affidavit to Staff Bar Counsel Henley accompanied by a request that, pursuant to his ethical obligation (i.e., not to suborn perjury and to refrain from putting on a crooked case), he ask the PDJ to strike the relevant portion of Caples' testimony.

Unethically, Henley refused. His two emails to that effect, dated February 16 and 17, 2012, are reproduced in Appendix 6-12 *infra.*

In the hearing, Henley not only suborned witness perjury but also misrepresented Klaiman's employment history. Trying to convince the panel that Klaiman was on a pathological quest to sue all her previous employers, Henley falsely introduced evidence whereby he hoped to persuade the panelists that Klaiman had been a plaintiff in a case against a certain hospital because she was a disgruntled ex-employee. This was a mean-spirited fabrication on Henley's part. The case at issue was the suit arising due to the wrongful death of Klaiman's husband. Klaiman says that Henley appeared to her to be eager, even gleeful, to try to insinuate this misstatement into the record, as if in a bloodlust—like a witch at a black sabbath—to tear at the heart of Klaiman, still a grieving widow.

On March 19, 2012, the PDJ issued a "Report and Order Imposing Sanctions" in PDJ-2011-9060/Bar disciplinary File No. 10-0329, sentencing Klaiman to a year's suspension to be followed by two years' probation. The Bar also imposed a fine of $1200.

Immediately thereafter, on March 23, 2012, as if to make it clear beyond doubt that the Bar's and its employees' motive in pursuing disciplinary formalities was wholly pecuniary, Presiding Disciplinary Judge O'Neil sent Klaiman a separate invoice for *his own* "costs." This invoice appears in Appendix 6-13 herein.

As shown in this document, "Office of the Presiding Disciplinary Judge's Statement of Costs and Expenses," O'Neil demanded $717.43 for his and his "acting clerk's" personal "costs" and "expenses" plus those of the other two hearing panelists—who, by Supreme Court rule, serve in a voluntary capacity.

It is a stretch to imagine that any other Arizona professional licensing organization, upon disciplining a member, empowers an employee to bill the member for his or her personal "costs" of showing up and doing the work.

In the March 19, 2012, "Report and Order" (*see* n. 231 *supra*), the PDJ pronounced that Klaiman would be subjected to another round of the "Member Assistance Program" once her suspension was complete and probation commenced. Not awaiting the prospect of further manhandling by the Bar's "Member Assistance Program" Director, Howard Murray "Hal" Nevitt, on June 28, 2012, Klaiman initiated a complaint against Nevitt alleging a previous act of sexual misconduct (*see* Appendix 6-7 *infra*). The complaint became AZBBHE File No. 2013-0002, discussed in Ch. 5 *supra*.

Staff Bar Counsel Henley, evidently considering himself on a roll in pursuing one charge after another against Klaiman, did not wait for the outcome in PDJ-2011-9060. Rather, in September, 2011, he proceeded to bring another complaint against Klaiman, PDJ-2012-9039/Bar disciplinary File No. 11-1698. It stemmed from the wrath of Pima County Superior Court Probate Judge Charles V. Harrington over being inundated with four pleadings from opposing counsel on the eve of a hearing in a probate case, Pima County Superior Court case no. GC-2010-0663.

This matter is alluded to in nn. 36 and 111 *supra.* Klaiman represented a client who was the subject of a relative's petition for a guardianship and conservatorship. Klaiman had requested the hearing after filing motions asking Judge Harrington to appoint a fiduciary for her client.

Harrington, enraged by the shower of last-minute pleadings, showed up in court and improperly ordered R. 11 sanctions (*see* n. 126 and accompanying text *supra*) against both attorneys—not only against the opposing counsel, but also against Klaiman—levying a court charge of $500 on each. Harrington evidently notified the Bar as well.

In bringing the complaint in File No. 11-1698, Henley seriously misstated facts in his Report of Investigation. He named eight different pleadings that, he untruthfully indicated, Klaiman had filed in the probate case. Of the eight pleadings, the opposing counsel had filed six.

Moreover, of the two pleadings for which Klaiman was responsible, neither had been filed on the eve of a hearing. Both were filed for the protection of the client, asking the judge to appoint a licensed fiduciary.

The client suffered from dementia, resided in a nursing home, and lacked responsible relatives in Arizona. A granddaughter who lived in an adjacent Arizona county with the client's son, a felon convicted of drug dealing, petitioned for guardianship and conservatorship. Klaiman filed documents in court showing that the son was seeking control over his mother's income to secure a mortgage on a residential property for himself, his two daughters (one of whom was the petitioner), his two minor grandchildren, and supposedly, the client ("Grandma").

Klaiman filed other documents showing that at the time of petitioning, the petitioner and her father, the felon, were living in a mobile home owned by another drug dealer (imprisoned at the time the petition was filed). The mobile home had no running water. The petitioners would have had no suitable place to house, let alone care for, an incontinent, demented woman with multiple organic medical problems. For the hypothetical home they hoped to purchase to house the family, they would have had no way to finance a mortgage without regular income (income from a non-welfare source), which none of them could demonstrate. The client, however, had an ample income—income that went to support her care in the nursing home.

And Klaiman showed the court evidence in the form of a police report that, with the help of their counsel, and without authorization, the petitioner's family tried to remove the client from the nursing home during the pendency of their own petition. The petitioner and her family appeared interested in taking the client across county lines to refile the petition for guardianship and conservatorship in a different venue.

It would appear that, in vilifying a lawyer for seeking to protect an incapable adult client who was in a precarious social position, Harrington was acting in accord with the philosophy of the Supreme Court of Arizona's "Committee on Improving Judicial Oversight and Processing of Probate Matters" of which he was a member. Its mission never was to assist vulnerable members of the public. This has been discussed in n. 29 and accompanying text *supra*.

Despite the written protestations of Klaiman's disciplinary defense counsel, Henley never corrected nor withdrew his untruthful allegation about the eight pleadings. Fed up with the Bar's unethical and dishonest discipline, Klaiman asked Henley in writing to consider her a resigned Bar member.

For pecuniary reasons, Henley did not pursue Klaiman's request but, in February, 2012, persuaded the PDJ to order an additional sanction of six months' and a day's (*see* n. 120 *supra*) suspension, to run concurrently with her one-year suspension stemming from PDJ-2011-9060. This occasioned another order of $1200 in "costs" imposed on Klaiman for Bar discipline.

It was said *supra* that Henley acted out of pecuniary motives. This would appear to be so, since he could only charge fees of Klaiman by progressive discipline. So he did not then accede to her suggestion to terminate her Bar membership.

Instead, in yet another maneuver in the Bar's campaign of personal harassment by discipline, on September 18, 2012, in a new file, PDJ-2012-9098/Bar disciplinary File No. 12-2152, Henley arranged for Klaiman to be disbarred for purported "unauthorized practice of law."

Henley had no evidence or information that Klaiman was continuing to accept or service clients after the imposition of the previous order of suspension. Rather, according to Henley, the sanction was merited by the fact that, on the very day she had been suspended, Klaiman had failed to arrange to take down a website advertising her law practice. It had remained online until a few weeks later.

The State Bar of Arizona issued a press release announcing the disbarment. In publishing the press release online, it inserted Klaiman's name prominently in the website address.[238]

By separately handling Klaiman's departure from the Bar from its action in PDJ-2012-9039, the Bar was able to impose on Klaiman yet one more $1200 fine. It was noted in the press release.[239]

According to the Rules of the Supreme Court of Arizona, "[N]o person shall practice law in this state or represent in any way that he or she may practice law in this state unless the person is an active member of the state bar."[240] The Arizona

---

[238]   *See* http://www.azbar.org/newsevents/newsreleases/2012 /12/klaimandisbarment. See also www.azaacpr.org, webpage "Inquisitional Discipline" [2] paragraphs 26ff.

[239]   *Id.*

[240]   Rules of the Supreme Court of Arizona R. 31 (b) "Regulation of the Practice of Law."

Bar has used this provision as a ruse to amplify charges against numerous members who it has disciplined by suspension. The Bar acts disingenuously in these cases by not advising the victim—just as the Bar did not advise Klaiman—that he or she will be considered in violation of the rule upon failing to cancel advertising in all media, including electronic media. Instead of mentioning this to the sanctioned attorney—who usually had his or her hands full right after being slapped with an order of suspension trying to arrange alternative representation for clients, and is not thinking immediately about his or her professional website or participation in social media—the Bar remains silent. It lays in wait for a few days, checks for the predictable oversight on the member's part, then pounces and initiates a new and more severe disciplinary outcome—just as it did in Klaiman's case.

Disciplining a member so severely—with disbarment—over failure to take down a website is excessive and unusual discipline even by the State Bar of Arizona's draconian standards. Klaiman believes this discipline was imposed on her pretextually. She believes she was disbarred in retaliation because, as mentioned *supra*, three months before the Bar prepared the order of disbarment, on June 28, 2012, she had complained of sexual misconduct against "Member Assistance Program" Howard Murray "Hal" Nevitt to the Arizona Board of Behavioral Health Examiners.

As discussed in Ch. 5 ii *supra*, in 2013, Klaiman addressed letters to Nevitt and the State Bar of Arizona after her disbarment, demanding to see the grounds on which she had been subjected to conditional admission to the Arizona Bar in 2006. Furlong's two responses are reproduced in Appendix 5-2 and 5-4 *infra* and Nevitt's in Appendix 5-5 *infra*.

As these documents show, together with its protégé Nevitt, the Bar is engaging in a shell game to unlawfully withhold information from Klaiman about its illegal admission policies and practices which occasioned so much suffering and such injustice to her.

As a Bar member, Klaiman served a number of clients. No client of Klaiman's *ever* complained about her to the Bar. All the discipline that the Bar imposed on her was for its own edification and that of its favorites.

185

Appendices

The only thing necessary for the triumph of evil is for good men to do nothing.
Edmund Burke

Help me to avoid shameful speech, as well as shameful silence.
Amidah (Jewish) Prayer

Snell & Wilmer
L.L.P
LAW OFFICES

One Arizona Center
400 East Van Buren Street
Suite 1900
Phoenix, Arizona 85004-2202
602.382.6000
602.382.6070 (Fax)
www.swlaw.com

DENVER
LAS VEGAS
LOS ANGELES
LOS CABOS
ORANGE COUNTY
PHOENIX
SALT LAKE CITY
TUCSON

John F. Lomax, Jr.
602.382.6305
jlomax@swlaw.com

November 30, 2011

Michele Flick
~~REDACTED~~

Dear Ms. Flick:

I understand you contacted Meredith Larrabe in our office several times yesterday. We represent the State Bar of Arizona. As you recall, you provided the State Bar with information about an employee of the State Bar. The State Bar asked us to obtain complete copies of public files associated with the claims you made regarding its employee. The State Bar is not contemplating bringing a lawsuit against you.

In your calls to Ms. Larrabe yesterday, you expressed concerns about your safety and implied you may be in need of mental health assistance. We strongly encourage you to reach out to the police and any mental health professionals or hotlines. Enclosed we have provided you with several resources.

Very truly yours,

Snell & Wilmer L.L.P.

John F. Lomax, Jr.

JFL:mbb
Enclosures

14097151.1   Snell & Wilmer is a member of LEX MUNDI, The Leading Association of Independent Law Firms

Appendix 3-2

-----Original Message-----
From: John F. Phelps <John.Phelps@staff.azbar.org>
To: 'Michele' <█████████████████>
Sent: Wed, Nov 30, 2011 12:34 pm
Subject: RE: Nevitt

Ms. Flick: Thank you for your note. Regarding the Snell and
Wilmer request—we retained that firm to review all of the
information and documents that you provided us as well as the
records associated with the Behavioral Health Board
proceedings. The firm was been hired to provide an
independent review of this information for us so that we can
resolve this matter. The firm has not been hired for any other
purpose. As part of that review, my understanding is that the
firm sought relevant police reports and I can only guess that
you must have been notified consistent with police department
policy and procedure.

I apologize if this has caused you additional anxiety or
concern.

Sincerely,

John

Response to Email

Aug 1, 2012

<u>John F. Phelps</u>
john.f.phelps@staff.azbar.org

To;

To Bartus Trust:

I am responding on behalf of the State Bar of Arizona to your email to State Bar President Amelia Cramer.   Your email contains a number of inaccurate statements regarding our Member Assistance Program (MAP) and Mr. Nevitt, too numerous to address in an email.   I will make myself and appropriate staff available to answer your questions or concerns at your earliest convenience.

My contact information is below.   I look forward to meeting with you.

Sincerely,

John Phelps

John Phelps, CEO/Executive Director

4201 N. 24th St., Suite 100 | Phoenix, AZ   85016-6266

602.340.7200   fax 602.416.740

John.Phelps@staff.azbar.org

www.azbar.org

Serving the public and enhancing the legal profession.

Date: July 30, 2012 4:25:45 PM MST
From: Bartus Trust
To: "amelia.cramer@pcao.pima.gov"
<amelia.cramer@pcao.pima.gov>
Subject: FYI

<u>Summary of the State Bar of Arizona Scandal</u>

The Member Assistance Program is a part of the State Bar of
Arizona's disciplinary armamentarium. MAP forces SBA
members into mental illness treatment as a condition of
obtaining or retaining their licenses to practice law.   For
several years the longstanding Director of MAP, Howard ("Hal")
Murray Nevitt, has been the subject of repeated agency
complaints and other reports to civil and criminal authorities
for sexual misconduct.   SBA has been aware of the
complaints.   It has failed to publicly dissociate Nevitt from
SBA.

This failure raises substantial issues of SBA corruption.   MAP
sanctions are imposed with astonishing frequency, whether
the attorney-victim has a prior mental illness or substance
abuse history or not.   For this reason, MAP has long been
integral to the SBA disciplinary apparatus, so much so
that SBA cannot publicly respond or react   to complaints
against its Director without drawing attention to its own
motives, policies and conduct toward its members.   In
addition, there must be a great deal known to Nevitt
about abuse in the SBA disciplinary apparatus, which could be
at risk of exposure should the ruling class of SBA hang Nevitt
out to dry.   Public money is not involved.   The SBA discipline
operation is funded by impositions on Bar members.   In other
words, Bar members pay.   SBA members are paying for the
cover-up of Nevitt's misconduct, and when targeted by the SBA
office which he directs, they pay again.   They pay to be
publicly humiliated and discredited, and they pay again for the
privilege of risking sexual assault by an SBA official.   SBA's
disciplinary policies and practices are a fraud on the public
trust, in addition to a fraud, financially and otherwise, on
members of the Arizona Bar.

In an "Adverse Action," File No. 2011-0063, the organization
that licenses "master's-level therapists," the Arizona Board of

Behavioral Health Examiners, sanctioned Nevitt on November 15, 2011. The sanction included a $1000 fine and a requirement to temporarily refrain from engaging in "clinical supervision." (*See* http://www.azbbhe.us/investigations/2011advaction.pdf, scroll to p. 29 [or go to the website, then use the command "Find" and type in "Nevitt"].) In sanctioning Nevitt on one allegation, AzBBHE dismissed a second allegation against him in the same file, alleging sexual misconduct.

Since January 18, 2012, Howard ("Hal") Murray Nevitt, his private company and his marital community have been named Defendants in a civil suit brought by a woman plaintiff in Maricopa County Superior Court, CV2012-001509, alleging counts of assault and battery, among others. (*See* http://www.superiorcourt.maricopa.gov/docket/CivilCourtCases/caseInfo.asp.) In a Phoenix Police Department report, DR No. 2010 01588991, dated November 5, 2010, law enforcement authorities document a criminal investigation of Nevitt on allegations of sexual assault and stalking.

In the criminal investigation, Nevitt hired and was represented by a Phoenix attorney Joe Chornenky, a criminal defense lawyer. On the other hand, in Case No. 2011-0063, the formal proceedings before the Arizona Board of Behavioral Health Examiners, Nevitt was represented by counsel Frederick Cummings of Jennings, Strouss & Salmon, PLC. It seems likely that this representation was not funded by Nevitt personally, since the Consent Agreement dated November 14, 2011, states that a copy was being provided to one Marc H. Harris, Assistant Attorney General of the Arizona Attorney General's Office. This would imply that SBA, as a governmental agency bearing a measure of responsibility for its official, Nevitt's, misconduct, involved itself in the matter. That would, in turn, suggest that SBA procured and may also have paid for the services of a Jennings Strouss attorney to represent Nevitt. In addition, there is evidence that SBA hired the services of the mammoth Snell & Wilmer L.L.P. law firm as a consultant to evaluate SBA's potential culpability in the criminal matter. Assuming it is true that SBA has been paying lawyers at Jennings, Strouss and Snell & Wilmer to engineer a cover-up and damage control, this has occurred at the expense of the Bar, since members' impositions alone fund the activities of SBA. Since July 16, 2012, the Arizona Board of Behavioral Health Examiners have opened a new file (File No. 2013-0002) investigating Nevitt on an allegation of sexual misconduct unrelated to the allegation investigated in its previous file.

   The above information and more appears on the website of Arizona Attorneys against Corrupt Professional Regulation, AZAACPR, at: http://www.azaacpr.org.

Appendix 5-2

 STATE BAR OF ARIZONA

June 14, 2013

Miriam Holly Klaiman

Re: Request for Records

Dear Ms. Klaiman,

In response to the letter we received from you on May 1, 2013 requesting "medical records", please be advised that the State Bar of Arizona does not qualify as a "health care provider" under the statute you have referenced. In addition, Rule 37(c), Ariz. R. Sup. Ct. indicates that certain "admission" records are confidential and therefore cannot be provided. Finally, pursuant to Rule 70(b)1 and 4, Ariz. R. Sup. Ct., bar counsel work product is also privileged and protected. Nonetheless, without waiving these objections, we are providing you with the balance of these records.

If you have any questions please feel free to contact me.

Sincerely,

John A. Furlong
General Counsel, Deputy Executive Director
State Bar of Arizona

JAF/ps

Enclosures

Appendix 5-3

BY CERTIFIED MAIL
return receipt requested

June 21, 2013

John A. Furlong, General Counsel/
  Deputy Executive Director
State Bar of Arizona
4201 N. 24th St., Ste. 100
Phoenix AZ 85016
(602) 252-4804

On April 30, 2013, I wrote to John Phelps, CEO of State Bar of
Arizona (SBA) requesting the following:

> Copies of all writings, documents, records, and tangible
> things about and pertaining to me collected by the State
> Bar of Arizona under the rubric of its "Member Assistance
> Program" supervised by the Bar's employee/licensed
> therapist, Howard M. "Hal" Nevitt.

On or about June 17, 2013, I received a mailing with a cover
letter from you, Mr. Furlong, dated June 14, 2013, which
purported to be a response to my request. I have inventoried
the contents. I enclose the inventory herewith.

I find that the contents of your mailing do not include (a)
copies of writings, tangible things, materials, documents,
correspondence or communications dated 2005-2006 between
MAP Director Nevitt/SBA and the Committee on Character and
Fitness of the Arizona Supreme Court apropos of its directing
him to conduct a meeting with me (a "therapeutic evaluation")
for purposes of addressing purported mental health issues. I
also don't find (b) copies of Mr. Nevitt's notes and written
summary or any other documentation of the "evaluation"
which Mr. Nevitt conducted on me at the SBA's premises on
December 23, 2005. And I don't find (c) copies of any
communications by Mr. Nevitt/SBA or the said Committee

resulting from and forming a record of findings and recommendations arising from the December 23, 2005, meeting.

I want copies of <u>all</u> such writings, documents, materials, tangible things and records. You will please provide them no later than July 1, 2013.

For the record, I have never seen any documents, materials or records whereby Mr. Nevitt obtained information from the Committee apropos of its reasons for recommending that I undergo such an "evaluation." After the "evaluation," Mr. Nevitt issued a written edict that my Bar admission be conditioned on mental health intervention. Whatever information, documents and materials provided to him by the Committee apropos of the December 23, 2005 "evaluation," and whatever report, records and documentation of that "evaluation" were composed by Mr. Nevitt, been available to the Committee itself, to SBA, and to Mr. Nevitt. There is absolutely no valid reason why such materials have been withheld all these years from me.

I demand that you furnish all of them.

In rounding out the context in which I issue this demand, I point out the following facts. I am not interested in engaging you, Mr. Furlong, in any discussion of these, at least not at this time. Please be so kind as to resist any impulse to rebut them.

    a. Neither SBA nor the Committee ever offered me a hearing on the conditions which Mr. Nevitt, acting under the aegis of SBA, required me to accept being labeled with a mental illness and to undergo "therapy" as a condition of joining the Bar. I was afforded no opportunity to attend any proceeding concerning conditions imposed on my Bar admission. Nor at any time did SBA or the Committee afford me an opportunity to confront either information or witnesses adverse to my Bar membership application. SBA is a licensing body and has no valid basis for withholding from an applicant the evidence based on which SBA decides to impose conditions on or to deny a license.

b. As the outcome of the December 23, 2005 "evaluation," Mr. Nevitt nevertheless issued a written edict requiring me to be "treated" for mental illness as a condition of my Bar membership. Because I was afforded no hearing and no chance to confront adverse information or adverse witnesses, the demand that I participate in purported mental "therapy" as a condition of Bar membership was presented to me as a take-it-or-leave-it proposition. Nevitt never even produced a document for my inspection expressing any opinion of his own as to what DSM-IV mental illness category I was supposed to be suffering from. Yet he insisted that I had a mental illness that required "treatment," and over the years since, SBA has repeatedly made public disclosures to the effect that I purportedly have such an illness.

c. Nevertheless, at the time I applied for Arizona Bar membership in 2005, I had passed the age of 50, had earned Ph.D. and M.D. degrees, had taught college for twelve years, had published a book with Cambridge University Press, and had neither been diagnosed with, nor ever treated for, any mental illness.

d. I have no history of misuse of any drug, intoxicant or substance. The only imaginable legitimate purpose of MAP is to deal with Bar members' and applicants' substance impairment. SBA is a licensing body and has no valid basis for taking an interest in purported "mental health" issues of applicants and members outside of their on-the-job conduct as law professionals. Accordingly, the unwarranted secrecy with which SBA has withheld from me information about so-called "therapy" and "mental illness" information that, in 2005-2006, it accumulated about me, including "mental illness" documentation it charged its employee Nevitt to produce and compile about me, raises a question whether, when he met me on December 23, 2005, Mr. Nevitt had already been provided with libelous and untruthful information to the effect that I had substance abuse issues.

e. In addition, it is my impresson that, at the December 23, 2005 meeting (supposed to give him an opportunity to "evaluate" my mental health), Mr. Nevitt, by virtue of materials and/or information he collected from a source other than my Bar application, felt emboldened, once he had me alone in a curtained room with himself on the SBA premises, to take indecent liberties with me.

f. The only possible source of any such information would have been the Committee on Character and Fitness, which obviously communicated with Mr. Nevitt prior to the date of that "therapeutic evaluation" (see the attached Inventory, item 25).

g. Although I was not afforded any opportunity to question or challenge the conditions imposed on my Bar membership, repeatedly in subsequent years, SBA has issued as public information the intelligence that in connection with my joining the Bar, I was made to participate in the Member Assistance Program, having been labeled as "mentally ill" and in need of "therapy." SBA's publications to this effect have included press release statements. SBA's purpose and the effect of these unlawful disclosures have been to destroy my reputation in the community and to shame, harass and personally persecute and humiliate me.

h. Over the years I was a Bar member, and prior to my acceding to a demand by Staff Bar Counsel to consent to disbarment, SBA repeatedly brought disciplinary proceedings against me. In each proceeding, as an "aggravating factor," the information was cited that SBA had gotten me to participate in MAP and that I had allowed myself to be labeled as "mentally ill" and in need of "therapy" as a condition on my Bar membership. I spent tens of thousands of dollars to defend myself in such disciplinary proceedings, only to learn that SBA does not prosecute in accordance with any standard of truthfulness. In proceedings against me, Staff Bar Counsel repeatedly presented conclusions that were unsupported factually. Said Counsel also relied on perjured testimony on the part of people it called as its witnesses.

i. In addition to costs of defense, from the time I was forced to accept the attentions of the MAP program to the end of my Bar licensure, I was also required to pay thousands of dollars in "costs" and "fees," purportedly for the administrative costs of MAP and other disciplinary administrative costs. I made payments to SBA, to "Hal" Nevitt, and even to SBA's Presiding Disciplinary Judge, William J. O'Neil. In pecuniary terms of my out-of-pocket expenses alone, leaving aside any other bases of claim, my damages due to the State Bar of Arizona's and its employees' illicit and wrongful actions amounts to a quarter of a million dollars.

j. I remind you, Mr. Furlong, that throughout the period during which I applied to and was a member of SBA, Mr. Nevitt was its employee; and I need not instruct you, Mr. Furlong, in the doctrine of *respondeat superior.* Your June 14, 2013 letter's comment, Mr. Furlong, to the effect that SBA is not a health care provider, is inaccurate. The accurate fact is that SBA has not complied with its obligations under Arizona statutes and administrative regulations in regard to patient rights such as the right of patients to copies of their medical records and their right to privacy of their medical information. If SBA were not a health care provider, it would not have had the privilege all these years of employing a licensed mental "therapist" (Mr. Nevitt), whose duties of "diagnosis" and "treatment" of State Bar members is disclosed in many public records of disciplinary proceedings which SBA has published and continues to publish.

Mr. Furlong, I am not interested in your response to points (a)-(j) above; rather, I have set them forth for the purpose of amplifying on my reasoning in seeking the materials I am demanding.

At this time, I reiterate my demand that by July 1, 2013, you furnish me with:

(a) copies of all writings, tangible things, materials, documents, correspondence and communications dated 2005-2006 appurtenant to the Committee on Character and Fitness' instructing Mr. Nevitt to "evaluate" me for mental health purposes and appurtenant to its complicity with his written recommendation that I submit to "therapy" as a condition of Arizona Bar membership; and (b) copies of all writings, documents, records and tangible things produced by Mr. Nevitt in connection with or as a result of his "evaluation" meeting with me at the SBA premises on December 23, 2005.

Miriam Holly Klaiman

Appendix 5-4

June 28, 2013

Miriam Holly Klaiman

Re: Request for Records

Dear Ms. Klaiman,

In response to your recent letter of June 24, 2013, please be advised that we have provided you with all of the documents that we are able to release in accordance with the Supreme Court Rules and applicable law.

Also, per your specific request, I am not responding to any of the alleged facts in your letter, even though I disagree with many of your allegations, representations and conclusions.

Finally, to the extent that your letter is an attempt to threaten me or the State Bar of Arizona, I would simply ask that you refrain from such unprofessional conduct.

I trust you understand our position. However, if you do have any additional questions, please feel free to contact me.

Sincerely,

John A. Furlong
General Counsel, Deputy Executive Director
State Bar of Arizona

JAF/ps

Innovative Workplace Solutions
13835 North Tatum Boulevard; #9-178
Phoenix, Arizona 85032

July 9, 2013

Ms. Klaiman,

I am in receipt of your letter dated July 5th, 2013 requesting that I furnish you with various records related to your evaluation and monitoring by the Member Assistance Program of the State Bar of Arizona.

As you are aware, the records you have requested are maintained by the State Bar of Arizona. Furthermore, I am no longer an employee of the State Bar of Arizona.

You will have to contact the State Bar of Arizona at 4201 North 24th Street, #100, Phoenix, Arizona, 85016-6266.

Sincerely,

Hal M. Nevitt
LCSW/LISAC/CEAP

Innovative Workplace Solutions
13835 N. Tatum Blvd; #9-178
Phoenix, Arizona 85032
602-885-4533

July 11, 2013

Lawyer Assistance Program
State Bar of Arizona
4201 N. 24th Street; #100
Phoenix, Arizona
85016-6266

To Whom It May Concern:

I recently received the enclosed letter requesting records. Because I no longer work with the Member Assistance Program and have no access to any of the records being requested, I am forwarding the request to you.

Thank you.

Sincerely,

Hal M. Nevitt
LCSW/LISAC/CEAP

cc Miriam H. Klaiman

203

ARIZONA PSYCHOLOGICAL SERVICES

2432 West Peoria Avenue, Suite 1007
Phoenix, Arizona 85029
(602) 997-6622

Harold Abramsky, Ph.D.
Director of Psychology

Bruce Kushner, Ph.D., P.C.
Clinical Psychologist

PSYCHOLOGICAL EVALUATION

NAME:	Hal Nevitt
DATE OF BIRTH:	10/11/56
AGE:	29 years
ETHNICITY:	Caucasian
REFERRED BY:	O. Joseph Chornenky, Esq.
DATE OF EVALUATION:	3/29/86
EVALUATOR:	Bruce Kushner, Ph.D.

REASON FOR REFERRAL

Mr. Nevitt was originally referred for evaluation in order to
assess his potential for suicide. At that time Mr. Nevitt had been
incarcerated on charges related to conspiracy to distribute cocaine.
He was interviewed for approximately three hours, and administered
a number of psychological tests, including the Minnesota Multiphasic
Personality Inventory, the Rorschach technique, Thematic Apperception
Test, and Projective Drawings.

Subsequent to his release from jail Mr. Nevitt has been seen on
an approximately weekly basis in order to assist him through the
present circumstances.

BACKGROUND

Mr. Nevitt was born in Mississippi, and raised in New Hampshire,
Alaska, and Arizona. He is one of three siblings, with one sister
residing in the present area, and another residing in Texas. He
reports being close to both of them. His parents presently reside
locally, and Mr. Nevitt is now living with them. Apparently he and
his wife had moved in with his parents pending the close of the home
they had purchased just prior to his current legal difficulties. Mr.
Nevitt describes his childhood as being essentially within normal
limits, noting that he spent most of his life in Scottsdale. He
denies that he was physically abused as a child. Initially, Mr.
Nevitt reported that both parents were social drinkers and that
his grandparents were not heavy drinkers. Later, however, he reported
that his father had been a heavy drinker in the past, and that
history was positive on his mother's side of the family for heavy
alcohol ingestion.

Mr. Nevitt attended Scottsdale High School where he received average to above average grades and attended regular classes. He reports no suspensions or expulsions while attending. Subsequent to high school he joined the Marines where he served for approximately two and a half years in Southeast Asia. He reports no disciplinary action while in the Marines, and received an Honorable Discharge. He subsequently attended Scottsdale Community College where he received an Associates Degree in Criminal Justice.

In 1978 Mr. Nevitt joined the Scottsdale Police force as a police assistant, becoming a police officer in 1979. He served as a patrol officer until approximately 1982 at which time he was transferred to narcotics, where he worked as an undercover officer until approximately January of 1984.

Mr. Nevitt is married to a woman he met in 1976. She is presently pregnant with their first child. They dated for approximately three years before marrying, with the course of the marriage being somewhat unstable until recently. His wife presently works as a claims adjuster for an insurance company.

PSYCHOLOGICAL FINDINGS

Mr. Nevitt appears to be a man who is well in contact with reality, and who displays no signs of psychotic processes. Thought patterns are logical, coherent and goal directed with no intrusions noted. He is oriented in all spheres, and denied the presence of any hallucinations and/or delusions.

Mr. Nevitt is situationally anxious and/or depressed, and while there has in the past been some suicidal ideation he was initially judged to be a low suicide risk, and continues to be seen in this manner. While presently under an enormous amount of stress, this related to not only the present charges but other recent events, he has managed to cope at reasonable levels. There have been times when he has been plagued by an inability to sleep, a lack of concentration, and nightmares, though these appear to be somewhat transitory and he has adequately coped with such symptoms.

In essence, Mr. Nevitt would appear to be a man who has had difficulty relating to others, and who has been prone, via history and personality makeup, to abuse substances in an effort to counteract periods of intense stress. He began to drink alcohol in his junior year in high school, though he tended to avoid heavy use of substances at that time due to his involvement in athletics. While in the Marines his alcohol use increased, to the extent where, when he was overseas, he drank some two to three times per week to the point of being drunk. Upon returning to the United States his drinking decreased, only to increase again when he joined the police force. His level of drinking increased over the years and from approximately 1973 to 1980 he would spend considerable time in bars or drinking at home. In 1980 he stopped drinking for approximately one year, although he began drinking again when assigned to narcotics duty. He reported that he would be

0021

allocated money to go to bars in order to meet drug contacts, and at that point began drinking again.

Interestingly, Mr. Nevitt's level of drug use prior to joining the police force was relatively negligible. There was some sporadic use of marijuana, but no use of LSD, PCP, heroin, or other hallucinogens. Moreover, he reports that he did not use any cocaine prior to joining the police force. While working as an undercover narcotics agent, Mr. Nevitt began to use cocaine, this spiralling into a period of heavy cocaine abuse from which he saw no way out. He describes himself as having literally slipped into his cocaine use without realizing the extent or nature of his difficulties, subsequently being unable to extricate himself once he realized the ill effects of his abuse.

It is interesting to note that with regard to his work as an undercover narcotics officer, Mr. Nevitt had difficulty separating or differentiating his undercover identity from his out of work identity. He tends to describe his undercover identity in a "macho" manner, and he clearly derived great pleasure from the sense of power and effectiveness that he derived from playing this role. There is a real need in this man to seek excitement, and his work as an undercover narcotics officer offered him the chance to succeed in this regard. Indeed, when describing his work there is a definite driven quality, this likely contributing greatly to his subsequent substance abuse. The job as described by Mr. Nevitt entailed dealing with enormous levels of stress and fear for which his use of substances helped. Moreover, Mr. Nevitt appears to have immersed himself in his street role, to the point where his main source of gratification was his ability to perform in that role at very high levels of efficiency. It is interesting, moreover, to note that in this regard there is some hint of underlying feelings of inadequacy which may have been counteracted by adopting this role as an undercover narcotics officer. In other words, there is a distinct possibility that Mr. Nevitt's feelings of inadequacy were dealt with by immersing himself in the role of a drug user, this allowing him to bolster feelings of low self esteem by overachieving on the job.

Since his marriage, Mr. Nevitt has had difficulty maintaining stability in that relationship. They have split up on a couple of occasions, initially in 1982. At that point he described himself as "very irresponsible as far as being a husband." He stayed out excessively, and was involved in other relationships. In 1984 they again split up, this time for approximately two months. It was at this point that he was working narcotics detail and was having difficulty maintaining stability. The split up apparently effected Mr. Nevitt to the point where he decided to cease his drug use and attempt to reconcile his marriage, and he reports that "our marriage has never been better." As previously reported, he and his wife were attempting to buy a house, and had been attempting to have a child.

Hal Nevitt
page 4

As has been noted previously, Mr. Nevitt continues to experience transitory and somewhat intense periods of depression and anxiety. He is extremely worried over the possibility that he could be incarcerated, and is realistically concerned about the possibility of being identified as a police officer while incarcerated. Additionally, he is concerned about his wife's ability to cope adequately with being a mother without his financial and emotional support. He has some bitterness that he is presently being investigated and punished for events which he feels have been put behind him. In other words, Mr. Nevitt reports that the events for which he is presently being tried are approximately two years old, and he feels that he has made great strides towards obtaining some stability in his life over the last two years. As a result he is somewhat resentful that he has only now lost his job and that his life is being disrupted after the events over which he lost control. There are times when he cries, feels that he has disappointed members of his family, and that he has lost the respect of others.

DIAGNOSTIC IMPRESSION

Axis   I: Adjustment Disorder with Mixed Emotional Features
              Cocaine Abuse, In Remission
              Alcohol Abuse, In Remission
Axis   II: Antisocial Traits
Axis   III: No Information

SUMMARY AND RECOMMENDATIONS

Mr. Nevitt is a 29 year old Caucasian male who shows signs of an adjustment disorder marked by anxiety and depression, this relative to his present set of circumstances. He appears remorseful and upset about not only his own situation but the extent to which he feels that he has punished others by his own inability to adequately control his impulses. The anxiety and depression are currently being coped with in an adequate fashion, and to the best of this examiner's knowledge he is not presently abusing any substances. He still, at times, has difficulty sleeping and concentrating, this compounded by a recent shooting incident during which Mr. Nevitt shot and killed a man. This aspect of his situation has, in my opinion, not been fully explored due to the fact that his subsequent arrest on the present charges have taken precedence over that event.

History, as well as job related difficulties, likely produced a man who was unable to adequately handle the intense levels of stress associated with his job, and the enormous need to succeed in the job further added to this man's willingness to abuse cocaine. He describes himself as having slipped into heavy cocaine abuse, indeed likely addiction, without realizing the extent and nature of his actions. He appears at present to be truly remorseful about his use of such, and indeed the loss of his career has effected him greatly. There is some evidence to indicate that Mr. Nevitt's self esteem was largely

207

based on his ability to perform as an undercover narcotics officer,
and as a police officer in general, the result being that the loss
of his job has effected him greatly. Moreover, the periods of
instability in his marriage had apparently been, at least to some
extent, ameliorated, the present set of circumstances only causing
further trauma in this regard. Furthermore, he is presently attempting
to deal with the fact that he may be separated from his not yet born
child during the period with which he and this child would become
attached to each other. Mr. Nevitt claims to have been drug free over
approximately the last two years, and there is some resultant bitterness and resentment that he is presently in these circumstances
because of events which he has attempted to handle on his own.

Mr. Nevitt appears to realize the extent and nature of the damage
he has done not only to himself but to others. He has expressed a
great deal of remorse over the disappointment he has caused in his
family, especially to his mother with whom he feels especially close.
He feels that he has disappointed others extensively, and has lost
the only career in which he was particularly interested.

In my opinion, there would appear to be little to be gained from
Mr. Nevitt's incarceration. He appears able to learn from his
mistakes, and in my opinion is unlikely to act out in an antisocial
manner so long as he is free of all substances. In this regard, he
is presently becoming involved in treatment specific to his substance
abuse, and has been attending sessions regularly in order to cope with
present levels of stress.

While his present treatment has been mostly crisis oriented, and
geared towards attempting to keep him stable and lessen the situational
anxiety and depression, long term treatment is likely necessary in
order to fully explore his need for increased levels of excitement, and
to explore the possibility that his feelings of inadequacy were being
coped with via his almost compulsive need to succeed in his job.
Indeed, this compulsive need likely played a strong role in his having
become heavily involved in cocaine use.

With continued treatment, both specific to his substance abuse
as well as his continued adjustment, there is, in my opinion, a
reasonable chance that Mr Nevitt could be precluded from any other
illegal activities and become an asset to his family, to himself,
and to his community.

If the court should decide against incarceration, Mr. Nevitt's
probationary period should include strict monitoring of ingestion
of substances, this perhaps best accomplished through random drug
screens. He also needs to be involved in a support group setting

such as AA or NA, this in conjunction with individual and/or group therapy. He is prone, by history and psychological makeup, toward alcohol and/or drug abuse and should be precluded from all future ingestion of such.

Bruce Kushner, Ph.D.

5-22-86

STATE OF ARIZONA
DEPARTMENT OF PUBLIC SAFETY
DISPOSITION REPORT

SID NUMBER	NAME	DOB	
AZ0	NEVITT HAL M		

ARRESTING AGENCY ORI NUMBER	ARREST NUMBER	DATE OF ARREST

FBI NUMBER	HENRY FINGERPRINT CLASSIFICATION

CHARGES/REDUCED CHARGES	OFFENSE CODE	ARIZONA REVISED STATUTE									
CONSP TRAF NARC DRUGS		13-3408									
OBSTRUCT CRIM INVEST		13-2409									
RACKETEERING											
SELL NARC DRUGS											
SELL NARC DRUGS											

FURTHER EXPLANATION OR MODIFICATIONS OF PRECEDING

SENT. TO RUN CC.

SUBMITTED BY BWB

DISPOSITION AGENCY ORI AZ 007035 J

AGENCY NAME: VIVIAN KRINGLE
Clerk of the Superior Court
STREET: 201 W. Jefferson Street
CITY, STATE, ZIP: Phoenix, Az. 85003

COURT CASE NUMBER		DISPOSITION DATE
LOWER COURT		
SUPERIOR COURT CR -	156528	6-27-86
APPEALS COURT		
SUPREME COURT		

DISPOSITION REPORT

CONTRIBUTOR OF FINGERPRINTS

RIGHT FOUR FINGERS TAKEN SIMULTANEOUSLY

Appendix 5-7

May 21, 1986

Gary L. Kiombhamm, M.D.
President

Neil O. Ward, M.A.
President-Elect

Robert A. Hilsert, M.D.
Vice President

Richard L. Collins, M.D.
Secretary

Mark Ivey, Jr., M.D.
Treasurer

Earl J. Ryker, M.D.
Past President

Ernest E. Kohlmann
Executive Vice President

O. Joseph Chornenky
4800 North Central Ave., Suite 100
Phoenix, AZ 85013

RE: Hal Murray Nevitt

Dear Mr. Chornenky:

At your request I saw Mr. Nevitt on May 15th for two hours. I spent an additional hour with him on May 21st. I conferred briefly with you, and between my two sessions with him conferred at length with Bruce Kushner, Ph.D. That was done to make sure that my advice to Hal would not be in conflict with the help Dr. Kushner is providing him. I also reviewed carefully the records that you provided. Without going into great detail, I will attempt to summarize my perceptions of what has occurred in relation to Mr. Nevitt's present circumstance.

Mr. Nevitt's family history is positive for alcoholism (father and paternal grandmother). It has been clearly demonstrated scientifically that the predisposition to addictive disease is hereditary. Hal began to drink as a teenager. His initial reactions to alcohol were not normal, but did not immediately create any serious problems. There was some perfectionism and high personal expectation evident, which is common in addiction-prone people. This led him to be very hard working in his career as a police officer. When he was transferred to narcotics squad he very much wanted to be "the best," which was his nature. In the process of his undercover work, in order to maintain his cover (and his safety), he found it necessary to "do" cocaine on occasion. In his undercover role he learned how to do and deal drugs which clearly was a necessity of his work. I suspect that many undercover narcotic officers find this necessary. At any rate Mr. Nevitt clearly felt that he had to as part of his job.

Unfortunately, Hal found that he liked the effect of cocaine. Very rapidly, and before he was aware of it, he became addicted to cocaine. As the addiction progressed it very naturally began to interfere with his work. Ultimately it made him so ineffective as a narcotics agent that he was transferred back to uniform patrol. This took him out of the environment and job which had been his drug supplier. All addicts, when faced with the necessity (it is urgent to understand that to the addict it truly is a necessity) to obtain their drug, will use the skills they know to obtain their drug. Some prostitute, some steal, wealthy addicts buy, physicians write prescriptions, airline pilots smuggle, and former narcotics officers buy and sell. Hal had learned his job well. He knew how to, and at that point in his life was too ill to realize that there was anything else he could do.

Ultimately his addictive use of cocaine so devastated his life that he discontinued cocaine and replaced it with alcohol. At that point his addiction improved only to the extent that he began to use a "legal" drug. His drinking was immediately heavy, destructive and clearly alcoholic. After a period of serious problem drinking, Hal was able to taper down considerably on the alcohol. Circumstances have forced him to almost entirely cease drinking.

During the period of heavy cocaine and alcohol use Hal's problems with work and family (multiple separations, at least one fairly serious family fight) were typical to the disease.

At the present time I feel Hal has made considerable progress in dealing with the tremendous stressors in his life. Dr. Kushner has been most helpful for him in that area. In addition I feel very strongly that Hal must become much more actively involved in dealing specifically with his addictive disease. I have urged him to begin to attend Alcoholics Anonymous (A.A.) with a close friend of his who is active in A.A. In addition I have introduced Hal to a friend and physician colleague of mine, a recovering alcoholic and cocaine addict, who has already taken Hal to one Cocaine Anonymous (C.A.) meeting and who is willing to spend more time working informally with Hal. Because of his rather unique life experiences I feel this physician may be very helpful to Hal. Mr. Nevitt has CIGNA health insurance at the present time, and I have urged him to seek formal addiction treatment through their alcohol and drug abuse program. He has made an appointment to see Dr. David Greenberg, the medical director of that program. _SEE NOTE

I do not believe that Mr. Nevitt's addictive disease was caused by his work. He was born with the predisposition, and at some point in his life circumstances would have triggered the disease anyway. However, I do believe that the pressures of wanting to be "the best" narcotics agent and his exposure to cocaine as part of his work were primary trigger events in the precipitation of the active phase of his disease. It is my medical opinion that the acts that he is accused of, as I understand them, were the result of his disease process rather than basic criminal intent. Clearly the acts were illegal. At the time they occurred Mr. Nevitt's disease rather than criminal intent was the underlying motive. The disease prevented him at that time from seeing his disease and from seeking some alternative course of action.

At the present time Hal seems willing to do whatever it takes to get his life back in order. Obviously his legal status has something to do with that. Mr. Nevitt (like my physician friend) has had some unique and devastating experiences as a result of his disease. He is now willing to do the things necessary to recover from his disease process. A prolonged legally supervised status with serious consequence for noncompliance can be most helpful

212

THE ARIZONA MEDICAL ASSOCIATION, INC. • CONTINUATION

May 22, 1986
Page Three

for his continuing recovery. I feel that he and his wife (who is pregnant with their first child) deserve that chance. If Hal recovers he will be in a position to be a productive and useful citizen, with life experiences which will allow him to be uniquely helpful to others. In that sense we all stand to gain. If he is incarcerated Hal's recovery process will be interrupted and possibly destroyed, in which case we all lose.

If there is any further help I can provide in this case please let me know.

Sincerely yours,

Donald L. Daenstra, M.D.
Chairman
Physician's Health Committee
and Medical Director
Chemical Dependency Program
St. Luke's Behavioral Health Center

DLD:mp

CURRICULUM VITAE

DONALD L. DYKSTRA, M.D.
Phoenix, Arizona

DATE OF BIRTH: June 4, 1933
PLACE OF BIRTH: Grand Rapids, Michigan

EDUCATION

June, 1955   Hope College, Holland, Michigan, A.B.
June, 1959   Northwestern University Medical School, M.D.

INTERNSHIP

May 1, 1959 -   Decatur and Macon County Hospital
April 30, 1960   Decatur, Illinois

POST GRADUATE EDUCATION

1961   Midwest Institute of Alcohol Problems

1963   Rutgers Summer School of Alcohol Studies

1964   University of Utah, Department of Post Graduate
                      Medicine (Courses for treatment and rehabilitation
                      for patients with alcoholism)

1965 - 1968   Intermittent Post Graduate Courses in selected
                      topics in Psychiatry and Internal Medicine,
                      University of Michigan and Wayne State University
                      Medical Schools.

PROFESSIONAL EXPERIENCE

June 1960 - June 1962   General Practice

October 1960-June 1962   Half-time physician, Alcoholism Clinic, Kent County
                         Health Department

June 1962-November 1964 Medical director, Brighton Hospital for Alcoholics

1964 - 1968   Consultant, Battle Creek Veteran's Administration
                        Hospital, Alcoholism Treatment Program, Battle Creek,
                        Michigan.

1968 - 1972   Attending Physician, Maricopa County General Hospital,
                        Alcohol Detoxification

1968 - 1972   Alcoholism Consultant, Arizona State Health Department

1968 - 1972   Alcoholism Consultant, Maricopa County Health Department

1969 - 1974   Adjunct Professor, University of Arizona College of
                        Pharmacy

22 X

214

MEMBERSHIP IN PROFESSIONAL ORGANIZATIONS

1. Member - North American Association of Alcoholism Programs
2. Member - American Medical Society on Alcoholism
3. Member - Civil Aviation Medical Association (inactive)
4. Member - American Academy of Medical Directors
5. Member - Maricopa County Medical Society
6. Member - Arizona Medical Association (ArMA)
7. Member - American Medical Association

PAST PRESIDENT

Michigan Institute of Alcoholism Programs

PRESENT POSITION

1. Director, Alcohol and Drug Abuse Section, Behavioral Health Services, St. Luke's Behavioral Health Center. Medical Director Detox and Outpatient Rehab Units, Tempe St. Luke's Hospital.

2. Alcoholism Consultant, Phoenix and Prescott Veteran's Administration Hospitals.

3. Adjunct Professor Addiction Studies, Department of Allied Health Sciences, University of Arizona.

4. Chemical Dependency Consultant, Arizona Board of Medical Examiners.

5. Behavioral Health Consultant to AEMS (Arizona Emergency Medical Systems, Inc.)

6. Member Arizona Department of Transportation, Medical Advisory Board.

7. Chairman Arizona Medical Association, Physician Health Committee.

LICENSURE

Illinois, Arizona

Appendix 5-8

LAW OFFICES
O. JOSEPH CHORNENKY, P.C.
ATTORNEYS AND COUNSELORS AT LAW
301 E. BETHANY HOME ROAD
SUITE A-209
PHOENIX, ARIZONA 85012

#002782 & #012736

Attorneys for Defendant

ARIZONA SUPERIOR COURT

MARICOPA COUNTY

STATE OF ARIZONA,	No. CR 156528A
Plaintiff,	**APPLICATION TO SET ASIDE JUDGMENT OF GUILT, DISMISS CHARGES, RESTORE CIVIL RIGHTS AND RESTORE RIGHT TO POSSESS WEAPONS**
v.	(Oral Argument and Evidentiary Hearing Requested)
HAL MURRAY NEVITT,	
Defendant.	

Defendant, HAL MURRAY NEVITT, acting through his undersigned counsel, pursuant to A.R.S. §13-907, §13-912, and the authorities cited in the attached Memorandum of Points and Authorities, respectfully requests that this Court enter an Order setting aside the judgment of guilt, and dismissing the charges in the above-entitled matter, restoring Mr. Nevitt's civil rights, and restoring his right to possess weapons. Mr. Nevitt has fulfilled all of the conditions of his sentence, including serving his prison sentence, serving his time on parole, and paying all of his fines.

Respectfully submitted this 5th day of August, 2003.

O. JOSEPH CHORNENKY, P.C.

By _____
O. Joseph Chornenky
Olin R. Hale
Attorneys for Mr. Nevitt

1

Facts:

On June 27, 1986, after his plea of no contest, the Court sentenced Hal Nevitt to prison. Mr. Nevitt pleaded no contest to charges that he conspired with others to traffic in narcotic drugs, a class 2 felony, and that he obstructed a criminal investigation, a class 5 felony. After serving approximately three (3) years of his prison sentence, Mr. Nevitt (hereinafter "Hal") was paroled in 1989.

Before he was sentenced to prison, from July 1, 1979 until April 11, 1986, Hal served as a Scottsdale police officer. During that service, while working undercover as a narcotics detective, Hal became addicted to cocaine.

Hal has made a remarkable comeback since being released from prison, as shown by his autobiography, which is attached hereto and noted as Exhibit A. Even the former Deputy County Attorney who prosecuted Mr. Nevitt, the Honorable James Keppel now "enthusiastically supports Hal's Application to Restore his Civil Rights." See Exhibit B attached hereto. Once Hal was released from prison, and transferred to work furlough status, he swallowed his pride and went to work unloading pre-packaged sawdust at horse farms in Scottsdale. In doing so, Hal worked for retired Scottsdale Police Sergeant Peter Wooster, a man whom Hal had trained as a police officer. Sgt. Wooster's character letter is attached hereto and noted as Exhibit C.

In May of 1989, Hal was able to begin work in his chosen field as an alcohol/drug counselor. Hal began working as a Counselor Technician for Phoenix Adolescent Recovery Center (PARC Place). He worked for PARC Place for the next six years. In December of 1989, Hal saved a man, who had attempted to hang himself in a public park. For this act of heroism and compassion, Hal received a Life Saving award from the Phoenix Police Department in February of 1990.

In May of 1990, Hal began attending classes at Arizona State University, majoring in Social Work, and graduating with honors in 1992. On May 22, 1992, Hal married Ellen Johnson and they reared three children, Kevin, Collin, and Mariah. At PARC Place, Hal was promoted several times, from Shift Leader to Case Manager.

In August of 1994, Hal began working for St. Luke's Behavioral Health Center, where he developed an Adult Partial Hospitalization Program. At the same time, Hal was accepted into the

2

1   Masters of Social Work Program at A.S.U, graduating in May of 1996. Additionally, Hal holds an

2   Independent Certification in Social Work, and a Certification in Substance Abuse Counseling, through

3   the Arizona State Board of Behavioral Health Examiners. In 1998, Hal accepted a position with the

4   Employee Assistance Program (EAP) at St. Luke's Behavioral Health Center. In this capacity, Hal

5   was able to realize his dream of assisting employees of public service agencies, such as the City of

6   Surprise, the City of Chandler, and the National Forest Service, with substance abuse and mental

7   health problems. Accordingly, Hal's life has now come full circle, from suffering with a drug

8   addiction, to helping others cope with their problems.

9   Hal is trying to use his education, training, and life experiences to help other public servants

10 who face the same problems which caused him to fall. Now, in addition to his busy counseling

11 practice, Hal teaches Sociology, Group Dynamics, and an Executive Fire Leadership classes at Grand

12 Canyon University. In 2001, Hal was asked by Diane Ellis, the Director of the Members Assistance

13 Program for the State Bar of Arizona, to conduct training presentations for members of the Peer

14 Monitoring Program on Substance Abuse and Behavioral Health issues. Hal also performs

15 assessments, and counsels members of the State Bar. Diane Ellis has written a letter for Hal which

16 is noted as Exhibit D and attached hereto.

17   Hal now holds the position of Clinical Supervisor for a Residential Treatment Center for

18 adolescent clients. He supervises three Master's level therapists and approximately 25 Behavioral

19 Health Technicians, who provide services to 20 clients and their families. Attached as Exhibit E are

20 numerous character letters which attest to the good things Hal has done for others. These letters,

21 from friends and co-workers, are the best evidence that Mr. Nevitt is rehabilitated and has earned the

22 privilege of having his conviction set aside and his rights restored.

23 Law and Argument:

24   A.R.S. §13-907 reads as follows:

25   Except as provided in subsection B of this section, **every person convicted of a** h
           criminal offense may, upon fulfillment of the conditions of probation or sentence
26   and discharge by the court, apply to the judge, justice of the peace or magistrate
           who pronounced sentence or imposed probation or such judge, justice of the
27   peace or magistrate's successor in office to have the judgment of guilt set aside.
           The convicted person shall be informed of this right at the time of discharge. The
28   application to set aside the judgment may be made by the convicted person or by his

                                    3

attorney or probation officer authorized in writing. If the judge, justice of the peace or magistrate grants the application, the judge, justice of the peace or magistrate shall set aside the judgment of guilt, dismiss the accusations or information and order that the person be released from all penalties and disabilities resulting from the conviction other than those imposed by the department of transportation pursuant to section 28-445 or 28-446, and except that the conviction may be used as a conviction if such conviction would be admissible had it not been set aside and may be pleaded and proved in any subsequent prosecution of such person by the state or any of its subdivisions for any offense or used by the department of transportation in enforcing the provisions of section 28-445 or 28-446 as if the judgment of guilt had not been set aside. (*Emphasis added*).

Based on the foregoing, Mr. Nevitt respectfully requests that this Court enter an Order setting aside the judgment of guilt and dismissing the charges in the above-entitled cause number and removing any and all disabilities imposed by the above-noted conviction. The proposed Order is predicated on a finding that Mr. Nevitt has successfully complied with all the terms and conditions of his sentence and has been rehabilitated.

Respectfully submitted this 5th day of August, 2003.

O. JOSEPH CHORNENKY, P.C.

By _____
O. Joseph Chornenky
_____ R. Hale
Attorneys for Hal Nevitt

Copy of the foregoing
mailed/delivered this
_5_ day of August,
2003, to:

The Honorable Thomas W. O'Toole
Criminal Presiding Judge
101 W. Jefferson, Suite 514
Phoenix, Arizona 85003-2302

Mr. Richard M. Romley, Esq.
Maricopa County Attorney
301 West Jefferson, 8th Floor
Phoenix, Arizona 85003-2151

_____

4

Appendix 5-9

19649 North Twelfth Place
Phoenix, Arizona 85024-1766
March 21, 2003

Mr. O. Joseph Chornenky
Attorney at Law
301 East Bethany Home Road
#A-209
Phoenix, Arizona 85012

Re: Hal Nevitt

Dear Mr. Chornenky:

It is my pleasure to lend my ardent support to efforts to secure expunction of Hal's conviction. I have known Hal for three years, personally and professionally, both in my capacity as Director of the State Bar of Arizona's Lawyer Assistance Programs and as a member of the Phoenix Chapter of the Employee Assistance Professionals Association.

The following is background information on myself. I have been employed by the State Bar of Arizona for ten years. For the first seven years, I was Director of the Law Office Management Assistance Program, which provides management consulting services to lawyers throughout Arizona wh. request such services on a voluntary basis; lawyers who are referred in connection with disciplinary proceedings by the State Bar's Lawyer Regulation Department, the Arizona Supreme Court Disciplinary Commission, or the Arizona Supreme Court; lawyers who are referred by the Arizona Supreme Court Committee on Character and Fitness in connection with conditional admissions; and lawyers who are referred by judges in the Superior Courts or other jurisdictions. Three years ago, I also assumed responsibility for directing the State Bar of Arizona's Member Assistance Program, which provides services to lawyers who suffer from chemical dependency, mental health issues, or other personal issues that affect their ability to practice. The two departments were combined under one umbrella known as the Lawyer Assistance Programs, and I was named Director.

Prior to joining the State Bar staff, I was employed for ten years in administrative positions with medium-sized Phoenix law firms; I was with one firm for six years and another firm for four years. My education includes a Bachelor of Arts degree from Arizona State University and a Master of Business Administration in Management degree from Western International University. I am currently enrolled in a graduate program in Employee Assistance Counseling at Ottawa University and expect to be granted a master's degree in that field in 2004. I have also successfully completed the examination to gain designation as a Certified Employee Assistance Professional.

In addition, I completed a number of legal assisting courses at Phoenix College and public relations coursework at Arizona State University. My first career was as a journalist. I completed three years in the University of Missouri Journalism School before transferring to ASU, and I held reporting positions with the Springfield (Missouri) Daily News and with the Phoenix Gazette.

I am a member of both the Phoenix and Tucson chapters of the Employee Assistance Professionals Association and of the American Bar Association's Commission on Lawyer Assistance Program's Annual Conference Planning Committee. I have been a member of the American Bar Association Law Practice Management Section's Practice Management Advisors Committee since the Committee's inception in 1994 and served as chair for three years beginning in 1998. I also am a member of the Association of Legal Administrators and have served as an officer and newsletter committee chair of the local chapter, as well as a member of the national Editorial Advisory Board.

I am a frequent author and speaker on management topics and issues related to lawyer impairment. I am the author of "A Decade of Diversion: Its Impact and Implications for the Arizona Lawyer Regulation System," which is scheduled for summer 2003 publication in shorter form in the American Bar Association Center for Professional Responsibility publication Professional Lawyer and in the Emory University Law Journal. I was a presenter at the following conferences: National Organization of Bar Counsel 2003 Mid-year Conference, Emory University Law School's 2003 Ethics and Professionalism Symposium, American Bar Association 2003 Ethics and Professionalism Conference, National Association of Law Placement 2003 Annual Conference, Missouri State Bar's Sole Practitioner and Small Firm 2003 Annual Conference, State Bar of Arizona 2003 Annual Convention, American Bar Association TechShow 2002, Washington State Bar Association 2002 Management and Technology Conference, State Bar of Arizona Annual Convention 2002, and Washington State Bar Association 2001 Lawyer Assistance Programs Annual Conference. I also present to numerous specialty bar associations, as well as other lawyer and legal staff groups within Arizona.

I have had extensive contact with Hal since first meeting him in 2000, when he was selected as a featured speaker for the annual retreat of the State Bar of Arizona's Member Assistance Program and Member Assistance Committee. Hal's selection was based on strong recommendations from my colleagues, and they were correct that he is a speaker with great breadth and depth of knowledge in his field, as well as an authoritative and engaging presentation style. Since that time, I have engaged Hal's services as a speaker on several additional occasions. He made two presentations at the 2002 Fall Conference of the Member Assistance Program and Member Assistance Committee and has also presented at several offerings of the State Bar of Arizona Department of Lawyer Regulation's Ethics Enhancement Program.

In addition, Hal taped a program on chemical dependency issues that is used in training monitors for the State Bar of Arizona's Law Office Management Assistance Program and Member Assistance Program. He also videotaped a presentation on the same topic that is offered on the State Bar of Arizona's Internet web site as on-line continuing legal education. Hal is also on the professional referral list maintained by the Member Assistance Program, and he frequently provides professional consulting services to program staff.

State Bar of Arizona members to whom I have referred Hal speak highly of his skills in helping them improve their situation or condition and teaching them coping techniques. Perhaps more importantly, they are impressed by his professionalism, compassion, practical problem-solving approach, and lack of judgmental attitude.

Hal also served as my professional advisor in connection with my pursuit of designation as a Certified Employee Assistance Professional (CEAP). The Employee Assistance Credentialing Commission requires that each applicant engage in 24 hours of advisement with a qualified CEAP over a period of at least six months. Because of our mutually busy schedules, Hal and I completed the advisement sessions over a period of more than one year, meeting at least twice each month. Hal's advice and instruction were invaluable to me in successfully meeting the requirements to become a CEAP.

During the first two years that I was a member of the Phoenix Chapter of the Employee Assistance Professionals Association, Hal served as treasurer. He is currently vice president and will serve as the next president. I have had contact with Hal virtually every month at the organization's educational programs. I also want to mention that he has been selected to make educational presentations to his EAPA peers. Hal is recognized by his peers, myself included, as being knowledgeable and an outstanding professional resource.

If I can provide additional information or answer any questions about my professional or personal opinions of Hal's qualifications and qualities, please be sure to let me know.

Sincerely,

Diane Ellis

Diane M. Ellis, MBA, CEAP

DME:

From the Desk of
Marc H. Harris

March 31, 2003

O. Joseph Chornenky
301 East Bethany Home Road, #A-209
Phoenix, Arizona 85012

RE: *Hal M. Nevitt*

I am writing personally on behalf of Hal Nevitt. As the Health Unit Chief for the Licensing and Enforcement Section of the Office of the Attorney General, I provide legal services to a variety of health regulatory boards, including representing the state in matters involving allegations of unprofessional conduct.

Recently, the Board of Behavioral Health Examiners issued a formal complaint against a certified substance abuse counselor. Because the hearing involved technical standard of practice issues, it was necessary to use the services of an expert witness. The person identified by the Board to serve in that capacity was Hal Nevitt, CISW. It was my first opportunity to work with Mr. Nevitt and I came away from the experience highly impressed.

As indicated, the case involved the conduct of a certified substance abuse counselor who engaged in unprofessional conduct. In order to successfully prosecute the case, I needed to utilize the skills of a professional who could both address the applicable standards of practice and apply those standards to the facts. I could not have asked for a more qualified person than Mr. Nevitt. From our first meeting, Mr. Nevitt proved to be a valuable asset. He quickly became familiar with the facts and because of his professional expertise, was able to persuasively apply the standards of practice to the facts and convey in a meaningful manner why the conduct constituted a serious threat to the public's health, safety and welfare.

What impressed me most about working with Mr. Nevitt was his work ethic and his passion for his profession. Mr. Nevitt was always well prepared and displayed a sincerity for the professional of certified substance abuse counseling that made it easy for the judge to find him to be a very capable and credible witness. Again, it was a pleasure working with Mr. Nevitt and should the facts warrant, I would welcome the opportunity to work with him again.

Sincerely,

Marc H. Harris

223

Greenberg & Sucher, PC

PO Box 2243
Scottsdale, AZ 85252
(480) 990-3111
FAX (480) 990-3114

March 18, 2003

Dr. Joseph Chornenky
5011 E. Bethany Home Road, # A-209
Phoenix, AZ 85012

RE: Hal Nevitt

Dear Mr. Chornenky:

I practice addiction medicine and am certified by the American Society of Addiction Medicine. I serve as the medical director of the monitoring programs for the Arizona Medical Board, Arizona State Board of Dental Examiners and the State Bar of Arizona. I also serve as the medical director of chemical dependency for Banner Behavioral Health Hospital in Scottsdale.

I first became acquainted with Hal in 1986. He was referred to me by Dr. Don Damstra who was his treating physician at St. Luke's Hospital in Phoenix. He was just entering recovery at that time and was going through numerous legal and personal issues. He dealt with those issues by being honest and straightforward. He has demonstrated consistent and high quality recovery since that time. We stayed in touch during his early recovery and during his period of incarceration. Since his release from jail we have had very regular contact. During the past five years our relationship has grown and I have served as a mentor and colleague of Hal's. We have had and continue to have at least weekly contact by phone and/or in person.

I have watched Hal grow significantly both personally and professionally. He has maintained sobriety through incarceration and divorce. He has built a new career and family despite significant obstacles and flourished. He is an inspiration to many and he continues to reach out and help others. His professional reputation is excellent. He maintains an attitude of humility in all areas of his life. He is someone I respect and admire more than words can say. I am proud to call him my friend and colleague. I certainly would recommend that his conviction be expunged based on his personal traits, strong character, resilience and his giving back to individuals and the community.

Hal Nesbit-Page 2

Please do not hesitate to contact me if you have any questions or if I can provide additional information.

Sincerely,

Michel A. Sucher, MD

May 1, 2003

To Whom It May Concern:

I was the prosecutor who prosecuted Mr. Nevitt in this cause and wish to take this opportunity to enthusiastically support his Application to Restore Civil Rights. Since his conviction, Mr. Nevitt has been a model citizen, has turned his life around and is very active in drug counseling for both our youth and adults.

Accordingly, to his credit, I believe that restoration of his civil rights is appropriate and well deserved. If you have any questions concerning my knowledge of Mr. Nevitt, please do not hesitate to contact me at 602-506-4251. Thank you for your time and consideration.

Sincerely,

James H. Keppel

JHK/ak

226

AN RYA
ized Investi

February 27, 2003

To Whom it May Concern:

My name is Daniel F. Ryan and I am the owner of Specialized Investigations in Phoenix, Arizona. I have served my country and community as a Marine Captain, FBI Special Agent, ATF Special Agent, Criminal Investigator in the Maricopa County Attorney's Office Major Felony Bureau and as a volunteer at St. Patrick's Parish in Scottsdale, Arizona.

Hal Nevitt and I have known each other for over ten years and I count him as a capable professional and a good friend. I have worked with Hal professionally on several cases and have observed him to be compassionate, intelligent and forthright. I feel strongly that when Hal makes a recommendation about a client that his decision is grounded in good sense, vast life experience and a strong sense of right and wrong.

I see Hal about twice a week over the last several years around the neighborhood and it's always a pleasure to see him because of this infectious enthusiasm about people and recovery and mental health. His sense of commitment approaches a ministry level as evidenced by his concern for his fellow man. As an example of this, I recall that he volunteered and went to New York City after 9/11/2001 to offer his counseling expertise to those people deeply touched by this national tragedy.

I am proud to say that Hal is my friend and feel that he is exemplary of the good people that we are fortunate to have in the community.

Very truly yours,

Daniel F. Ryan

DFR:khs

714 North Third Street • Phoenix, Arizona 85004
Phone (602) 258-8158 • Fax (602) 258-8159 • E-mail: specializedinvestigations@hotmail.com

227

Appendix 6-1

Supreme Court
STATE OF ARIZONA

COMMITTEE ON CHARACTER AND FITNESS
1501 W. Washington Street, Suite 104
Phoenix, Arizona 85007-3231
602-364-0371

November 28, 2005

PERSONAL AND CONFIDENTIAL

Miriam Holly Klaiman

Dear Ms. Klaiman:

As a continuation of our review of your application for admission to practice law in Arizona, the Committee is referring you to the Member Assistance Program (MAP) of the State Bar of Arizona for an evaluation of mental/emotional stability. This referral is made as a part of the Committee's continuing investigation as to whether you meet the standards for admission to the practice of law in Arizona (reference Supreme Court Rule 36(a)2).

MAP offers confidential assistance and evaluation to individuals with situations of work-related stress, anxiety or depression, career problems, family conflicts, chemical dependency, mental and emotional problems, financial difficulties, and other areas of concern. Although MAP's clients are primarily those already admitted to practice in Arizona, this Committee of the Supreme Court refers to MAP when we believe it will be of benefit in our review process.

Would you therefore contact the MAP Program at 602-340-7219 or 602-340-7313 to make arrangements for evaluation and assessment by Mr. Hal Nevitt. Please be advised you are responsible for all fees related to this process.

Sincerely,

C. de Looper, Attorney Admissions
Character & Fitness/Examinations

cc: MAP

Stephen M. Weiss, Co-Chair · Ann Birmingham Scheel, Co-Chair
Howard D. Sukenic, Vice-Chair · J. Russell Skelton · Tobin Rosen · Timothy R. Hyland
David F. Gaona · James H. Dyer · Troy P. Foster · Lee Marshall Holtry
Henry C. Manuelito · H. Christina Hill · Ronald Ross Watson, Ph.D.

Appendix 6-2

6 December, 2005

C. de Looper, Attorney Admissions
Character & Fitness/Examinations
Arizona Supreme Court
1501 W. Washington, Ste. 104
Phoenix AZ 85007
(602) 364-0371

Dear Ms. de Looper:

Thank you for your letter of November 28. I wonder if I may inquire as to reasons which have prompted the determination that I should undergo a psychological evaluation as a condition for further consideration of my application for Bar admission. I do not question that the Supreme Court has the right to regulate the profession and set standards for admission. On the other hand, I am unaware that this particular requirement is often imposed.

Because I am 52 years old with no history of treatment for psychiatric or psychological problems, no history of substance abuse, nor a history of being a public charge, I am wondering what information received by the Supreme Court has prompted this requirement. If there is information that it would not be improper for you to share, I hope you will not mind replying. Thank you.

Sincerely,

Miriam H. (Mimi) Klaiman
J.D., 2005, University of Arizona College of Law

Appendix 6-3

Previous | Next | Back to Messages

Delete | **Reply** | **Forward** | **Spam** | **Move...**

This message is not flagged. | Flag Message - Mark as Unread | Printable View

Folder [Add - Edit]

Inbox (15)
Draft
Sent
Bul [Empty]
Trash [Empty]

Subject: Contractor and Fitness
Date: 15 Mar 2006 15:53:39 -0700
From: "Stanley Feldman" <sfeldman@hmpmlaw.com> Add to Address Book Add Mobile Alert
To: "M. Harrigan"

My advice to you is to sign the contract (if you haven't already), get admitted to the bar, and leave the past behind.

Stanley G. Feldman
Haralson, Miller, Pitt, Feldman & McAnally, P.L.C.
One South Church Avenue, Suite 900
Tucson, Arizona 85701-1620
Tel: 520.792.3836
Fax: 520.624.5080
E-mail: sfeldman@hmpmlaw.com

Delete | **Reply** | **Forward** | **Spam** | **Move...**

Previous | Next | Back to Messages

Save Message Text | Full Headers

Check Mail | **Compose**

Search Mail | Search the Web

RE: Bar issue

Tuesday, June 13, 2006 5:01 PM

From: "J. J. Rico" jrico@azdisabilitylaw.org
To: "Mimi Klaiman"

Mimi

After review of the new information you provided at the conclusion of our phone call I have detrmined that the ACDL will not be able to represent you and write the letter on your behalf. This decision is based on your disclosure that the information shared with the counselor was not truthful.

If you would like to discuss further or need clarification please do not hesitate to contact me. Thanks.

J.J. Rico
Managing Attorney, Access Unit
Arizona Center for Disability Law
            (520) 327-9547
www.azdisabilitylaw.org

Note that my email address has changed. It is now
jrico@azdisabilitylaw.org

This Communication is confidential and is intended only for the use of the individual or entity named above.   If you have received this communication in error, please immediately destroy it and notify the sender by reply e-mail or by telephone at 1(800) 922-1447.

Appendix 6-5

STATE BAR OF ARIZONA

December 9, 2005

Ms. Miriam Holly Klaiman

~~[address redacted]~~

Re: Character & Fitness

Dear Ms. Klaiman:

Per our discussion, I am enclosing some forms I need you to complete. The Confidential Information Sheet, the Consent to Release of Confidential Information authorizing the Member Assistance Program to disclose information to the Supreme Court Committee on Character and Fitness, and the Consent to Release of Confidential Information authorizing the Member Assistance Program to disclose information to the Lawyer Regulation department upon your admission to the State Bar of Arizona should be returned to the address on this letterhead.

I have also enclosed a HIPPA and an Informed Consent. You may either return these forms with the others, or give them to me at our appointment on December 23, 2005.

I am also enclosing an invoice in the amount of $350.00 for the assessment.

Thank you for your cooperation. If you have any questions, please call me at (602) 340-7334 or toll free at 1 (866) 482-9227, ext. 334.

Sincerely,

Hal M. Nevin, LCSW, CEAP
Director
Member Assistance Program

HMN:tw
Enclosures

Appendix 6-6

INFORMED CONSENT FOR ASSESSMENT AND TREATMENT

Welcome to Innovative Workplace Solutions, an independent counseling practice, offering counseling and consultation services to members of The State Bar of Arizona. A counseling situation offers a unique relationship between the therapist and client. In order to start our relationship in a healthy way, I have put together this document to ensure that there are no misunderstandings about the various aspects of the counseling and psychotherapy services.

Background and Services

I am a Licensed Clinical Social Worker, and a Licensed Independent Substance Abuse Counselor; licensed by the Arizona Board of Behavioral Health Examiners. In addition, I am a Certified Employee Assistance Professional; certified nationally through the Employee Assistance Certification Commission. My educational background includes a master's degree in social work.

I offer counseling, psychotherapy, and consultation services to individuals, in the areas of mental health, and employee assistance.

The primary focus of my practice is the evaluation of State Bar members presenting with a variety of mental health and substance abuse situations, which affect their practice and personal lives. This service is not meant to be a long term counseling service; most members are assessed and referred to a therapist, treatment program, or appropriate resource depending on the clinical situation assessed.

Financial

Payment is expected at the time the service is rendered unless other arrangements have been made. By signing this document, you are agreeing to pay for the services rendered and any additional expenses that may be accrued in collecting said fees. Currently, the fee for an initial assessment is $150.00 (if you are also participating in LOMAP) or $350.00 (if you are only participating in MAP), additional office visits are $20.00 made payable to The State Bar of Arizona. There may be other fees for additional services such as development of a MAP contract. The fee structure is maintained by The State Bar and information is available upon request. You have the right to be informed of all fees that you are required to pay, please discuss these with me if you have a concern.

Availability of services

The Member Assistance Program has a limited capability to respond immediately to counseling emergencies. True emergencies should be directed to the community emergency services (911) or to the local hotlines (Empact–480-784-1500, Banner Help line–602-254-4357, St. Luke's Behavioral Health System–602-251-8535, or ValueOptions–602-222-9444). Established clients with an urgent need to make contact may call me, but an immediate response is not guaranteed. A quick or immediate response in one situation does not constitute a commitment of rapid response in another situation. Finally, the State Bar maintains a 24-hour crisis hotline for its members in need of emergency mental health services. The number is 1-800-681-3957.

Appointments

Regular attendance at your scheduled appointments is one of the keys to a successful outcome in counseling. I reserve an hour or more for each appointment with a client. Appointments canceled at the last minute are very detrimental to my practice. Therefore, I ask that you notify me a minimum of one full business day (24 hours, Monday through Friday) prior to your appointment if you need to cancel. **You will be billed for appointments you fail to cancel in accordance with this policy. Currently, the fee billed for this is $20.00. Repeated late cancellations or missed appointments will be billed at the full fee of $75.00 and may result in termination of treatment.** Appointment availability varies with the client load at the time.

Privacy, confidentiality, and records

Ordinarily, all communications and records created in the process of counseling are held in the strictest confidence pursuant to Arizona Supreme Court rule and federal statute. However, there are exceptions to confidentiality defined in the state and federal statutes. The most common of these exceptions are when there is a real or potential life or death emergency, when the court issues a subpoena, or when child/elder abuse or neglect is involved. I also participate in a process where selected cases are discussed with other professional colleagues to facilitate my continued professional growth and to get you the benefit of a variety of professional experts. While no identifying information is released in this peer consultation process, the dynamics of the problems and the people are discussed along with the treatment approaches and methods.

There are also numerous other circumstances when information may be released including when disclosure is required by the Arizona Board of Behavioral Health Examiners, when a lawsuit is filed against me, to comply with worker compensation laws, to comply with the USA Patriot Act and to comply with other federal, state or local laws. The rules and laws regarding confidentiality, privacy, and records are complex. The *HIPAA NOTICE OF PRIVACY PRACTICES*, included in this packet of information, details the considerations regarding confidentiality, privacy, and your records. This packet also contains information about your right to access your records and the details of the procedures to obtain them, should you choose to do so. Periodically, the *HIPAA NOTICE OF PRIVACY PRACTICES* may be revised.

Any changes to these privacy practices will be posted in my office, but you will not receive an individual notification of the updates. *It is imperative that you read and understand the limits of privacy and confidentiality before you start treatment.*

	I have read the *HIPAA NOTICE OF PRIVACY PRACTICES*, and have had my questions about privacy and confidentiality answered to my satisfaction. I understand that the *HIPAA NOTICE OF PRIVACY PRACTICES* is incorporated by reference into this agreement.
ssNK **Initials**	

Purpose, limitations, and risks of treatment

Counseling, like most endeavors in the helping professions, is not an exact science. While the ultimate purpose of counseling is to reduce your distress through a process of personal change, there are no guarantees that the treatment provided will be effective or useful. Moreover, the process of counseling usually involves working through tough personal issues that can result in some emotional or psychological pain for the client. Attempting to resolve issues that brought you to therapy in the first place may result in changes that were not originally intended. Psychotherapy may result in decisions about changing behaviors, employment, substance use, schooling, housing, relationships, or virtually any other aspect of your life. Sometimes a decision that is positive for one family member is viewed quite negatively by another family member. Change will sometimes be easy and swift, but more often it will be slow and even frustrating. There is no guarantee that psychotherapy will yield positive or intended results.

Treatment process and rights

Your counseling will begin with one or more sessions devoted to an initial assessment so that I can get a good understanding of the issues, your background, and any other factors that may be relevant. When the initial assessment process is complete, we will discuss ways to treat the problem(s) that have brought you into counseling and develop a treatment plan. You have the right and the obligation to participate in treatment decisions and in the development and periodic review and revision of your treatment plan. You also have the right to refuse any recommended treatment or to withdraw consent to treat and to be advised of the consequences or such refusal or withdrawal.

Our relationship

The client/counselor relationship is unique in that it is exclusively therapeutic. In other words, it is inappropriate for a client and a counselor to spend time together socially, to bestow gifts, or to attend family or religious functions. The purpose of these boundaries is to ensure that you and I are clear in our roles for your treatment and that your confidentiality is maintained. If there is ever a time when you believe that you have been treated unfairly or disrespectfully, please talk with me about it. It is never my intention to cause this to happen to my clients, but sometimes misunderstandings can inadvertently result in hurt feelings. I want to address any issues that might get in the way of the therapy as soon as possible. This includes administrative or financial issues as well.

Consent for evaluation and treatment

Consent is hereby given for evaluation and treatment under the terms described in this consent document and the *HIPAA NOTICE OF PRIVACY PRACTICES*. It is agreed that either of us may discontinue the evaluation and treatment at any time and that you are free to accept or reject the treatment provided. In the case of a minor child, I hereby affirm that I am a custodial parent or legal guardian of the child and that I authorize services for the child under the terms of this agreement.

Signature: _____ Date: _2/22/05_

---

or office use only - verification that client has read and understands informed consent document
Authorized Representative: _____ Date: _____

Exhibit 6-7

June 28, 2012

Complaints
Arizona Board of Behavioral Health Examiners
3443 N. Central Av. Ste. 1700
Phoenix AZ 85012   (602) 542-1882

I am writing to lodge a complaint against a licensee of AzBBHE. I would prefer that my identity as reporter be kept confidential from the licensee complained of and from the licensee's employer, the State Bar of Arizona (SBA).

Since the date of my encounter with the licensee (December 23, 2005) may also be identifying, I ask that it also be withheld.

I am reporting a sexual assault, wherein I was the victim, by a licensee of your agency to whom I was required to submit to for mental health "evaluation." He is Howard "Hal" Murray Nevitt, LCSW-3406 and LISAC-0837. I ask AzBBHE to investigate Nevitt.

As a lawyer, I joined SBA in mid-2006, conditioned on my being evaluated and supervised by Nevitt in his capacity as "Director" of the "Member Assistance Program" (MAP) of SBA. I had no prior substance abuse nor psychological/psychiatric history. A committee evaluating my SBA membership application, the Committee on Character and Fitness, recommended this condition on my admission. To this day, and despite my several written inquiries, no one has shown me any evidence which supported the Committee's determination that this was necessary. I still do not know why I was directed to meet with Nevitt.

Nevitt sent me a letter stating I must pay a charge in advance for his "evaluation" and that I must provide signed forms, including an "informed consent" to the "evaluation." A copy of his letter is enclosed.

On the aforementioned date, about 1 or 2 pm, directed by Nevitt in advance as to where and when to appear for the supposed "evaluation," I went to the SBA offices at 4201 N. 24th St., Phoenix, 2d floor. Across from the receptionist desk was a small enclosed room. I was instructed to sit inside there and wait. Mr. Nevitt entered and from then on for the next hour, he and I were alone and he kept the door closed. His "evaluation" included detailed questions about my sexual habits: was I homosexual or heterosexual, was I or had I been married, how many times had I been married, when had I first and how recently had I had sexual relations, how frequently on average did I engage in sexual relations, through which orifice(s) and/or with what objects did I engage in sexual acts, and several other sex-related questions.

I do not consider these as questions appropriate to mental health provider's first professional meeting with a subject who has not complained of sexual dysfunction and where the goal is (supposedly) to determine whether that person has the mental stability to engage in the practice of law.

At the conclusion of the "evaluation" I rose from my chair and made for the door, at which point Nevitt stepped between me and the door, blocking my exit. He put out his right hand, fondled the left side of my neck and my left shoulder, and then moved his hand so that the palm made contact on the clothes over my left breast. I immediately took two steps backward, breaking the contact. Nevitt stopped himself and frowned. Evidently he was considering the potential risk, the room containing us being just off SBA's busy main lobby. He stepped away and I rushed out of the room.

Nevitt then retaliated by issuing a letter to the Committee stating that he considered me as needing mental illness treatment during my "difficult" first year of membership in SBA for the purpose of "relationship dynamics."

However, I was not required to submit to any further in-person meetings with Nevitt. The subsequent MAP supervision of the supposed "therapy" was conducted long-distance, inasmuch as I live hours away from Phoenix. Nevitt did phone my home several times over the year following the "evaluation," however, threatening me that if I were not "nice" to him, my MAP supervision period might be extended. But to my relief, he stopped short of demanding that I see him again in person.

AzBBHE may wonder why I am reporting this sexual assault so many years after it happened. The reason is that recently, SBA got a court order issued demanding that as a condition of practicing law, I undergo further MAP "evaluation and supervision." Since Nevitt is still directing the MAP program of his employer SBA, this entails that I again submit—this time knowingly and voluntarily—to the likelihood of Nevitt's groping—again, under the pretext of "evaluation" and/or "therapy." I am not up for this.

I will appreciate being notified if AzBBHE will investigate.

Miriam H. Klaiman, Ph.D., M.D., J.D.

Appendix 6-8

Supreme Court
STATE OF ARIZONA
COMMITTEE ON CHARACTER AND FITNESS
1501 W. Washington Street, Suite 104
Phoenix, Arizona 85007-3231
602-364-0371

January 30, 2006

PERSONAL AND CONFIDENTIAL

Miriam Holly Klaiman

Dear Ms. Klaiman:

The Character and Fitness Committee has authorized the State Bar's Member Assistance Program to prepare a therapeutic contract for you in accordance with the terms set forth in their report.

The Committee will receive the contract after you have signed it, at which time an overview of your file, including a copy of the contract, will be prepared for review by the Supreme Court justices. You will receive a copy of the overview. At that time, you may contact the Clerk's office at 602-542-9396 to inquire when your matter will be scheduled. Please note the filing of your matter is via the Clerk's office of the Supreme Court and is therefore public record.

The Court will subsequently issue an Order as to their decision, which will be sent to you and the Committee concurrently. The Committee will then confirm with you, in writing, as to the decision and your admission status. Therefore, please advise the Committee if you change your address or telephone number.

If you have any questions regarding the foregoing procedures, please call me at 602-364-0363.

Sincerely,

C. de Looper, Attorney Admissions
Character & Fitness/Examinations

cc: MAP

Stephen M. Weiss, Co-Chair · Ann Birmingham Scheel, Co-Chair · Howard D. Sukenic, Vice-Chair
J. Russell Skelton · Tobin Rosen · Timothy R. Hyland · David F. Gaona
James N. Dyer · Troy P. Foster · Lee Marshall Holtby · Evelyn Patrick Rick
Henry C. Manuelito · H. Christina Hill · Ronald Ross Watson, Ph.D.

Exhibit 6-9

Supreme Court
STATE OF ARIZONA

NOËL K. DESSAINT
CLERK OF THE COURT

402 ARIZONA STATE COURTS BUILDING
1501 WEST WASHINGTON STREET
PHOENIX, ARIZONA 85007-3231

TELEPHONE (602) 542-9396

KATHLEEN E. KEMPLEY
CHIEF DEPUTY CLERK

April 21, 2006

RE: In the Matter of MIRIAM HOLLY KLAIMAN
     Arizona Supreme Court No. SB-06-0029-C

GREETINGS:

The following action was taken by the Supreme Court of the State of
Arizona on April 20, 2006, in regard to the above-referenced cause:

ORDERED: Findings of Fact and Recommendations of Conditional
Admission /Letter of Understanding = REVIEW DECLINED. The
Committee's recommendation for admission with conditions is final.

Noel K Dessaint, Clerk

TO:
Miriam Holly Klaiman
James H Dyer, Committee on Character and Fitness
Carolyn de Looper, Director, Committee on Character and Fitness

tel

Exhibit 6-10

STATE BAR OF ARIZONA

TO: Supreme Court Committee on Character and Fitness

CC: Carolyn de Looper and Miriam H. Klaiman

FROM: Hal M. Nevitt, Member Assistance Program   DATE: January 9, 2006

RE: Miriam H. Klaiman

Ms. Klaiman met with MAP Director Hal M. Nevitt, LCSW, CEAP on December 23, 2005, at her request and in response to the Committee's letter dated November 28, 2005. Mr. Nevitt provided a written report to the Member Assistance Program ("MAP").

As a result of her interview and assessment with Mr. Nevitt, he has indicated he believes Ms. Klaiman is a candidate for the MAP Monitoring Program. Mr. Nevitt recommends a Therapeutic Contract with duration of one (1) year.

The proposed Therapeutic Contract, which will be drafted by MAP for signature by all parties, would include the following minimum requirements:

      1.   Applicant shall make and attend appointments with a therapist, approved by MAP, for the purpose of refining conflict management skills and life adjustment throughout the difficult first year of life as a practicing attorney. Applicant shall meet with her therapist at least once a month or as recommended by her therapist, or any successor treatment professional, as outlined below.

      2.   Applicant shall make and attend a psychiatric/psychological assessment by a psychiatrist/psychologist approved by MAP and follow any recommendations made by her psychiatrist/psychologist.

      3.   If medications are prescribed by her doctor or any successor treatment professional, Applicant shall continue on the medications as prescribed.

      4.   Applicant shall authorize and direct her psychiatrist and therapist, or any successor treatment professional, as outlined below, to provide a written progress report to the MAP every ninety (90) days verifying that Applicant has met with him/her and is following his/her recommendations. The first progress report shall be due ninety (90) days after Applicant's admission to the State Bar of Arizona.

5.   Applicant shall be assigned and shall maintain regular contact with a Monitor. Applicant shall NOT be required to pay for support and monitoring activities provided by the Monitor.

6.   Applicant shall meet with the Monitor at such date, time and place as set by the Monitor at least once each month and maintain weekly telephone contact with the Monitor. These contacts are for the purpose of reviewing Applicant's progress and compliance with this agreement. Missing two (2) meetings in a six-month period will constitute a breach of this agreement.

7.   Member shall, at the MAP Director's discretion, schedule and hold an exit interview within 30 days of the date this agreement is scheduled to expire. There shall be no charge to Member for this interview. However, Member will not be considered to have successfully completed this agreement until she has met this requirement.

8.   Applicant shall execute all necessary releases for communication between MAP, Dr. Sucher, her therapist and psychiatrist, the Committee, and the Monitor.

9.   Applicant is solely responsible for any and all expenses, costs and fees incurred in carrying out the provisions of this agreement including, but not limited to, evaluation, hospitalization, in-patient or out-patient treatment, counseling or therapy, preparation and distribution of reports and records, etc.

10.   Applicant shall be responsible for payment of all fees related to her treatment by any treatment professional, as outlined previously in this document.

11.   Applicant shall pay $50 per month to MAP for services rendered in monitoring Applicant's compliance with the terms of this agreement.

Please contact me at (602) 340-7334 if the Committee has any questions. If the Committee approved the proposed terms, I will prepare the Contract.

Appendix 6-11

1   Georgia A. Staton, Bar #004863
    Russell R. Yurk, Bar #019377
2   JONES, SKELTON & HOCHULI, P.L.C.
    2901 North Central Avenue, Suite 800
3   Phoenix, Arizona 85012
    Telephone: (602) 263-1752
4   Fax: (602) 200-7854
    gstaton@jshfirm.com
5   minuteentries@jshfirm.com

6   Attorneys for Defendants Santa Cruz County
    Board of Supervisors and George Silva, Santa
7   Cruz County (Arizona) Attorney

8

SUPERIOR COURT OF THE STATE OF ARIZONA

9

COUNTY OF SANTA CRUZ

10

11 MIRIAM KLAIMAN,	NO. CV 08-630
12 Plaintiff,	**NOTICE OF *VIDEOTAPED* DEPOSITION**
13 v.	(Assigned to the Honorable Anna M.
14 SANTA CRUZ COUNTY (ARIZONA), a	Montoya-Paez, Div. 2)
governmental entity; SANTA CRUZ	
15 COUNTY (ARIZONA) BOARD OF	
SUPERVISORS, a governmental entity; and,	
16 GEORGE SILVA, SANTA CRUZ COUNTY	
(ARIZONA) ATTORNEY, ex officio,	
17	
Defendants.	

18

19   YOU ARE HEREBY NOTIFIED that, pursuant to Ariz. R. Civ. P. 26 and

20 30, the *videotaped* deposition will be taken upon oral examination of the persons whose

21 names and addresses are stated below at the time and place stated below before an officer

22 authorized by law to administer oaths. If the names are not known, a general description

23 sufficient to identify those persons or the particular classes or groups of which those

24 persons belong is given below.

25 **PERSONS TO BE EXAMINED:**   Custodian of Records
                                     State Bar of Arizona
26   4201 N. 24th Street, Suite 200
                                      Phoenix, Arizona 85016-6288

27 **DATE AND TIME OF THE**   Wednesday, May 27, 2009
    DEPOSITION: at 9:30 a.m.
28

```
 1    LOCATION OF DEPOSITION:        State Bar of Arizona
                                     4201 N. 24th Street, Suite 200
 2                                   Phoenix, Arizona 85016-6288

 3              DATED this 13th day of May, 2009.

 4                                   JONES, SKELTON & HOCHULI, P.L.C.

 5

 6                                   By
 7                                      Georgia A. Staton
                                        Russell R. Yurk
 8                                      2901 North Central Avenue, Suite 800
                                        Phoenix, Arizona 85012
 9                                      Attorneys for Defendants Santa Cruz
                                        County Board of Supervisors and George
10                                      Silva, Santa Cruz County (Arizona)
                                        Attorney
11

12    COPY of the foregoing mailed
      this 13th day of May, 2009, to:
13

14    Miriam H. Klaiman, in pro per

15

16

17    Lea, Sherman and Habeski
      834 North First Avenue
18    Phoenix, Arizona 85003
      Court Reporters
19

20

21

22

23

24

25

26

27

28
```

245

From: Craig Henley [mailto:craig.henley@staff.azbar.org]
Sent: Friday, February 17, 2012
11:38 AM **To:** **Cc:** Donna Stephens; Amy Rehm; David Sandweiss
Subject: RE: Klaiman

I anticipate that this will be my last e-mail regarding this topic. Needless to say, I disagree with your characterization of the State Bar's actions and intent. If you feel that you must pursue this matter further, please feel free to file the appropriate documents with the court.

While I will not reiterate my prior e-mails, I feel it prudent to address a couple of your allegations.

First, as all trial lawyers know, differences in testimony does not mean that one of the witnesses has committed perjury. Differences in testimony merely gives rise to credibility issue(s) that are ultimately resolved by the trier of fact, not post-trial by the attorneys.

Second, as you know, I have _significant concerns_ about your client's credibility and her ongoing attempt to pursue her personal issues with Ms. Caples. With that in mind, I reject your contention that a post-hearing affidavit purportedly obtained by your client under unknown circumstances is absolute proof of perjury. Again, there were various remedies available at the time of trial to challenge Ms. Caples's credibility. If memory serves me correctly, you did address Ms. Caples's credibility in both your cross examination of Ms.

Caples and during your client's testimony.

Third, while you would have no reason to know it, you should be aware that I did contact Ms. Caples and verified that she stands by her testimony. More importantly, I was able to obtain additional information supporting Ms. Caples's recollection and testimony on this issue. Therefore, I have no knowledge that the testimony is false – in fact, I have significant reason to believe that the testimony is absolutely true.

Hopefully, this explains the State Bar's position regarding this issue.

STATE BAR OF ARIZONA

Craig Henley, Bar Counsel
4201 N. 24th St., Suite 200 | Phoenix, AZ   85016-6288
T : 602.340.7272   **F :** 602.416.7470
EMAIL: craig.henley@staff.azbar.org
www.azbar.org

Serving the public and enhancing the legal profession.

From: Craig Henley [mailto:craig.henley@staff.azbar.org]
Sent: Thursday, February 16, 2012
5:05 PM **To:** Cc: Amy Rehm; David Sandweiss
Subject: Klaiman

You should be aware that, as promised, I discussed your proposal with Amy <u>and</u> David. Both agreed with my prior rejection of the proposal, particularly given the Court's ruling(s) which allowed Nina's testimony, your client's testimony regarding the [Mr. Sesile] representation and your client's ability to call [Mr. Sesile] as an impeachment witness at trial instead of through a post-trial affidavit or stipulation in the finding of fact. As you know, the State Bar has been consistent in this case regarding any attempt to submit affidavits/letters in lieu of live testimony.

Additionally, and more importantly, just because [Mr. Sesile] purportedly does not remember the events the same as Nina doesn't necessarily change anything. Different people are able to interpret events differently. Again, this is why I believe that it was incumbent to produce any impeachment witnesses at trial.

STATE BAR OF ARIZONA

Craig Henley, Bar Counsel

4201 N. 24th St., Suite 200 | Phoenix, AZ   85016-6288
T : 602.340.7272   F : 602.416.7470
EMAIL: craig.henley@staff.azbar.org

www.azbar.org

Serving the public and enhancing the legal profession.

Exhibit 6-13

Statement of Costs and Expenses

In the Matter of a Member of the State Bar of Arizona,
Miriam Holly Klaiman, Bar No. 024299, Respondent
PDJ-2011-9060
File No. 10-0329

Travel and expenses costs incurred by Darin Cody Hufacker, Acting Clerk of the Office of the Presiding Disciplinary Maria Salapska, Attorney Member and Judge William J. O'Neil, Presiding Disciplinary Judge of the Office of the Presiding Disciplinary Judge to travel to and from the hearing on the merits and lunch for the panel members at the Court of Appeals, Div. II, 400 W. Congress, Tucson, Arizona 85203-4810 scheduled on Thursday, February 2, 2012 and concluding on Friday, February 3, 2012.

TOTAL COSTS AND EXPENSES INCURRED

02/02/2012 Travel to Tucson, Arizona and overnight stay at The Hotel Arizona, for Maria Salapska, Attorney Member   **$ 237.49**

02/02/2012 & 02/03/2012: Travel to Tucson, Arizona and parking for Acting Clerk, Darin Cody Hufacker   **$213.52**

02/02/2012 & 02/03/2012: Travel to Tucson, Arizona for Presiding Disciplinary Judge, William J. O'Neil, parking for Acting Clerk on 2/02/2012 and Judge O'Neil's vehicle for 2/02/2012 and 2/03/2012and and lunch for the panel members on 2/02/2012 and 2/03/2012   **$266.42**

TOTAL COSTS AND EXPENSES DUE   ($717.43)

_____   3/23/2012
Laura L. Hopkins   Date
Disciplinary Clerk, Office of the PDJ

Nina Lou Caples, Never-Disciplined Arizona Bar Member

Bar member no. 013513, Nina Lou Caples, has been the subject of several complaints to the State Bar of Arizona. The Bar is aware of the following.

Caples filed a suit *in pro per* in Pima County Superior Court, case no. C-2000-1568. The case became a model for Caples' pattern of engaging in frivolous litigation, dishonesty in formal proceedings, and/or misuse of court process.

Caples' March 16, 2000, complaint stated that the defendant, Mr. J., was her ex-employee and that she had hired him to service her law office computers. She alleged he had misconducted himself in several ways, including removing a computer with client data on it.

Caples did not inform the Superior Court that she had been representing Mr. J. in a DUI case in Tucson Municipal Court, case no. M-1041-CR-99270634. Through counsel, on April 14, 2000, Mr. K filed a Counterclaim and Answer to which he provided an Exhibit called "Work for Hire Agreement." For representing Mr. J., Caples had taken Mr. J's services in lieu of full payment in cash. Thus Caples gave access to confidential client records stored on her computer to another client, Mr. J— who was at that, a defendant in a DUI proceeding.

Caples and Mr. J. did not work out any settlement of their opposing claims. Caples filed no further papers in the case; she did not file an Answer to the Counterclaim. The case was dismissed for want of prosecution on August 13, 2001.

This case is also discussed on the website www.azaacpr.org, webpage "Inquisitional Discipline" [4] [iv].

In another case in Cochise County Justice Court (small claims) J-0205-CV-20051363, Caples claimed against a former client, Ms. B., for outstanding payment for Caples' legal services. Caples won judgment and an order of garnishment. Caples proceeded to garnish the client's wages. Ms. B. was an unmarried mother and was in financial distress, earning very little. Another local attorney (John Kelliher, who at the time of this writing is a Cochise County Superior Court Division II judge) undertook to assist Ms. B. because Caples failed to stop the wage garnishment after her judgment against Ms. B. was satisfied. Rather, Caples continued to take wage deductions when there was no further justification. Mr. Kelliher's office complained to the Arizona Bar, noting that because of Caples' excessive monetary impositions, the ex-client and her minor children were being evicted from their living accommodations. The Bar opened a disciplinary investigation against Caples, Bar disciplinary File No. 06-1393. It failed, however, to discipline Caples.

This case is also discussed on the website www.azaacpr.org, webpage "Inquisitional Discipline" [3] [c] [ii].

Caples' untruthful witness testimony in a hearing in Arizona Bar disciplinary case PDJ-2011-9060 has been discussed in Ch. 3 i c 2 and Ch. 6 "Attorney D" *supra*, and is also alluded to on the website www.azaacpr.org, webpage "Inquisitional Discipline" [3] [b]]iii].

Ch. 6 "Attorney D" *supra* also recounts Caples' response to a small claims suit for unpaid wages.

Caples was the subject of complaint by an ex-husband in a Domestic Violence case, Tucson Municipal Court, case no. M-1041-DV-99279545.   This is also discussed on the website www.azaacpr.org, webpage "Inquisitional Discipline" [4] [ii].

Over several years, Caples handled several legal matters on behalf of a Mr. Padilla.   Originally, Mr. Padilla's family engaged Caples to defend him in a domestic violence matter (wherein his wife was of record as a "victim") in case no. J-0201-CR-20060523 in Cochise County, Bisbee, Arizona, Justice Court.   Caples subsequently represented Mr. Padilla in his divorce in Cochise County Superior Court, case no. S-0200-DO-200700477. Then, on June 11, 2009, Caples and Padilla were married in Nogales, Arizona, in Santa Cruz County, Arizona, Superior Court (S-1200-ML-2009-0164). Back at Cochise County Superior Court, there appeared in the divorce record a letter addressed to the court by the ex-wife complaining that she had become destitute and homeless because Padilla had not complied with the property settlement. Presumably, this would be a property settlement that his lawyer, Caples, had arranged. Padilla was subsequently the subject of a paternity/child support action brought by the Arizona Attorney General in Cochise County Superior Court, case no. S-0200-DO-200901145.   In 2013, Caples divorced Padilla in Graham County Superior Court, case no. S-0500-DO-201200151.   This history is alluded to on the website www.azaacpr.org, webpage "Inquisitional Discipline" [4] [ii], [iii].

Caples' past husbands include Messrs. Davis, Finley, Whalen, Glanville, Fimbres and Padilla. The record of her marriages and divorces is spread over public records of superior courts in at least three Arizona counties, including Pima, Santa Cruz, and Graham. Caples has been divorced at least six times.

Traditionally, our scholars marked their redemption
from persecution by writing books.

Genizah Service Text, Congregation Anshei Israel

COLOPHON

Since 2012, the organization Arizona Attorneys Against Corrupt Professional Regulation has dedicated itself to educating the public about corruption in the Arizona Judicial Department, concentrating on policies and practices of the State Bar of Arizona that harm the legal profession and abuse the civil rights of its practitioners. AZAACPR has maintained its purpose while safeguarding the privacy and anonymity of its supporters and correspondents. AZAACPR's website is www.azaacpr.org. For directions on how to make contact anonymously, consult the website's "Contact" form: http://www.azaacpr.org/contact-azaacpr.html.